Praise for Citizen of a Wider Commonwealth

"By contrast with most Grant biographers, Edwina Campbell chronicles Grant's travels with the understanding that he was on a U.S. government-sanctioned diplomatic mission—in fact, the first diplomatic mission ever undertaken by a former U.S. president." —*The Foreign Service Journal*

"Campbell does a wonderful job of detailing how Grant dealt with the portentous decorum of the British Empire, which worked to downplay his mission by providing him with all of the ceremony of an ex-sovereign but denying him that same dignity as he ventured into areas of the empire east of the Suez."

—**Dustin McLochlin**, *Presidential Studies Quarterly*

"In her lucid and fast-paced book, Campbell makes clear that as his country's 'ambassador at large,' Grant pioneered the practice of public diplomacy. . . . This volume both adds to the growing revisionist scholarship on Grant and confirms that those who dismiss the contributions and legacy of the eighteenth president do so at their own peril."

—**John David Smith**, author of *Lincoln and the U.S. Colored Troops*

"This is an important book, not only for scholars of Grant but also for students of U.S. foreign policy, the latter part of the nineteenth century, and the evolution of the role of presidents in and out of office."

—**Kenneth B. Moss**, professor emeritus, National Security Studies, National Defense University

"*Citizen of a Wider Commonwealth* is the untold story of Grant's post-presidential 'world tour,' a diplomatic mission that sought to position the United States for the power and influence it would wield in the twentieth century. A must-read for anyone interested in the forces shaping American foreign policy as the continental power took its place on the world stage." —**Charlotte Ku**, Texas A&M University School of Law

THE WORLD OF ULYSSES S. GRANT

SERIES EDITORS

John F. Marszalek & Timothy B. Smith

Citizen of a Wider Commonwealth

Ulysses S. Grant's Postpresidential Diplomacy

Edwina S. Campbell

Southern Illinois University Press
Carbondale

Southern Illinois University Press
Mail Code 6806; Southern Illinois University;
Morris Library, 605 Agriculture Dr.,
Carbondale, IL 62901
siupress.com

Cloth edition 2016.
Paperback edition 2025.
Printed in the United States of America

Paperback edition first printed November 2025.

Jacket illustrations: *Top*, world map of 1871 showing actual and projected undersea routes of telegraph lines (G. W. & C. B. Colton & Co.); *center*, Ulysses S. Grant and Li Hung-chang, China's northern viceroy (author's collection, *Harper's Weekly*, October 4, 1879); *bottom*, USS *Richmond*, which was to have met Grant in France during the winter of 1879 but caught up with him only off the coast of China in June of that year.

Frontispiece: From December 1877 to March 1878, the Grants toured the eastern Mediterranean aboard USS *Vandalia*, disembarking in Naples on March 18, 1878, for a month-long visit to Italy. Julia, Ulysses, and Jesse Grant (*left to right*) are seated, while John Russell Young is on the far right, holding a hat in his left hand. Photo NH 61138; courtesy of US Naval History and Heritage Command Photo Archives.

ISBN 978-0-8093-4002-6 (paperback)
ISBN 978-0-8093-3478-0 (cloth)
ISBN 978-0-8093-3479-7 (ebook)

The manufacturer's authorized representative in the EU for
product safety: Mare Nostrum Group B.V., Mauritskade 21D,
1091 GC Amsterdam, The Netherlands. gpsr@mare-nostrum.co.uk

Printed on recycled paper ♻

SIU
Southern Illinois University System

From the Address of American Citizens, resident in Peking, to General Ulysses S. Grant

US Legation, Peking, June 3, 1879

Read by Dr. W.A.P. Martin

Twenty years ago, the American flag for the first time entered the gates of this ancient Capital. For the greater part of that time your countrymen have been residing here under its protecting folds; and it is with feelings of no ordinary type that we gather ourselves beneath its shadow this day to welcome your arrival; because to you, Sir, under God, it is due that its azure field has not been rent to fragments and its golden stars scattered to the winds of heaven. . . .

. . . [W]e reflect with pride that you have shown the world how a great man can descend from a lofty station and yet carry with him the homage of the people and the admiration of mankind. As you travel from land to land, everywhere welcomed as the citizen of a wider commonwealth than that of our native country, we cannot forget that your visits to their shores possess an international character of which it is impossible to divest them.

You are honored as the highest representative of our country who has ever gone beyond her borders; and America is the more respected for having given birth to such a son.

Contents

Illustrations

Gallery Two begins on page 171

Preface

I first saw a photograph of Ulysses Grant, near the end of his 1877–79 world tour, seated next to one of the principal foreign policy figures of late nineteenth-century China, the northern viceroy, Li Hung-chang (Li Hongzhang), when I visited White Haven, Ulysses S. Grant National Historic Site, in early summer 2010. A map showed the extent of Grant's travels, and there was a photo of Ulysses, his wife Julia, and son Jesse Grant on the Mediterranean aboard USS *Vandalia*, surrounded by the ship's officers. The White Haven exhibit brilliantly covers the whole of the Grants' life together ("as true" to each other "as the thread to the needle," in the words of William Tecumseh Sherman that are the leitmotif of the exhibit); but it was the photos of Grant with Li and aboard *Vandalia* that stayed with me long after my visit.

In the 1970s, I was a member of the United States Foreign Service. After I left the State Department to teach, initially at the University of Virginia in the 1980s, my research and writing focused on US foreign policy toward Europe since World War II. But my undergraduate degree was in Far East Language and Area studies, and I had studied Japanese for three years, in addition to French and German. I knew the dire strategic situation of China that Li Hung-chang tried, but ultimately failed, to master. If he made time to meet with Grant, it was not mere courtesy or curiosity; there was a foreign-policy purpose behind everything Li did. And if Grant was aboard a warship of the US Navy, it was because the American government had foreign-policy reasons to desire his presence there. The secretary of the navy had to have been involved in any such invitation to the former president, with the concurrence of the secretary of state and under the authority of President Hayes. The Navy and State Departments were not in the business of rewarding ex-presidents with a grand pleasure tour around the world.

Until I visited White Haven, I had not thought that I might make a contribution to understanding the life and work of Ulysses Grant. After that visit I began to think that my background in the practice and study of diplomacy meant that I had something worth saying about a relatively unknown and largely misunderstood aspect of Grant's service to the United States.

From 1877 to 1879, Ulysses Grant was his country's ambassador at large, the first practitioner of postpresidential diplomacy. He did a lot of diplomatic heavy lifting for the United States at a moment when it was weakly represented overseas, relative to its growing foreign-policy interests. But when I began to reread the scant portions of the secondary literature on Grant that dealt with the world tour, I found that with rare exceptions, the principal one being Joan Waugh's *U.S. Grant: American Hero, American Myth*,[1] the authors treated his travels as a self-indulgent boondoggle focused on wining, dining, and shopping. Nothing could be farther from the truth. Thanks to the generous hospitality of the U.S. Grant Presidential Library (USGPL), Mississippi State University, Starkville, I have been able to work with the primary sources that show the nature, the extent, and the achievements of Grant's diplomacy.

Housed in MSU's Mitchell Memorial Library, led by Dean Frances Coleman, the Grant Library contains a wealth of resources on all aspects of the life of the nation's eighteenth president. But the most extensive collection of documents is only as valuable as the archivists and librarians who create and maintain it and help researchers navigate their way through it. No thanks can adequately repay the creative and collegial group of professionals who welcomed me on my many research visits to the Grant Library; chief among them were John Marszalek, Ryan Semmes, Michael Ballard, Amanda Carlock, Elizabeth Coggins, Aaron Crawford, Louis Gallo, Meg Henderson, and David Nolen.

While doing my research, I was greeted with the same level of enthusiasm and hospitality by those working at sites around the country concerned with the life and legacy of Ulysses Grant. My thanks to Bob Conner, Jonathan Duda, David Hubbard, Melissa Trombley-Prosch, and Tim Welch of Grant Cottage Association (Mount McGregor), Saratoga, New York. Melissa took time from working on her own book, *"For You, Julia": The Final Victory of U.S. Grant*, to help me with mine. I am grateful for the expertise and encouragement of Robert Boyd, Brett Griffith, Ned Lodwick, Nancy Purdy, Stan Purdy, Lee Schweickart, and Joye White of Grant's birthplace, boyhood home, and school, Point Pleasant and Georgetown, Ohio.

On a return visit to White Haven in 2013, I finally had the pleasure of meeting the two people who created the exhibit that set in motion the research for this book, National Park Service site historian Pam Sanfilippo and site curator Karen Maxville, and seeing again their colleague, Terry Orr, who led my first tour of the Dent-Grant home in 2010. I owe the greatest debt to Pam and Karen; while there would be no book without the assistance of all those named above, without Pam and Karen there would have been no idea for a book. It all began with their exhibit.

I have not had the pleasure of thanking in person Rebecca Stockbridge, Reference Librarian, New Hampshire State Library, Concord; Laura Dimmock-Jones, Librarian, Royal United Services Institute (RUSI), London, UK; and Rev. John Beach and Helena Mbele-Mbong, Emmanuel Church, Geneva, Switzerland, for their assistance with my research. Ulysses Grant laid the cornerstone of Emmanuel Church in July 1877; RUSI, founded by the Duke of Wellington, hosted a dinner for Grant earlier that month; and New Hampshire played a prominent role in the former president's travels. On the China coast in 1879 his home was USS *Ashuelot*, named after a river in the Granite State and captained from Hong Kong to Canton (Guangzhou) by one of its most prominent seamen, Commander (later Commodore) George H. Perkins.

Marc Flores created the maps for this book, for which he would accept nothing in return except my thanks; he certainly has that, as well my affection for him and his family, Heather, Summer, Savannah, and Josh.

I am grateful for the invitation to speak about my research at the May 2014 annual meeting of the Ulysses S. Grant Association, and for the encouraging words of my fellow USGA members, especially those of Ulysses Dietz, Claire Telecki, and USGA president Frank Williams, as well as to Jim Kroll and Jennifer Dewey for the invitation to discuss Grant's post-presidential diplomacy in an April 2015 talk at the Denver Public Library.

My thanks to all the friends who have traveled vicariously with the Grants and me over the past few years, especially to Naomi and Paul De Mayo, Judy and Bob Fralish, David and Christy Weas, Morgan and Chandra Mackey, K. Michael Prince, and Sarah Archer. Thanks also to J. D. Benson, Cory Bulris, Larry Chalmer, Richard Fagan, Lewis Griffith, Karl Hjembo, Christopher Holmes, Brent Lawniczak, Jody Rose Platt, Mark Rizzieri, Mark and Joyce Smith, (the other) Tim Smith, Aubrey Sterling, Ronnie Taylor, Jim and Molly Toth, and Tom Weaver. My friend Paul De Mayo did not live to see this book completed, but like the American citizen-soldier who is its subject, Paul was, in the tradition of the two services in which he served, *semper fidelis* and *semper paratus.*

Two friends again deserve more thanks for more reasons than I can possibly list: Charlotte Ku, Professor of Law and Assistant Dean for Graduate and International Legal Studies at the University of Illinois Urbana-Champaign College of Law, and Michael D'Ambrosio, recently retired from the United States Senior Executive Service. More than four decades ago Charlotte, Michael, and I were graduate students at the Fletcher School of Law and Diplomacy. In the years since, they have been there for all the important personal moments of my life, generously contributing their time, their own professional experiences and expertise, and their constructive criticism to make me a better scholar and person. Michael drove several hours to join me on my visit to Grant Cottage and acted as a sounding board, patiently listening to me describe my research and asking insightful questions, as he has since 1971, that stayed with me as I wrote this book.

Before joining the UIUC faculty, Charlotte was, for more than a decade, executive director of the American Society of International Law, founded in 1906 by Grant's spiritual heir, and Ulysses S. Grant III's father-in-law, Secretary of State Elihu Root. Today recognized as one of the world's experts on the development of international law in the twentieth century,[2] Charlotte wrote her doctoral dissertation on the late nineteenth-century encounter of China with the western international system. Throughout this project she offered historical perspectives, secondary literature suggestions, and thought-provoking questions about two of the issues most important to Ulysses Grant, the peaceful settlement of international disputes and the United States' role in the Pacific. Charlotte was the first person to read the entire manuscript, and her questions, comments, and insights were, as always, invaluable.

Finally, my thanks to the editors of *The World of Ulysses S. Grant* series, John F. Marszalek and Timothy B. Smith; to the two anonymous readers whose comments and perspectives were invaluable in revising and improving the manuscript; to my editor at Southern Illinois University Press, Sylvia Frank Rodrigue; and to all of her SIU Press colleagues, especially Linda Buhman, Amy Etcheson, Wayne Larsen, Lynanne Page, Karl Kageff, Judy Verdich, and my copy editor, Ryan Masteller. Their judgment, expertise, and dedication have certainly made this a better book, but I appreciate most of all their patience, good humor, and humanity. I am especially grateful to Sylvia for her professional advice and her personal collegiality, even while handling the Massachusetts blizzards of 2015 and me at the same time.

Unfortunately, I never had the privilege of knowing the editor of the *Papers of Ulysses S. Grant* (*PUSG*), the late John Y. Simon; but like all those who study Grant's life and career, I owe the greatest debt to him. In his introduction to the final volume of *PUSG*, John Marszalek wrote:

> The result [of Professor Simon's work] has been the recognition by historians that Ulysses S. Grant was one of the most significant figures in all of American history. No longer can any historian repeat the cruel myths that Grant was an insensitive military butcher, an inveterate alcoholic, and an incompetent failed president. Today the historical profession has come to recognize Grant as a military genius and the nation's first modern president. Unfortunately, the general public still believes the myths, but this too is changing, as historians dispute such inaccuracies.[3]

Because of the primary resources now readily accessible at USGPL as a result of the work of Professor Simon and his colleagues, most notably his wife, Harriet Simon, I was able to learn that John Russell Young's description of Grant was no overstatement. The former president was, when "he returned home in 1879 the most accomplished and best informed statesman of his time. The book of the world had been opened to him. He saw the relative proportion of things, the true place of America in the economy of nations, and, under wise, intrepid statesmanship, the magnificence of her opportunities."[4]

I have been fortunate to travel the late nineteenth-century world with the eighteenth president, who represented the government and people of the United States in countries where no American president had ever been seen before and, in many cases, would not be seen again for nearly a century. I hope that this book contributes to recognition of Grant's post-presidential diplomacy as a major contribution to US foreign policy that paved the way for the nation's global role in the twentieth century. It could not have been written without the professional expertise, personal encouragement, and patient friendship of all the individuals here named, but they are not responsible for any errors, which are my own.

A Note on Names of People and Places

Many of the places visited by Ulysses Grant now have different names than they had in 1877–79, and the names of many individuals he met in the non-English speaking world are now romanized differently than they were at the time. For consistency with the primary sources, the place names and romanization used by Grant and John Russell Young (for example, Li Hung-chang, rather than Li Hongzhang) are used in this book. No political or ideological point of view should be inferred from such usage. Romanized Chinese and Japanese names are rendered as in those languages, last name first: for example, Yoshida Kiyonari. At the first reference to a place name contemporary to Grant, the modern name, if different, is given in parentheses: for example, Christiania (Oslo), Norway.

Citizen of a Wider Commonwealth

Introduction

On Saturday, May 17, 1879, Ulysses and Julia Grant, accompanied by their eldest son, Lieutenant Colonel Frederick Grant, journalist John Russell Young, former secretary of the navy Adolph Borie, and Borie's physician, Dr. John Keating, arrived in Shanghai, China, aboard the US Navy gunboat USS *Ashuelot*. Exactly two years before, the Grants and their youngest son, Jesse, had departed for Europe from Philadelphia, "the only port in the country from which [they] could have sailed under the American flag,"[1] on the steamer *Indiana*. The former president returned home through the Golden Gate aboard the Pacific Mail steamer, *City of Tokio*, on September 20, 1879. In more than two years overseas, Ulysses Grant invented key aspects of the foreign-policy role of the modern American presidency and created an image abroad of the United States that endures to this day. The Japanese emperor Meiji was "said to have been impressed in his forty-four-year reign by no one more than by the unassuming bourgeois Civil War hero and president."[2] He was far from alone in this opinion at the time, but in the intervening decades it has been hard to understand why he felt that way. Grant's world tour has not so much been mischaracterized, as have other aspects of his life, as it has not been characterized at all.

To military historians, the former president's years abroad have been of interest chiefly for the opportunity they gave him to ruminate on the course of the Civil War with John Russell Young. East of Suez, Grant had long hours aboard ship to review his own decisions, comment on the conduct and personal qualities of other Union generals, and assess the successes and failures of both sides in the war. Some of these conversations were published in the *New York Herald* while Grant was still abroad, and they eventually constituted a large part of Young's 1879 book *Around the World with General Grant*. For presidential historians, had Grant been reelected to the presidency in 1880, his experiences overseas would have been of interest as the background to the foreign policy of the third term. Since he was not, they have paid little attention to his travels. And historians of American diplomacy have paid even less attention to the world tour than have their military and presidential counterparts. Aside from the general lack of interest, until very recently, in the development and conduct of American foreign policy in the years after the Civil War until 1898, they have taken at face value that Grant was a private American citizen enjoying the opportunity to see the world. But he was not, even if he had originally intended to be a tourist.

Jesse Grant, who accompanied his father and mother during their first year abroad, wrote a memoir nearly fifty years later in which he described what happened to his expected family holiday the moment they arrived in Britain. Although not always reliable in his recollections of whom Grant met and where, Jesse, precisely because he was not pleased with the way things developed, remembered vividly the diplomatic tasks that his father found waiting for him in Europe. The former president's welcome in Liverpool was tumultuous; as Jesse wrote, "Thus in the beginning the character of our tour changed unexpectedly." His father "stood up with unflagging interest under a round of social and civil ceremonies" that Liverpudlians had prepared for him, and things only got worse (from Jesse's point of view) from then on. "We had anticipated a natural curiosity," he remembered, but "[b]efore we left Liverpool for London we began to realize that, while father was [in his own mind] a private citizen traveling for pleasure, he was scarcely more free to follow his own plans than if there officially in a representative capacity." Indeed, Grant discovered that, whatever his own intentions, for both the Hayes administration and the governments hosting him, he *was* overseas "in a representative capacity." The former president regarded his welcome in Britain as "a tribute to his country to which he must subordinate personal plans, inclinations, and desires." Jesse recalled unhappily that

> during the entire tour father declined every invitation of an official character, where the non-acceptance would not be misconstrued. . . . He did not go abroad to be feted. . . . But where his acceptance could be of possible advantage to his country, acceptance only could be considered.[3]

From Liverpool to Tokyo, this approach guided Grant's conduct for more than two years.

The vocabulary to describe Grant's diplomatic role had not been invented in the 1870s; such a role had not been possible before that decade. Grant was the first former president able to benefit from and to exploit the technological advancements that changed the nature of global intercourse in the decade after the Civil War: steamships, railroads, and intercontinental telegraphy.[4] Both the Suez Canal and the United States' transcontinental railroad were completed in 1869. The first transatlantic telegraph cable was laid in 1866. Looking back at its development more than three decades later, American diplomat John W. Foster, Benjamin Harrison's second secretary of state, wrote that the telegraph "has had a greater influence on the methods of diplomacy than any other physical fact of the century."[5] Moreover, no one had conceived a diplomatic role for a former president. Grant invented that role, as Jesse described, as he recognized that his actions and words overseas reflected on the United States:

> [T]o compensate for the loss of privacy and freedom upon which he first counted was the knowledge that he was advancing the interests of his country. It was a mission now as well as his personal tour. Everywhere his presence was directing the attention and thought of other countries to America. And the nation at home was following his triumphal progress with keen satisfaction. He could not turn back now even if he would.[6]

It did not take long for the American government to realize that something new was happening. As reports arrived in Washington of Grant's initial reception abroad, the Hayes administration recognized that the former president had become what would be called, in later parlance, a special ambassador of the United States, and it acted to see that he was given the support necessary to fulfill this mission. It was not accidental that Grant arrived in Shanghai in 1879 aboard USS *Ashuelot.* She was the second of three ships put at the former president's disposal by the US government: USS *Vandalia* in the Mediterranean; *Ashuelot* along the coast of China from Hong Kong to Tientsin (Tianjin); and USS *Richmond*, which was to have taken Grant from France to Japan, but, as events turned out, was his home for only a few weeks, from Tientsin through the Inland Sea to Yokohama. With the offer of *Richmond*, Grant's boyhood friend, Rear Admiral Daniel Ammen, wrote in his memoirs, "[I]t was the intention of the President so to arrange the visit of General Grant to the East as to make it one of importance diplomatically and commercially."[7]

But while the American government could and did offer the former president transportation on three US naval vessels while he was abroad, it had only the broadest guidance to offer him in terms of *what* it wanted him to accomplish and nothing at all to say about *how*. "[Y]our presence on board a Man-of-war," Secretary of the Navy Richard Thompson wrote to Grant in the fall of 1878, "will so arrest public attention as to bring prominently into view, not merely the character and extent of our commerce, but the nature and value of our institutions."[8] This was accurate, both as a description of the effect of Grant's presence on *Vandalia*'s Mediterranean cruise earlier that year, and as a prediction of what would happen in East Asia in 1879, but it was hardly guidance. President Hayes no doubt felt that it would be inappropriate for the government to "instruct" the former president, as it would a serving diplomat or military officer, but the effect of this polite discretion was to leave Grant on his own in deciding what to do and how to do it.

The diplomatic situation was unprecedented, since no former president had ever been asked to play such a role, but as a military officer Grant had been there before. As an unknown commander in the western theater in 1862, he had had to decide what needed doing and how to do it to achieve the strategic goals of the United States. "Where others perceived disaster, Grant saw opportunity"; he "possessed that most uncommon quality, common sense," and "the capacity . . . to make a decision and stick with it."[9] Grant had understood what Abraham Lincoln required of him, and he brought the same awareness and sense of duty to the diplomatic tasks necessary to accomplish Hayes's goals. The survival of the United States was not at stake in 1877, as it had been in 1862, but as the country became a principal actor in the international system dominated by the European powers, Grant's creative strategic genius shaped the conduct of American foreign policy in important ways. He also shaped other countries' expectations of what American foreign policy would mean to them. After 1865, the United States was regarded for the first time as "a power of the first class, a nation which it is very dangerous to offend and almost impossible to attack."[10] Grant was fully aware of this changed attitude, and he welcomed it. Far from shying away from a greater international role for his country, he told John Russell Young near the end of their travels together that

> [a]part from the triumph of the Union and the emancipation of the slaves, one of the great results of the war was the position it gave us as a nation among the nations of the world. That I have seen every day during my

residence abroad, and to me it is one of the most gratifying results of the war. That alone was worth making a great sacrifice for.[11]

As he circled the globe, Grant contributed to American diplomacy in three areas. First, he initiated the practice of *public diplomacy*—direct engagement with the people of another country, not only with its government and intellectual elites—that became widespread in the twentieth century but was unheard of in the monarchical and aristocratic diplomacy of Europe as it had been conducted for centuries. As often as he could, in countries where it was possible, Grant spent time not only with the elites who comprised the government, but with average people. In 1877, the US consul in London was Grant's biographer, Adam Badeau. Although his hyperbolic self-absorption was eventually the undoing of his relationship with Grant and his family, Badeau understood the revolutionary nature of Grant's appearance on the international stage. For the British people, the former president was "the realization of what they had heard of but never seen—that a plain man, without rank, or birth, or fortune" could lead a nation. Badeau described the startling newness of an experience no average Briton had ever had: Grant had been "a ruler of a great people—and they could shake his hand!" Unlike European heads of state on tour, his visit was to "both peoples and sovereigns." He represented "not only the Government [of the United States], but the plainest people in it from whom he sprang, whom he claimed as his fellows, whom he believed in as his political peers." Badeau asked, "[W]ho ever so represented a nation before?"[12]

While personifying the promise of the United States to average people, Grant also represented his country at the summit, to use a twentieth-century term, of international politics. Although steamships had reduced travel time across the Atlantic to about ten days, given an American president's short time in office, it still seemed unlikely that a serving American head of state would ever visit Europe. Grant was the first president since Andrew Jackson to serve two full terms, but even eight years seemed incredibly short to Europeans used to monarchs and prime ministers who led their countries for decades. Moreover, Americans were resistant to the idea that there was any good reason for their president to go abroad, where he might be unduly influenced by untrustworthy foreigners. Theodore Roosevelt was the first president to leave the country while in office, but his "excuse" was that he went to Panama to watch an American project, the building of the canal, take shape. The first serving president to visit Europe and participate in a summit conference there was Woodrow Wilson in 1919. Nor did nineteenth-century secretaries of state travel abroad while in office. If, after Appomattox, governments around the world wanted insight into what made Americans and their political leaders tick, and they did, then hosting Ulysses Grant was as close to a summit meeting with an American president as they were going to get.

After mid-1878, in receiving Grant, these governments believed they were hosting the future, as well as the past, chief executive of the United States. Given the reports he was receiving from home, Grant himself thought it not unlikely that he would return to the White House in 1881. Historians have long debated if he wanted a third term, but whatever the answer to that question, it is clear that he intended to prepare himself if he was reelected. Jesse wrote that his father endured "experiences [abroad] that to him, no less than to me, were ordeals," because "he was gaining understanding and knowledge that was fitting him for better service if his country again called." In describing Grant's activities as "ordeals," Jesse transferred his own feelings to his father, who regarded his diplomatic tasks as a lot of work but nevertheless enjoyed them a good deal. But he was right that Grant was developing a "conviction" that he could use "his intimate, personal contact with the rulers of the world, his new understanding of world thought, conditions and needs . . . perhaps, better than another without his experience [to] effect a more satisfactory adjustment of our foreign relations." As Jesse concluded, "[I]f called, there was further work he could do for the advancement of his country and of the world."[13] Because of this, Grant and his host governments had a common interest in "getting to know you" *summit diplomacy;* and he got to know every monarch and minister of importance in Europe and Asia.

Finally, while Grant practiced public diplomacy and summitry throughout his travels abroad, in Asia he dealt not only with the forms of diplomacy but also with a specific international issue that engaged him emotionally and intellectually arguably more than any issue had since emancipation, restoration of the American Union, and defeat of the French intervention in Mexico. That issue was what the twentieth century eventually called *self-determination* and what Grant called, simply, independence. In 1879, he spent weeks in the British Empire before arriving in Siam (Thailand), China, and Japan. He also paid brief visits to Portuguese Macao and to French Saigon and stayed, while in Canton, Shanghai, and Tientsin, in the foreign concessions gained by Europeans in the "unequal" treaties and exempt from local law (extraterritoriality).[14] While he recognized, particularly in India, Singapore, and Hong Kong, the practical improvements that European colonialism brought with it, including dredged harbors, railroads, and public sanitation, Grant was revolted by its racist arrogance and by the exploitation of Asians, particularly the opium trade imposed on China to change an unfavorable (to Britain) balance of trade in tea and take the burden of funding India off the British taxpayer.

Grant's reaction to what he saw from Bombay (Mumbai) to Yokohama was reflected in his comments to John Russell Young as they traveled along the China coast about the "most unjust" Mexican War. "The wickedness was not in the way our soldiers conducted it, but in the conduct of our government in declaring war," Grant said. The United States "had no claim on Mexico. Texas had no claim beyond the Nueces River, and yet we pushed on to the Rio Grande and crossed it. I am always ashamed of my country when I think of that invasion." Grant saw the same manufactured "grievances" in the Europeans' seizure of territory in Asia. "There is no investigation more unprofitable than this inquiry into the causes of the invasion of Eastern powers by the Western. The causes are the same. The Western powers want territory and glory, military and naval opportunities, and the rest comes." He was not against the acquisition of territory by the United States or any other power, but forty years before Woodrow Wilson's Fourteen Points and creation of the League of Nations mandate system, he believed that territorial changes should only take place "by the free will of the people. I would not fire a gun to annex territory. I consider it too great a privilege to belong to the United States for us to go around gunning for new territories."[15] Grant's attitude was a new one for the governments of Siam, China, and Japan. They were used to European powers that believed, as Young wrote of China, that "the only way of dealing with that government was to hammer and hammer, and always to hammer" to force Peking to accept western demands. "But the General had not come to China in a hammering mood."[16] Although out of office, Grant was the first western head of state to visit these countries, and he came to listen more than to talk. That alone confounded all their previous experience with western diplomacy.

The other reason that Grant received such a warm welcome from monarchs and ministers in Bangkok, Peking (Beijing), and Tokyo was that his hosts valued what he and his country had achieved from 1861 to 1865. But unlike the working people of Britain, what these leaders admired in the victory of the Union was not the triumph of republican values but the success of the United States in deterring European interference in the Civil War and emerging from that war an acknowledged, if embryonic, great power. Both China and Japan had recently fought civil wars of their own, and their governments still faced formidable challenges to central authority from local forces opposed to modernization and westernization. Unlike the United States, they had been unsuccessful at preventing European interference in their internal affairs. If Grant knew, as they supposed he must, the secret to American success, they wanted him to share it. And once he returned home and, they hoped, reentered the White House, they wanted him to speak for the equality of nations and revision of the unequal treaties. In Siam, China, and Japan, "[t]he welcome given to General Grant was something more than a personal tribute. It was an appeal to the friendship and generosity of the American government."[17]

The private citizen who left Philadelphia in 1877 returned home in 1879 as an experienced diplomat, having given a face and a voice to the United States around the world. Like Benjamin Franklin in France a century before, Grant projected a combination of confidence in the future, congeniality toward his fellow man, and commitment to the cause of republican democracy. Unlike Franklin, he did not represent thirteen disparate colonies aspiring to be a country, but that country itself at its century mark. Franklin's diplomacy had been based on the potential power and influence of the United States; Grant's was rooted in the demonstrated power and influence of his country. Because he did not win a third presidential term, his activities on the world stage have unjustly faded far into the background of his other services to the republic. They deserve recognition for the impact they had on the definition and practice of American foreign policy, and that of other countries, not only in the late nineteenth century but to the present day. Earlier than most people, and at the time perhaps uniquely among the world's political leaders, Grant saw the approaching twentieth century begin to take shape and understood the meaning of what was happening.

Given his prescience in recognizing the changing nature of warfare in the industrial age, it is no surprise that Grant was equally adept at recognizing the changing world order in which he traveled and the impact of the revolutions in connectivity, mobility, and firepower on all aspects of international relations, not only the waging of war. A special ambassador in every way except formal title, he brought to American foreign policy the practice of public diplomacy and summitry and a commitment to self-determination that became its hallmark in the twentieth century. Indeed, the acceptance of all three became universal, so commonplace in the discourse and practice of nations that it is difficult to recapture a moment when that was not the case. There was a time, however, when Ulysses Grant, circumnavigating the globe with his wife, a son, and a few friends, was required on his own to articulate their meaning and put them into practice. This is the story of how he did so.

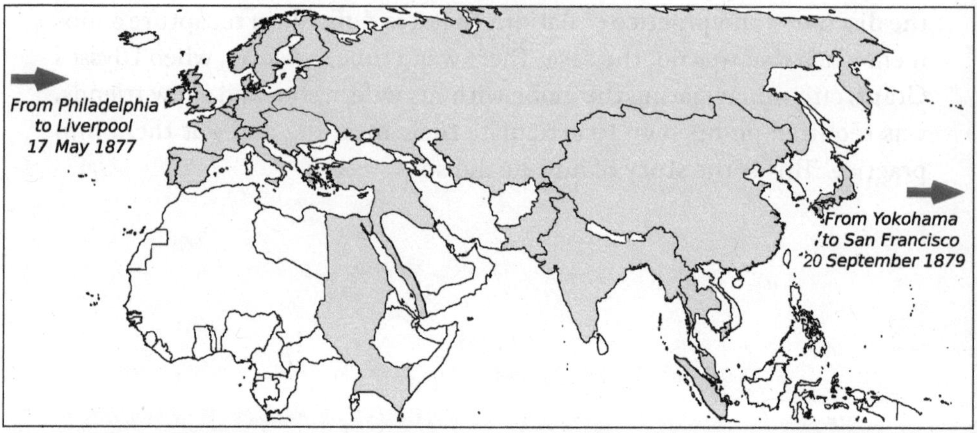

Overview of Grant's travels, May 17, 1877–September 20, 1879. Leaving Philadelphia in May 1877, Grant returned to San Francisco in September 1879, after visiting nearly every country north of the equator (*visited countries shaded*) and meeting with national leaders from London to Tokyo. Grant was the first American president that most of those leaders had ever seen, and in their discussions with him, they hoped to gain insight into the growing international presence of Americans and to assess the likely impact on their countries of the postbellum United States.

CHAPTER ONE

Europe Welcomes America's "Tyneside Skipper": 1877

On May 23, 1877, Secretary of State William M. Evarts sent the following message "to the Diplomatic & Consular Officers of the United States":

> General Ulysses S. Grant, the late President of the United States, sailed from Philadelphia on the 17th instant, for Liverpool. The route and extent of his travels, as well as the duration of his sojourn abroad, were alike undetermined at the time of his departure, the object of his journey being to secure a few months of rest and recreation after sixteen years of unremitting and devoted labour in the military and civil service of his country.
>
> The enthusiastic manifestations of popular regard and esteem for General Grant, shown by the people in all parts of the country that he has visited since his retirement from official life and attending his every appearance in public from the day of that retirement up to the moment of his departure for Europe, indicate beyond question the high place he holds in the grateful affections of his countrymen.
>
> Sharing in the largest measure this general public sentiment, and at the same time expressing the wishes of the President, I desire to invite the aid of the Diplomatic and Consular Officers of the Government to make his journey a pleasant one, should he visit their posts. I feel already assured that you will find patriotic pleasure in anticipating the wishes of the Department by showing him that attention and consideration which is due from every officer of the Government to a citizen of the Republic so signally distinguished both in official service and personal renown.[1]

Evarts's message was addressed to all US diplomatic and consular posts, not just those in Europe, indicating, as he explicitly stated, that Grant's stay abroad might be a lengthy one involving a wide swath of the globe. Its tone

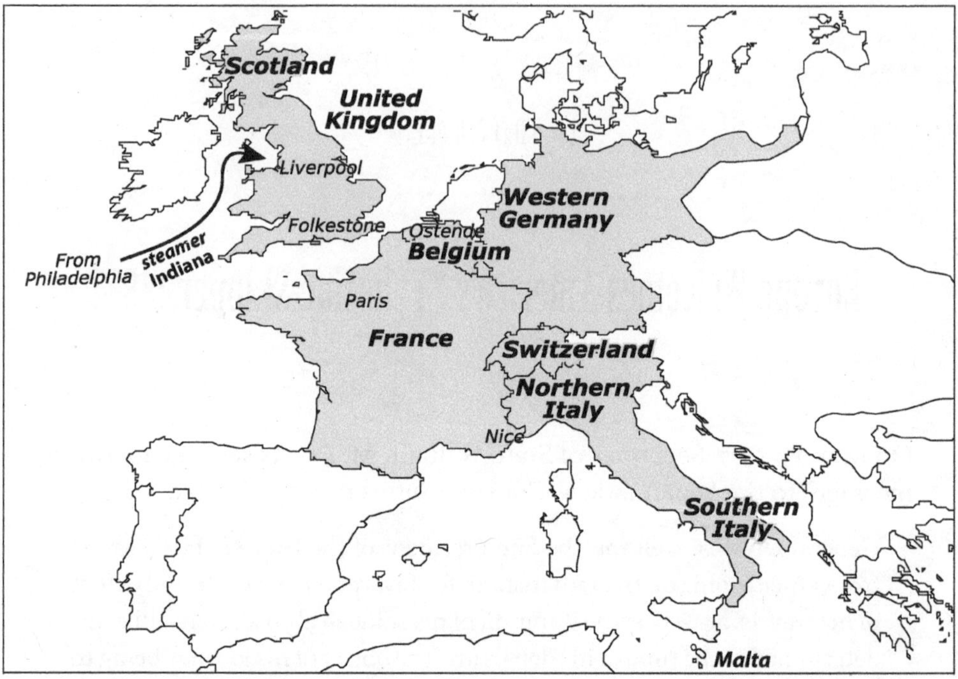

Western Europe, May 28–December 13, 1877. In his first few months abroad, Grant was greeted by enthusiastic crowds throughout England; toured Scotland, Belgium, the Rhine Valley, and the Black Forest; and visited Geneva and the Swiss and Italian Alps. He spent several weeks in Paris before departing for the south of France on December 1.

was not exactly directive, but it transmitted "the wishes of the President." Any minister or consul who missed its point would have failed "in anticipating the wishes of the Department," which, in that case, the implication is clear, might be made more explicit. The message identified Grant as the former president, but in its reference to his sixteen years of service, it emphasized the totality of his contributions to the country. The sending of the message reflected some concern on the part of the Hayes administration that not all American diplomats and consuls would exert themselves to welcome Grant, and as events were to show, that concern was not ill-placed.

Evarts's circular message was part of a flurry of correspondence with which the US government prepared the ground for Grant's stay abroad. On May 22 Evarts issued special passports to Ulysses, Julia, and Jesse Grant. Evarts's predecessor, Grant's secretary of state Hamilton Fish, had gone to Philadelphia to see the Grants off. He wrote to Evarts on May 19 that Grant had not procured a passport before leaving for Europe, "and suggesting that in view of the disturbed condition of affair[s] there [Russia had declared war on the Ottoman Empire on April 24], it may be necessary for him to have one." Evarts concurred. He wrote to Fish on May 26 that the passports were being forwarded to Grant in London, "with a copy of [the May 23] circular letter addressed to our Diplomatic and Consular Officers abroad." President Hayes had telegraphed Grant on his departure with "heartiest wishes that you and Mrs. Grant may have a prosperous voyage, and after a happy visit abroad, a safe return to your friends and Country." And as the Grants arrived in Liverpool on May 28, Secretary of the Navy Richard Thompson wrote to inform the former president "of the instructions given by the Department to the Commanders of the European, Asiatic, and North Pacific Squadrons to facilitate and make pleasant [Grant's] travels when appearing upon the waters embraced within their respective commands." Grant replied from London on June 17, that it was "most probable that I will avail myself of [the offer] this coming winter while visiting ports upon the Medeteranien [*sic*]."[2] Even more than Evarts's message, which might be interpreted as simple courtesy to the immediate past chief executive, Thompson's instructions indicated that the United States government saw foreign policy implications in Grant's stay abroad.

In the time it took Thompson's May 28 letter to reach Grant, the first press reports arriving in the United States from Britain confirmed that such expectations were well-founded. From the moment of his arrival in Liverpool, Grant was feted by the British public and government. He wrote to George Childs from London on June 6, 1877, of

> my surprise to find nearly all the shipping in port decorated to the last flag, and from the Mainmast of each ship the flag of the Union was most conspicuous. The docks were lined with as many of the population as could find standing room, and the streets to the hotel where it was understood my party would stop, were packed. . . . Pressing invitations were sent from most of the cities in the kingdom to have me visit them. . . . The same hearty welcome was shown at each place, and as you have no doubt seen, the press of the country has been exceedingly kind and courtious [*sic*] in its comments.

Grant was better prepared to play the diplomatic role that these attentions required of him than most Americans realized. During the Civil War he had recognized that the United States' military and diplomatic efforts were symbiotic, an understanding sadly lacking in many Union commanders, to the despair of President Lincoln and Secretary of State William Seward. And during his eight years in the White House, in a close working relationship and eventual personal friendship with Secretary of State Fish, Grant had developed an understanding of international issues that would only deepen as he traveled abroad. The 1871 Treaty of Washington providing for arbitration of the CSS *Alabama* claims had given expression to two of Grant's principal concerns, Anglo-American rapprochement and the peaceful settlement of disputes. In his letter to Childs, he reiterated his "desire to see all jealousy between England and the United States abated, and all sores healed up. Together they are more powerful for the spread of Commerce and civilization than all others combined, and can do more to remove cause of Wars by creating mutual interests that would be so much disturbed by war, than all other nations."[3] Nevertheless, Grant was no starry-eyed Anglophile, and his conviction that world peace could best be served by Anglo-American cooperation would be sorely tested when he encountered British colonialism in Asia.

His immediate role in Britain, however, was to allow himself to be lionized at private and public events throughout the country. In the industrial cities of the Midlands and the North, Grant was hugely popular as the "tanner from Galena" who had risen to the White House, and as a consistent advocate of free labor whose military victories and presidential policies had advanced that cause. In Manchester on May 30, Mayor Abel Heywood told him that "it had been his grateful duty to welcome the captain of the George Griswold relief ship, which had come from the United States laden with provisions for Lancashire during the Cotton Famine." Grant replied that "he was very well aware during the war . . . of the sentiments of the great mass of the people of Manchester . . . with regard to the struggle in which it fell to my lot to take a humble part." His "countrymen," Grant said, had "a feeling of friendship towards the people of Manchester, distinct and separate from that which they feel for all the rest of England."[4] The Manchester speech was a surprise to most Americans and Britons, since Grant's taciturnity was legendary in the English-speaking world, and he often made self-deprecating references to that reputation in his first few months abroad. In the years of his public fame since Fort Donelson fell in February 1862, Grant had not chosen to be a speechmaker, but in Manchester he recognized that had to change. Taciturnity overseas would not reflect on him, but on the United States. To be an effective practitioner of American public diplomacy, Grant had to give speeches, and so he did. His eloquence in Manchester showed his ability, with no staff support and almost always speaking without notes, to make well-chosen remarks tailored to the occasion. As Jesse Grant remembered, his father "at times became almost loquacious" while traveling abroad. He "carried on with unflagging interest, sustained, I know, by the conviction that he was making friends for his country."[5]

The other important aspect of the Manchester speech was that it reflected the distinction that Grant drew, in playing his public diplomacy role, between those who had genuinely supported the Union at a moment when its survival was in doubt and those who became friends of the United States only after it was clear that the Confederacy would fail. Grant never lost sight of who was who, and he often found subtle ways to draw the distinction without overtly offending his hosts. Indeed, he was so skilled at doing this that the British media and political elite seemed convinced that he was enthralled by all things English. In his speeches and meetings he sought to promote and cement Anglo-American amity, a process begun with the 1871 Treaty of Washington, in which the two countries agreed to binding arbitration of their decade-long dispute over the British role in building ships for the Confederacy. But personally, Grant knew full well what his interlocutors had said and done from 1861 to 1865 to support or thwart a Union victory. When hosted by those who had stood by the United States, as he was in Manchester, he found a way to express his appreciation, but in a way that could not possibly be taken as criticism of the United Kingdom. Grant's job overseas was to cement good relations between the governments hosting him and the United States, not to express his personal opinions, and he did that job as skillfully as any lifelong diplomat could have done, indeed, with greater skill than most.

Three days after disembarking at Liverpool, Grant arrived in London on May 31, and for more than a month maintained a schedule rivaling that of any modern president or secretary of state traveling overseas. Among his hosts were Queen Victoria, Prime Minister Benjamin Disraeli, the Prince of Wales (the future Edward VII), and the Duke of Wellington, the son of the victor of Waterloo. When not being hosted by the British, Grant attended functions given in his honor in London by US minister Edwards Pierrepont, Adam Badeau, and *New York Herald* journalist John Russell Young, who was based at the newspaper's Paris office. Over the next two years Young would spend more time in Grant's company than anyone except Julia Grant. At these and other venues, the former president met virtually every member of Britain's governing, business, and media elites, most of them on numerous occasions. One of the most important events took place on June 15, when he received the freedom of the City of London at a banquet at the Guildhall.

The chamberlain of the City, Benjamin Scott, welcomed Grant with the analogy that succeeding generations of British and American leaders often used to describe the Anglo-American relationship. According to Scott, it was one between parent and child, the latter having shown "a spirit of independence of parental restraint not unbecoming in grown-up sons of the Anglo-Saxon stock" that resulted in the American Revolution. But now "both children and parent [had] forgotten old differences and forgiven old wrongs," and "the children continue[d] to revere the mother country, while she [was] not wanting in maternal pride" in her American offspring. It was a cliché more flattering to the British ego than to the American one, since children, even grown ones, were products of their upbringing and owed a debt to their parents; it implied that the United States, in some ways, remained part of the British Empire. Scott captured the significance of Grant's presence in Britain; had he used modern terminology, he might have called the former president's meetings and engagements with the queen and prime minister the first Anglo-American summit—or as close as one could get to one. While, as Scott noted, "the unprecedented facilities of modern travel . . . have brought to our shores . . . rulers of empires both ancient and of recent creation[,] . . . we have not as yet received a President of the United States of America—a power great, flourishing, and free, but so youthful that it celebrated only last year its first centennial." Because "[a] visit from the ruling [American] President . . . is scarcely to be looked for, so highly valued are his services at home during his limited term of office," Scott asked Grant to "bear with us, . . . if we make much of an ex-President of the great Republic of the New World visiting the old home of his fathers."[6]

But what type of welcome was due to Grant? Although he had been a head of state and government, he was no longer. At the commemoration in 1888 of what would have been Grant's sixty-sixth birthday, Edwards Pierrepont recounted his efforts to assure a proper reception for the former president. Pierrepont, on his first visit to Britain in 1853, had witnessed the discourteous treatment of former president Martin Van Buren.[7] At a state dinner at Lord Clarendon's, "Not a man stepped forward to receive Mr. Van Buren with respect; they rather looked as though they wondered how he came there. When they went to dinner, he was put at the foot of the table. When he went out, he had to be the last to leave the room." And "[t]hree nights after that . . . the same thing occurred again" at a dinner hosted by Lord Derby. In 1877, Derby's heir had become foreign minister, and Pierrepont called, unofficially, on this Lord Derby to discuss how the British government planned to treat Grant. He asked if Britain was "going to see [Grant] as the representative of a Nation with whom you are in the closest relations, and whose relations are growing more and more important every year—or whether you are going to see him as a nobody." Derby replied that Grant's status was up to the United States: "[Y]ou know here everything is governed by rank. . . . You give him no title, and there is no precedent for giving him precedence without it."[8]

But Pierrepont believed he had a precedent, although one unlikely to please Ulysses Grant: Napoleon III. He told Derby that "[w]hen Louis Napoleon, the ex-Emperor [came to Britain]—he was an Emperor by the vote of the people, the same as General Grant was President by a vote of a much more powerful people—you treated Louis Napoleon as an ex-sovereign." He asked for equal treatment for Grant, and at Derby's request, put his case in writing to Prime Minister Disraeli and the cabinet. According to Pierrepont, with the support of Derby, Disraeli, and especially the Prince of Wales, and with the reluctant acquiescence of ambassadors accredited to the Court of St. James, who under the protocol regime adopted by the 1815 Congress of Vienna had precedence over all but sitting and former sovereigns, Grant was "treated as an ex-ruler of a great country, and [had] all the attention which the most sensitive American can desire." Because Britain had accorded him such treatment, "in every country he went to afterwards, [Grant] was treated in the same way."[9] In fact, this was not the case. The British government's treatment of Grant east of Suez differed from what it had been in Britain itself, and many of the countries he visited, particularly Siam, China, and Japan, did not model their reception of him on British practice.

Nevertheless, when the American minister went to the Foreign Office, the question of how to treat Grant once he landed on British soil was an immediate issue that the government needed to resolve. In pointing out to Derby the growing importance to London of its relationship with Washington, Pierrepont was only telling the foreign minister something he knew very well already. Diplomatic negotiations often consist of one side offering to the other a formulation that will enable it to shift its position on an issue *if it wishes to do so*, without acknowledging its underlying motives. Derby would have been fully justified in insisting on what he initially told Pierrepont, that it was up to the American government to give Grant a title that would establish his precedence; but he did not insist on it. The British government had lawyers perfectly capable of finding reasons to reject the comparison with Napoleon III, had Derby and Disraeli instructed them to do so; but they did not. In the wake of its dalliance with the Confederacy, with fresh memories of the bellicosity of the US Senate with regard to the CSS *Alabama* claims,[10] and with steamships and the transatlantic telegraph linking Britain ever more closely with the United States, London had no interest in offending American elite and public opinion by snubbing Ulysses Grant.

On the contrary, Britain had an interest in establishing the nature of what would in the future be called the "special relationship" before Grant traveled to the continent and was received by other countries with claims on the friendship of the United States: France, with Louis Napoleon gone, reasserting its role as the ally that had made possible American independence; Germany now united under Prussian leadership, a supporter of the Union, and whose emigrants to the United States had been the largest foreign-born portion of Grant's armies; and Russia, another friend of the Union cause and Britain's rival for control of central Asia, with its armies on the move to Constantinople. As the British government expected they would, all of these countries received Grant in a way designed to create a favorable impression in Washington, as did, in 1879, Siam, China, and Japan, their assertiveness in hosting the former president perhaps more of a shock to London. It was not Pierrepont's indignation or ingenuity that led to Grant being treated differently than Martin Van Buren, but the growing importance to London of good Anglo-American relations. The government cultivated American opinion by accepting Pierrepont's comparison and welcoming the former president as it knew Americans wished to see him welcomed.

Washington and London had a common interest in seeing that Grant's visit received favorable press coverage in both countries. The sincerity with which Britons welcomed him varied, however. On one end of the social and economic scale, what members of the British aristocracy wrote in their diaries and letters was often not what they said in public when they knew their words would make their way across the Atlantic. William Gladstone's diary entry was relatively benign, if stereotypical: Grant "fulfills his ideal as a taciturn, self-possessed, not discourteous, substantial kind of man. Mrs. Grant kind but alas 'dowdy.'" Queen Victoria also had unflattering things to say privately about both Julia and Jesse Grant after an unpleasant incident at Windsor Castle (unknown to the public at the time) when the Grants and Adam Badeau spent a night there in June 1877. But perhaps the clearest contrast between the government's public reception of Grant and its private comments about him was in the diary of the foreign minister himself. Derby described Grant as "certainly the roughest specimen we have yet had from the west. Any one who had seen him today [at Windsor] would have said that his manners & intelligence were about on a par with those of a bulldog."[11] In contrast, what working-class Britons said in public reflected their sincere admiration for Grant's accomplishments. They rightly saw him as a subversive figure; dine though he did with royalty and peers, he embodied the end of hereditary aristocratic government in the Anglo-Saxon world and the opening of a new meritocratic age.

This was never more clearly demonstrated than on the day that Grant received a delegation of British working men and was later honored at a dinner given by the United Services Institute, the military society founded by the first Duke of Wellington.[12] Henry Broadhurst of the Labour Representation League had asked Grant in a June 16 letter "to receive a deputation from the Working men of London" who had been "foremost in promoting the large meetings held . . . during the American War, and which did such good service in preventing this country taking the part of the Southern States." Grant agreed, and on July 3, "a deputation of forty men . . . representing altogether about one million English workingmen" expressed to him "the gratitude of a liberty loving people" who "looked upon your successes as our success." They would never forget "[t]he noble generosity of your countrymen, in the midst of their life and death struggle, in sending food to the starving operatives of Lancashire," and they lauded one of Grant's accomplishments as president of which he was most proud, "the reasonable and just settlement" through arbitration of the CSS *Alabama* claims, "a settlement which we feel convinced is destined to exercise a civilizing and lasting influence on International Relations." They eloquently expressed the universal significance of the Union's victory:

> It was not difficult for us to understand that although the scene of conflict was confined to the American States, its results would affect the whole world; the interests of the entire Human family, of whatever colour or race, were at stake; it not only gave freedom to the slave, and consolidated the power of a great nation, but it enobled labour of all countries, and broadened the liberties of the free.[13]

Some members of Britain's hereditary governing class who read the *Times* and *Daily Telegraph* reports of the delegation's meeting with Grant over their breakfast on July 4 were no doubt thoughtful enough to reflect on the "esteem and admiration" the men felt for the American leader. If they did, the address's implications for their class's control of the country and empire must have given them pause. Grant's reply was equally ominous for the future of inherited political power. A week after his visit to Windsor Castle and hours before he dined with aristocratic military officers, he told the delegation that "whatever there is of greatness in the United States, or indeed in any other country, is due to the . . . labourer who is the author of all greatness and wealth, and without whom there would be no governing, no leading classes, nor anything worth the trouble of preserving. . . . We [Americans] recognise that . . . whatever a man's occupation, he is eligible for any post in the gift of the people, his calling being left out of consideration when it is a question of electing him as a law maker or an executor of the law."[14] In the privacy of his diary, Lord Derby might take comfort in comparing Grant's manners and intelligence to those of a bulldog; had that been true, he and working men like him would have been less of a threat to the hold on power of men of Derby's class.

But whether the welcome that Grant received throughout Britain was sincere or not did not matter to the success of Anglo-American public diplomacy, which both sides conducted with subtle skill. Transatlantic press coverage was overwhelmingly positive and had the desired effect on American public and elite opinion. Victoria's invitation to the Grants to stay at Windsor Castle was particularly flattering to Americans, and provoked an immediately favorable reaction from the encampment of the Grand Army of the Republic in Providence, Rhode Island. On June 26 the governor of Pennsylvania, John Hartranft, telegraphed Grant that "[y]our comrades in National Encampment . . . send heartiest greetings to their old commander and desire through England's Queen to thank England for Grant's reception."[15] This good feeling was exactly what both London and Washington desired. The former president had written on June 17 to his son Ulysses Jr. (Buck) of the "most enthusiastic receptions" accorded to him throughout Britain. He elaborated in a June 22 letter to Hamilton Fish on the "invitations from all authorities connected with the Govt. from the Queen down to the Mayors and City Councils of almost every city in the United Kingdom," as well as "the hearty responces [*sic*] of the citizens of all the cities I have visited, or at which trains upon which I have been traveling have stoped [*sic*] even for a few minuest [*sic*]." Grant understood the mix of policy and sincerity among his British hosts:

> Many persons say to me quietly that they were our good friends in the day of our countries [*sic*] trial but they witness now many who were the reverse then that outdo their neighbors in respect and kindness of feeling for us now. Of course I know this is so, but . . . I believe now the real feeling of the majority is that it i[s] much better that the result should have been in favo[r] of the Union.[16]

As Pierrepont reported to Secretary of State Evarts, "These courtesies [the Guildhall reception and visit to Windsor], as well as those of the Prince of Wales and of the Queen's Ministers of State were intended as friendly compliments to our Country and have their uses."[17]

Grant's first stay in Britain ended on July 5, 1877, when he departed by ferry for Ostende, Belgium. In seeing him off, the mayor of Folkestone, John Sherwood, wished Britain and the United States "increased amity and prosperity," expressing the hope that commerce would be "the means of firmly cementing the friendly ties that exist between the Old Country and the New." Sherwood referred approvingly to the CSS *Alabama* arbitration, and in reply Grant reiterated "a feeling of mine of many years' standing, that the United States and Great Britain should be the very best of friends." But despite all the references, including his own, over the previous weeks to Britain and America as mother and daughter, parent and child, he also made clear that the equality of the two countries was the necessary basis of their friendship. He had pursued the *Alabama* arbitration, he said, because he had "no desire . . . that England should be humiliated in any sense, and there was certainly a determination on our part that we should not be humiliated, but we wanted a settlement that should be honourable to both nations."[18] The sentence was a fine example of Grant's mastery of diplomatic language. On the surface, it was a gracious response to a municipal official bidding him a temporary farewell; but it sent a message to the British government that Grant's policy of negotiation and arbitration had been one of strength, not weakness. As he traveled beyond Europe, to Egypt, India, and the Far East, the former president encountered many countries seeking to extricate themselves from humiliations inflicted on them by the United Kingdom. He came to realize that the success of the United States was for them the example of how to do so.

Grant sailed to Ostende, and not to one of the French channel ports, because of the political situation in France. His original intent had been to go directly from London to Paris, but a major crisis had broken out in the French capital on May 16, the day before the Grants departed Philadelphia. Crises were nothing new to Elihu Washburne, whom President Grant had named minister to the Second Empire in 1869. Little more than a year later, in September 1870, Prussian-German forces defeated Napoleon III's armies at Sedan and captured the emperor. While Leon Gambetta proclaimed a Government of National Defense and continued the war from Tours and Bordeaux, German forces besieged Paris, and in January 1871 the Prussian king was crowned Wilhelm I, emperor of the Second Reich, in the Hall of Mirrors at Versailles. Marxist-anarchist revolutionaries opposed to both monarchy and republic staged an insurrection in the capital in March, and the Paris Commune survived until put down in the "bloody week" of May 1871 by forces under the command of Marshal Patrick MacMahon. Through it all, Washburne stayed in Paris, where he was responsible for the repatriation of German nationals, as well as the safety of American citizens. The United States legation had been asked to represent German interests in France during the war.[19]

Washburne wrote as regularly as he could to President Grant and Secretary of State Fish about the startling events that, in a few short months, deprived France of its status as the great power of continental Europe. The Franco-Prussian War ended with the May 1871 Treaty of Frankfurt, but until he returned home in 1877, Washburne dealt with French leaders settling historic scores and divided among themselves on the question of which political institutions the country needed to deal with its new geostrategic situation. For four years, France seemed likely to restore the descendants of Louis XVI, as it had in 1815, to a post-Napoleonic throne. But with their intransigence toward maintaining the tricolor, the republican flag, monarchists lost their final opportunity to rule France again. Gambetta's republicans and the royalist Marshal MacMahon joined forces in 1875 to adopt the constitution of the Third Republic, with MacMahon as its president. The issue of France's future government was not yet settled, however. MacMahon dismissed the legislature and government on May 16, 1877, and seemed set to stage a coup against the republic that, if successful, might yet result in a reestablished monarchy.[20] As the May 16 crisis dragged on into the summer of 1877, the US minister became convinced that Grant must not come to Paris until it was resolved.

For three weeks in June, Washburne sent letters across the Channel to Grant, Pierrepont, and Badeau to keep them abreast of French political developments. In response to the idea that Grant visit Paris briefly in early July en route to Switzerland, Washburne told Badeau on June 9 that "I have very serious doubts whether it will be policy for him to come at the time you mention, and only to stay three or four days." There was in Paris an atmosphere of "intense political excitement, unfavorable to official and social festivities and attentions." Washburne counseled delaying Grant's visit until the fall, when he "hope[d] the present extraordinary crisis will be over, and if it should terminate in bringing in a Republican ministry, the reception of the General will be vastly more cordial than it will be now." The next day, June 10, the minister wrote directly to Grant that he had "conferred with many of our friends on the subject and they all confirm what I wrote [yesterday], and even more strongly," that no official visit to Paris should take place before the fall. But a week later, the fluid French political situation caused him to think that a brief, unofficial, summer visit might be possible. On June 18, he wrote to Grant that "a good time to come" would be "after the 4th of July," and "it should be understood that you are here briefly *en passant* and that it would be unwise to receive any demonstrations and to keep as quiet as possible." Ominously, though, in the same letter, he described the state of French politics:

> I hardly dare to speak out all I think in regard to the situation here, and I do not write anything to be quoted. I was at the chamber [of deputies] on Saturday and it seems to me that the scenes enacted there can but be the prelude of the most fearful events in France. No man not present can have an idea of the violence, the madness, and the ruffianism of the opposition to the Republicans. . . . The assembly is certain to be dissolved and for their demands the country be convulsed by the most terrible excitement. The new election must be within three months from the date of the dissolution.[21]

The idea of a short, private stay in Paris from July 5 to 9, during which the Grants would see no one but Americans from the legation, a "programme of quiet dinners," as Badeau called it, survived until the end of June. But on June 30, Washburne followed his own analysis to its logical conclusion. He sent a letter to Grant in London, hand-carried by the US consul general in Paris, Alfred Torbert, "who will explain to you the object of it more fully than I can do in writing." Washburne told Grant that

> it will be unwise for you to come to Paris at present even *in transitu*. Though we have never spoken of your coming, it has been announced in the Paris journals that you are to be here next week. It will be impossible for you to come here in anywise *incognito* and without having a demonstration, no matter how short a time you may stay. When it becomes known that you are here, and if you do not call on the President, the Republican papers will say it is because you are not in sympathy with his *Coup d'Etat*, and if you do call upon him the reactionary papers will claim that it is to signify your approval of his action. . . . [E]ach party will want to play you off on the other, and there is danger of much embarrassment following, and the effect of your visit at a later day will be much impaired.

Washburne expressed his disappointment that, if the Grants did not come to Paris before fall, he and his wife would not be there to receive them; "but knowing the situation of things, I should be unjust to you, as well as to the country which is so much interested in all that concerns your reception abroad, did I not speak frankly." By autumn, he "hope[d] the [French] political situation . . . will be greatly ameliorated," and "you will have a reception worthy of you and our country." The issue—"such a hitch about Paris," in Pierrepont's words—made its way into the British press. The *Times* (London) reported on July 7 that Washburne had advised Grant to delay his visit to France because, "there was a fear th[at] ex-President Grant would be played off against P[re]sident MacMahon."[22] Grant personified American republicanism and nationalism, and because of this, as in Britain, it was not possible for him to be a private tourist in Paris. This turned out to be true in many of the countries he visited in the next two years.

Briefly, though, having skirted the pitfalls of French politics with Washburne's guidance, Grant enjoyed a respite from the pace of his spring diplomacy. For a few weeks in the summer of 1877, he and his family had the opportunity to sightsee in parts of Europe where his presence had less political significance than it did in Britain and France. They toured Ghent and Brussels, dined with the Belgian royal family, and spent time with Henry Sanford and his wife, "charming Americans living in Brussels," as Julia Grant called them, but much more than that. During the Civil War, Sanford had run a surveillance operation of Confederate military procurement efforts in France and Britain, and he was later active in promoting American interest in the economic opportunities of the Belgian Congo.[23] From Brussels, the Grants went to Cologne, then up the Rhine to Bingen,

Wiesbaden, and Frankfurt, Germany. In Cologne, they missed Grenville Dodge and his family by a day, but Dodge wrote to Grant to "express my great satisfaction at the hearty and spontaneous reception you have received on this side of the 'Atlantic.'" Grant's travels were "bringing about a far better understanding between our country and these nations and cementing more solidly and lastingly their friendships." Dodge had been in France, and he told the former president, "[Y]ou did a very judicious thing in delaying your visit to Paris until the present political excitement is over."[24]

The Grants visited Heidelberg, where they met Richard Wagner, then traveled to Lucerne, Interlaken, Bern, and Geneva, Switzerland, where Grant laid the cornerstone of the American community's new church. They crossed the Simplon Pass and toured the lakes of northern Italy before returning to Britain in late August via Basel, Switzerland; Strasbourg and Metz, both part of Germany since 1871; and Antwerp, Belgium. After touring Scotland and parts of England they had not yet seen, including Stratford-upon-Avon, they spent the first two weeks of October visiting friends and their daughter, Ellen (Nellie), at her home on the south coast.[25] But despite the private visits, once the former president was back in England, tourism took a back seat to public diplomacy. Wherever he went, Grant was greeted, as he had been in the spring, by local dignitaries and crowds of people eager to see him. The enthusiasm at his public appearances in Birmingham and Newcastle upon Tyne was, if anything, greater than it had been in Manchester in May.

Birmingham was represented in Parliament by two of Britain's most influential Liberal politicians, one long famous, John Bright, and one at the beginning of his career, Joseph Chamberlain. Bright, "the foremost British champion of the Union," had never faltered in his support for the United States. His eloquently expressed opposition to British recognition of the Confederacy did not single-handedly prevent it, but it was one factor that kept the possibility at bay long enough for Grant's and George Meade's 1863 victories at Vicksburg and Gettysburg to tip the scales in favor of American minister Charles Francis Adams's diplomatic efforts in London.[26] Bright had met Grant in London earlier in the year, but could not be in Birmingham for his visit. He wrote his constituents that he knew they would "give to General Grant a reception which will show how much Birmingham has been in sympathy with himself and his country." The city did. Mayor George Baker and his predecessor, Chamberlain, welcomed Grant on October 16. The former president told Bright's constituents that he was happy to be in "a city that was so well-known in my country during the trying periods [of the cotton famine] that have been referred to by your worthy Mayor." He drew the same distinction he had in Manchester, praising the "warm feeling of fellowship between our citizens and the citizens of Birmingham" who stood by the Union from 1861 to 1865, even "when the feeling was not good between the United States and all parts of Great Britain." He was pleased that now "the feeling between the citizens of the United States and the citizens of this great Empire is good, is increasing, and is what it should be." As for Bright, "The name of your distinguished representative . . . is as familiar in my own country as in his own home."[27]

On the same day, Grant received a delegation representing Birmingham's working men. He thanked them for "the compliments you have paid to me for the efforts I have made in the cause of freedom and the North," and again spoke of the importance of free labor, as he had in July in London and in September in Newcastle. "I expressed [on the two earlier occasions] what I thought was due to the workingmen, not only of my country and of Great Britain, but to the workingmen all over the world. I said that we in our country strove to make labor respectable." Grant knew that the expansion of the franchise was a hot political issue in Britain in the 1870s, but he continued that, in the United States, "[t]here is no class of labor that disqualifies a man from any position, either in society or in official life."[28] Statements like these made his public appearances a sensation with average people. On the Tyneside, Jesse Grant recalled, "[E]nthusiasm for father was almost beyond belief." The crowd at Newcastle was estimated at eighty thousand, "workmen from all trades and thousands of pitmen from the mines of Northumberland," all of whom came to hear Grant speak of "the great question of freedom, of the rights of man, and the dignity and honor of labor." Grant's physical appearance was a crowd-pleaser. One newspaper described him as "'[l]ooking like an ordinary Tyneside skipper, open-browed, firm-faced, bluff, honest, and unassuming, everybody at once settled in his own mind that the General would do.'" When his father read the description, Jesse remembered, it "amused him greatly, but did not please mother so much."[29]

The former president's words about free labor and social and political opportunity touched on an issue of immediate domestic significance in Britain, but Grant delivered an equally important speech in Birmingham on the same busy day of October 16, when he addressed the Midlands International Arbitration Union about the peaceful settlement of international disputes. Grant thought a lot about war and the necessity to avoid it. He abhorred the slaughter of humans and animals, and he regarded war as a waste of the resources of a country that would otherwise be devoted to enhancing the prosperity of its citizens. As he traveled, he developed this theme in his speeches, linking it to education and free labor. Education made possible the skilled worker and informed citizen who, when needed, could be called upon by his country as a citizen-soldier. But his country should do all in its power not to call on him to make war. National prosperity, like individual prosperity, depended on the worker being able to devote his time to his trade; countries with large standing armies wasted the most productive years of their most productive citizens. At the time the most famous and successful military officer in the world, Grant often startled his more military-minded hosts, notably those in Berlin and Vienna, with such sentiments.

In Birmingham, the members of the Arbitration Union, honoring Grant for his commitment to peaceful settlement, were no doubt pleased, but not startled, when he told them that, "It has been my misfortune to be engaged in more battles than any other general on the other side of the Atlantic; but there was never a time during my command when I would not have gladly chosen some settlement by reason rather than by the sword." He wanted to "see the millions of men who are now [under arms] . . . return to industrial pursuits, and thus become self-sustaining, and take off the tax upon labor which is now levied for their support." This reply was responsive to the sentiments expressed by his hosts, but Grant went further, and in doing so, perhaps he did startle his audience. It is unlikely that they expected a victorious general and president, even one no longer holding office, to express sentiments that would not be heard again, with equal conviction, from another American chief executive until 1918. Grant did not desire only future ad hoc or even standing arbitration agreements between Britain and the United States but also "some sort of congress, which shall take cognizance of international questions of difficulty, and whose decisions will be as binding as the decision of our Supreme Court is binding on us. It is a dream of mine that some such solution may be found for all questions of difficulty that may arise between different nations."[30] Without diplomatic instructions, briefing memoranda, or talking points, when Grant described the need for a future universal "league of nations," it was because his own observations of the changing relationship of national governments to each other and to their own citizens had convinced him of its necessity. In a late nineteenth century dominated and enamored by the *Machtpolitik* of the Great Powers—"blood and iron"—Grant recognized where this would likely lead, and he tried in his conversations with world leaders to deflect them and their countries from that path.

The former president finally left Britain for his long-delayed visit to France in late October. Fortunately for Grant's diplomacy, although his plans had been affected by the Third Republic's political minefields, he no longer had to conceal his personal feelings about the Bonapartes. As a West Point cadet, Grant had been no admirer of Napoleon, who could have had peace but kept Europe at war for twenty years; but his lack of admiration for the first emperor was nothing compared to Grant's hatred of his nephew. It was bad enough that the popularly elected president Louis Napoleon had proclaimed himself emperor, suppressed freedom of expression, and dallied with the Confederacy. But worst of all, he had taken advantage of the Civil War to install the Austrian archduke, Maximilian, on the newly created throne of Mexico, flaunting the Monroe Doctrine and suppressing the republic of Benito Juarez. As Grant made clear in his conversations with John Russell Young while abroad, and later in his memoirs, after his own early service in the Mexican War, he felt very strongly about injustice practiced by other countries, including his own, on Mexico and Mexicans. Napoleon III's incursion not only posed practical problems for Grant as commanding general of the US Army and secretary of war in the 1860s, it offended him deeply. "In regard to Napoleonism," Young wrote, "though General Grant had never written a poem on the same subject, he entirely agreed with Victor Hugo."[31]

Spending over a month in the French capital, Grant saw a lot of the city, but in contrast to his public appearances in Britain, comparatively little of the French. For one thing, France's politics were still unsettled. For another, as Grant wrote to his son Buck on October 27, "I intend to have a more quiet time than when in England"; but "more quiet" was a relative term. Grant had fewer engagements than in Britain, and with a smaller circle of French political leaders and foreigners resident in the capital, but he was kept busy enough until he departed on December 1 for Nice. Washburne was gone, so Grant was received in Paris by the new American minister, Edward Noyes, who had arrived in the city only a few weeks before. There was no attempt to keep the French public from knowing about Grant's arrival. On the contrary, Noyes, US consul general Torbert, and a representative of President MacMahon boarded the former president's train outside the city and accompanied him into Paris, where a crowd was waiting at the station. Julia Grant was given two bouquets of violets tied with tricolor ribbons, which she later wrote "were very sweet, but I felt somewhat conspicuous with the ribbons."[32] In modern terms, this was a "photo opportunity," in which the former first lady of the United States was seen carrying the revolutionary republican colors that monarchists had refused to accept as the French flag.

In this sensitive political climate, the American legation took care with Grant's engagements. Demonstrating again that he was no ordinary tourist, his first call on October 25 was at the Elysee Palace, to pay his respects to President MacMahon. This professional soldier, like most of his continental counterparts, assumed that Grant shared his interests, "and offered him every facility for examining the military establishments in Paris and the Provinces." In his travels, Grant received many such invitations from his hosts, frequently from reigning monarchs who were both head of state and commander of their armed forces. When diplomatic courtesy required, he reviewed troops and visited military installations, but when free to exercise his own inclinations, Grant declined, as he did with MacMahon. Instead, the former president took time to walk the streets of Paris with John Russell Young. "I know the city 'like a native,'" Grant wrote to Adolph Borie on November 19.[33] He had the privacy to do so, for two reasons: his name was well-known in France, but his face was not; and even more importantly, to continental eyes, Grant looked not at all like a military officer. It was simply inconceivable that the man paying his own streetcar fare had been a general and a head of state.

Nevertheless, Grant had plenty of what diplomats call "representational" functions on his calendar while in the French capital. The Grants' first invitation to dine was with President MacMahon's family, and on November 6, they were the guests at a banquet given by the US minister and the American residents of Paris. On November 22, Grant wrote to his daughter, Nellie, that he had "accepted invitations for every evening but two up to the close of the month." That evening, the Grants were invited by the Talleyrands to "our first dinner," as Grant told Nellie, "with—exclusively—French people, since we have been here, except the dinner immediately after our arrival, given by the President, at which his Cabinet was present." Grant told Adolph Borie on November 19, "I have not seen much of the French people so far, no doubt because of the troubled condition of affairs. But every thing has been pleasant. . . . [F]inding from the press that I was the instrument of attacking—or through whom to attack—others, I have kept as much as possible with foreigners—to France—mostly Americans."[34] What this meant was that invitations to the Grants were almost exclusively extended by foreigners resident in the capital; but American diplomats had a hand in seeing that these supposedly purely social events took place, and that the appropriate French politicians were invited to them. On November 17, Robert Hitt, secretary of the legation, confirmed that the US minister had arranged Grant's engagements for the next ten days:

> General Noyes on yesterday, calling at Mrs. Sickles house, arranged with her that her dinner to you and Mrs. Grant should be on *Saturday, the 24th*; and subsequently at the house of Mr. Emile de Girardin who desired to give you a dinner, arranged that it should be on the *27th Tuesday*. Mr. Girardin, who is the leading editor of Paris (La France), and has been recognised for 20 years as one of the ablest friends of Republicanism, will invite Mr. Gambetta and several other leading Republicans to meet you. . . . The Girardin dinner is for *gentlemen* only. We now understand your engagements to be for the 17th (tonight), Monday, 19, afternoon at M. Meniers, then dinners on the 20th MacKays, 22nd Talleyrands, 23rd Laugels, 24th Sickles, and 27th Girardins.[35]

The legation did its job well; the dinners enabled Grant to meet and talk with all the leading players on the French political scene without attracting a great deal of press coverage or arousing hostility from any one particular political faction.

At the Girardin dinner, the former president met Leon Gambetta for the first time. Grant already knew a good deal about him from Washburne's admiring reports during the Franco-Prussian War. Gambetta had formed the Government of National Defense that continued to resist the Germans after the defeat of Napoleon III at Sedan; and for months, he was "all there [was] of the government of France," despite which he was "full of pluck and courage" and "the most superhuman energy." Seven years later, John Russell Young reported that "the French republican leader . . . impressed the General as one of the foremost minds in Europe."[36] At the Laugels' dinner, Grant met the Comte de Paris, the oldest grandson of Louis Philippe, who had lived in exile while Napoleon III was in power, served on George McClellan's staff during the Peninsular Campaign, and written a history of the Civil War. Elizabeth Bates Laugel, whose French journalist husband had covered the war in its last months, and was now Paris correspondent of *The Nation,* described Grant's meeting with the count in a May 1878 letter to Elihu Washburne:

> It was the first time I had ever seen the General, as I was not with my husband when he stayed with General Grant at his camp before Richmond. I need not tell you how much we all liked him and how much we were impressed by the dignity and perfect simplicity of his manner. . . . The General was most interesting and by no means silent, for he told many most curious things of his own experiences during the war and after; . . . he and the Comte de Paris had a very long conversation to which all listened with very great pleasure.[37]

Before he departed Paris on December 1, Grant paid a visit that responded to a French initiative that he had followed for the last six years of his presidency. In 1871, President Grant had received the French sculptor, Frederic Auguste Bartholdi, who had been asked, in an inspired moment of post-Napoleonic French public diplomacy, to design a statue as a gift from the people of France to the people of the United States. Bartholdi approached the president about locating that statue on Bedloe's Island, at the entrance to New York harbor. Five years later, the first completed section of his "Liberty Enlightening the World," the right arm holding a torch, was exhibited at the International Centennial Exposition in Philadelphia, opened by President Grant on May 10, 1876. In one of his last acts as president, on March 3, 1877, Grant signed a joint resolution of Congress authorizing the president to accept Bartholdi's statue and to select a site for it. Rutherford B. Hayes, in one of his first acts as president, selected the site recommended, Bedloe's Island. Eight months later, Grant visited Bartholdi's atelier outside Paris on November 20 and observed "with great interest the work now in progress." He wrote the next day to Edouard Laboulaye, president of the Committee of the Franco-American Union, whose idea it had been to present the statue to the United States, that "[t]he Statue of Liberty promises to be in every way worthy of its purpose and will fitly express the friendship of the two nations."[38]

This was diplomatic language appreciative of Laboulaye's goal, to celebrate the 1778 Franco-American alliance that had made possible the independence of the United States; but it was also a genuine expression of Grant's new regard for the French. Before coming to Paris, his attitude had largely been shaped by Napoleon III's support for the Confederacy and invasion of Mexico, and, to a lesser extent, by the pro-German bias of the reporting he received from George Bancroft, US minister in Berlin during the Franco-Prussian War. But as Grant wrote from Nice on December 10 to his old friend Daniel Ammen, "My opinion of their capacity for self-government has materially changed since seeing for myself. Before coming here I did not believe the French people capable of self-government. Now I believe them perfectly capable, and they will be satisfied with nothing less. They are patient 'and of long suffering,' but there will not be entire peace and quiet until a form of government is established in which all the people have a full voice. It will be more republican than anything they have yet had under the name of a republic."[39] Grant would return to Paris often in 1878. When he left for the final time in January 1879, it was with a far higher regard for the French and the future of their republic than he had had two years before.

Ulysses Grant never saw the completed Statue of Liberty. It arrived in New York City in June 1885, in crated pieces, just as Grant, dying of throat cancer, departed the city for the Drexel cottage on Mount McGregor, near Saratoga, New York. The former president died there on July 23, 1885. On August 11, three days after Grant's funeral in New York City, Joseph Pulitzer announced that his *New York World*'s fund-raising campaign had raised the $100,000 necessary to pay for the base of the statue.[40] The Statue of Liberty was reassembled and dedicated on Bedloe's Island on October 28, 1886, thirteen miles down the Hudson River from the final resting place of the president whose life had made it possible, in more ways than one, for liberty to enlighten the world.

CHAPTER TWO

On the Mediterranean with the US Navy: 1877–78

The second phase of Ulysses Grant's travels began on December 13, 1877, when he took up the invitation of Secretary of the Navy Richard Thompson and boarded USS *Vandalia* at Nice to visit Egypt and the eastern Mediterranean. It is difficult to capture, in a century accustomed to the sight of Air Force One around the world, what an unprecedented situation this was for all concerned. Outside American waters the US Navy was used to hosting foreign dignitaries and American diplomats, but not its commander in chief. Grant was no longer that, but he had been until nine months before, and as his host at the Guildhall had observed, President Hayes was not going to turn up in Europe. In 1877, Grant was as close as the European squadron was going to get to welcoming aboard a US president.

Not everyone was thrilled by the prospect of the former president venturing beyond Britain and France. Since the United States had not been a major player in European politics, the duties of American diplomats in Europe had not been onerous; many of them wrote books and traveled in a circle of aristocrats and intellectuals who did not share Grant's attitude toward the value of labor. In 1878, some of them, notably the American minister in Rome, made clear to the State Department that they regarded Grant's travels as an unwelcome intrusion on their time. They missed the point that his presence, first in Europe and then in South Asia and the Far East, was a sign of things to come. The communications and steam technologies that made his trip possible, and gave it a public diplomacy significance it could not have had in an earlier era, were about to deprive both diplomats and naval officers of their ability to operate "over the horizon," independent of instructions from their home departments that came too late or not at all. At the same time the United States was no longer the

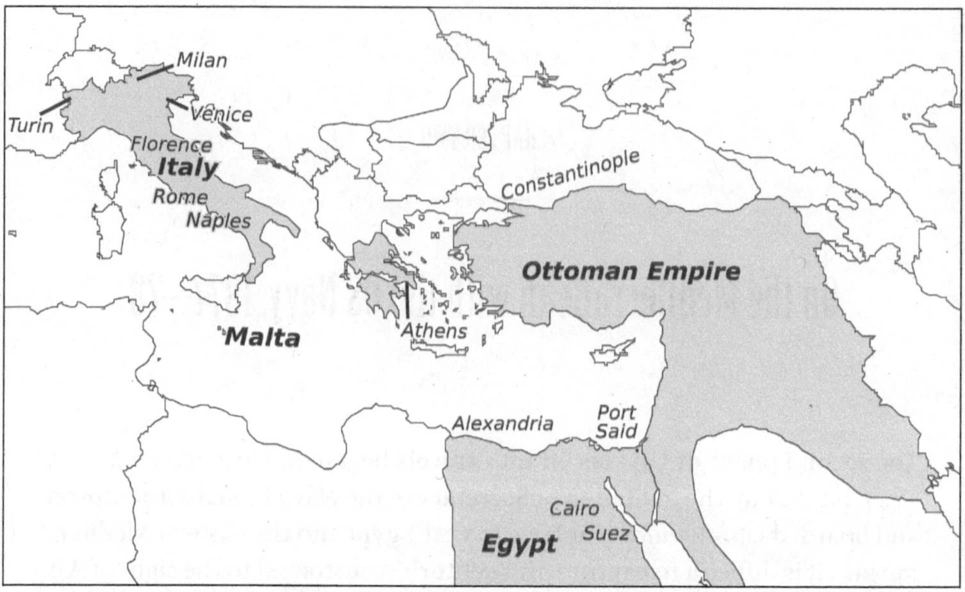

The Mediterranean, December 13, 1877–May 7, 1878. On December 13, Grant embarked on USS *Vandalia* for a three-month visit to the eastern Mediterranean, including southern Italy, Malta, Egypt, the Holy Land, Constantinople, and Athens. Disembarking at Naples on March 18, 1878, Grant spent several weeks in Italy before returning to Paris in early May.

country they had represented before the Civil War; it had begun to matter in the political calculations of the European powers, and European governments' interest in hosting Grant reflected that changed role.

But all of this was yet to become clear in December 1877, as Ulysses, Julia, and Jesse Grant, accompanied by John Russell Young, sailed from Nice on *Vandalia*. "The United States government had placed this beautiful ship at General Grant's disposal," Julia Grant remembered. "This was a great honor, and we appreciated it."[1] But Secretary Thompson's order was more than an honor; it was foreign policy. The Hayes administration's decision to have an American president, even if no longer in office, appear aboard an American warship in waters dominated by vessels of the European powers was an inspired stroke of diplomacy, if initially unwelcome to the officers of *Vandalia* herself. Lieutenant Commander Albert Gallatin Caldwell made no secret in letters to his family in Indiana that he did not welcome the prospect of having Grant on board. "We are to take the great ring-master about the mediterranean [*sic*]," he wrote home on November 30, 1877. "[I]t has cost me much annoyance and trouble already and I[']m in hopes that his money will give out before . . . we are to pick him up." Caldwell was frankly disgusted by what he regarded as a junket and a waste of his and the Navy's time. He hoped for "heavy gales . . . & then he will leave for good & all. We have a lot of his wine aboard & Govt has ordered certain expenses to be paid—(it comes out of contingent fund)."[2]

Three weeks later, the Grants had been on board for a week. In a December 20 letter Caldwell painted a picture of them for the folks back home that showed he had an open mind and an observant eye:

> Genl Grant is bluff & hearty weighs about 180 lbs—looks grim & does not talk when strangers are about but is quite chatty with us on board—I think he is a very capable man—bright & witty when he wants to be but diffident as a young girl in company & silent as a post before the world—is full of stories about the Mexican war & men of the times—some of his remarks are very terse & epigrammatical. Mrs Grant is about the height of Mama—not of graceful or Sylph like figure—must weigh as much as the Genl: has a pleasant motherly face—expects a good deal of attention—is not well up in history & geography—very cross-eyed: always kind & pleasant. Jesse is a good deal like his father—quiet but desires to be a swell—has been much flattered but on the whole is a nice young fellow—smart enough—always gentlemanly & gives no trouble. . . . Mr Young is a brick full of fun—just like a boy off for a holiday which indeed it is to him. I like him very much—is a Philadelphian by birth—lives in New York—5 ft 8 high—blue eyes brown hair an open countenance—red English whiskers—is full of information & is the confidant & personal friend of the Genl.

The Grants were equally pleased, even before they sailed, with their uniformed traveling companions. Grant wrote to Commodore Ammen from Nice on December 10 that "[w]e breakfasted the other day with Admiral [William] Le Roy [commander of the European squadron], and saw all of the officers then in port here. They seem to be a nice set of youngsters."[3] For the first couple of weeks, all of them were effectively on holiday together. Grant's first official function was at Malta, where he was welcomed by the British governor on December 28, 1877. Until then, it was the Christmas season, and *Vandalia* visited Genoa, Naples, and Sicily; from Naples, the Grants and the officers made a side trip to Pompeii.

Julia Grant was especially popular. Famously a one-man woman in her lifelong devotion to her husband, she was also an antebellum Southern belle who enjoyed the attentions of young naval officers. The former first lady was flirtatious, not fickle, and this served her well as she traveled the world in the company of men. She had particularly fond memories of Christmas Day in Palermo:

> The wardroom officers . . . gave a dinner . . . and were kind enough to say it was in my honor. They were always kind. This dinner is a very pleasant memory to me. The menu could not have been better, and the dinner was well-served by their waiters, who wore white canvas jackets and black silk scarfs [*sic*]. . . . You were very good, dear gentlemen and brave sailors, and I will never forget this, nor any of your kind attentions to me and mine!

The friendly familiarity established between the ship's officers and the Grants in the first two weeks of the voyage was captured in the former first lady's recollections of how she was teased one evening:

> The sea was calm, and we sat on deck watching the coming twilight, when two or three of the young officers came hurrying up to me and said, "Mrs. Grant, hasten and get out your cotton wool. We are nearing the Island of Calypso. Remember the fate of Ulysses of old. Take warning and bring out the cotton wool and fill the General's ears at once." "Oh," I said, "My Ulysses has no music in his soul. And am I not with him? Do you suppose that I, after such a lesson from dear old Penelope, would remain at home? No, indeed! I defy all outside enchantments." And so the fabled island was passed in safety.[4]

If anyone was enchanted, it was the officers of the US Navy, notably Lieutenant Commander Caldwell. He wrote home on January 10, 1878, that "my whole opinion of old USG has changed wonderfully—he is as pleasant & jolly as can be & I can see now how he had friends who stuck to him through thick & thin." As for the former First Lady, "One thing that makes me like the whole party is the affection existing between them all—the Boss and Jesse are as kind & attentive to the mother as if she were a sweet girl of 18 summers—she must have been a good mother & wife to have held on to their affection so strongly through all the temptations of their high life & that too against odds for she is very cross eyed."[5] But it was not only the officers who had taken a shine to the Grants. Jesse Grant overheard a conversation between two sailors, one of whom had apparently had enough of foreign dignitaries arrayed in their finery and was indignant on the former president's behalf. "[T]he old man," he said, "should get out his togs and show these foreigners what real medals [look] like." But his shipmate disagreed: "The old man's got enough decorations and medals . . . to load a ship. He don't need to wear 'em. He's just like me. These damn little kings make him sick!"[6]

Vandalia's route as she conducted her, in modern terminology, presence mission in the eastern Mediterranean, took her to Malta, Egypt, Ottoman Syria (the Holy Land), Smyrna (Izmir), Constantinople (Istanbul), Athens, and back to Naples, where she arrived on March 18, 1878. For the former president, until he arrived in Athens in early March, the trip was a mixture of summitry and tourism. Literacy was not widespread in the region, and public opinion was not a factor in shaping government policy. On Malta, the purpose of Grant's diplomacy was not to build a relationship with the people of the island, but to reinforce the importance of Anglo-American friendship by accepting the hospitality of the British governor. Victoria's second son, the Duke of Edinburgh, and his wife, the daughter of Alexander II of Russia, were visiting at the same time, and there were dinners, an opera excursion, and a twenty-one-gun salute. *Vandalia*'s officers were included in the governor's invitations, and Lieutenant Commander Caldwell reported home that he "met a crowd of distinguished people but had a slow stiff dinner."[7]

Vandalia arrived in Alexandria on January 5, 1878. Egypt was the first country on Grant's itinerary that had a cultural and religious heritage unfamiliar to him and the vast majority of Americans and Europeans. What most of them knew (or thought they knew) came from the Bible and from historical novels about sheiks and harems that painted a romantic picture of life but had very little to do with the reality of the Ottoman and Muslim world in the late nineteenth century.[8] Grant's party spent three days in Alexandria before leaving for Cairo in the private railcar of the Ottoman viceroy (khedive) Ismail Pasha on January 8. The former president's first impressions of the nonwestern world were not flattering. He wrote to his son Buck on January 7 of the "[i]nnate uglyness [*sic*], slovenlyness [*sic*], filth and indolence," and commented that "[a]ll the romance given to Oriental splendor in novels and guide books is disipated [*sic*] by witnessing the real thing." But after nearly a week in Cairo, where the Grants stayed in one of Ismail Pasha's palaces, and a trip up the Nile on the khedive's steamer, Grant had moved beyond his initial reaction and was fascinated by Egypt and its history. He displayed the diplomatic skills he had honed in Britain and France at a dinner hosted by US consul general Elbert Farman on January 10, declaring that he would leave Egypt "with recollections as pleasant as those—yes, second to none, he said—from countries he had already visited."[9] At that point, Grant had seen very little of Egypt, but he pleased Ismail Pasha, and sent a message to the leaders of Europe, by comparing the khedive's hospitality to that of his hosts at Windsor Castle and the Elysee Palace.

Grant's visit gave his Egyptian hosts the opportunity to send their own message to the European powers. For Egypt, how the United States had maintained its independence and freedom of action in a European-designed and dominated international system was of vital interest. The khedive, through the building of the Suez Canal, a series of wars, and a lavish lifestyle, owed money to European creditors that Egypt was unable to repay. In collusion with corrupt or overwhelmed local elites, European powers encouraged such indebtedness. It gave them an excuse for military interventions in which their technological superiority would almost inevitably prevail, and defeat meant the cession of territory and payment of indemnities that robbed a country, at least, of its independence of action and often of its existence. The khedive admired Grant's military career, but his visitor's personal history was not in and of itself relevant to Egypt's policy aims. What was relevant was that Grant clearly mattered to the current American president. After all, as Egyptian leaders could observe, the warships and diplomatic representatives of the United States were at his disposal. As the Hayes administration used Grant's travels to establish an American presence on the international stage, his hosts in Egypt (and eventually Siam, China, and Japan) used their reception of him to do the same. If they could attract American attention through press and diplomatic accounts of the welcome they accorded Grant, they might find an anticolonial ally in Washington. What Grant first encountered in Egypt was much on his mind a year later when he discussed with the leaders of Siam, China, and Japan, ways to avoid the vicious cycle of the loss of tariff and customs autonomy, extraterritoriality, and indebtedness that served European interests, but not their own.

For a month, Grant was an enthusiastic tourist in Egypt. He wrote to his son Buck on January 25 that "Egypt has interested me more than any other portion of my travels." He was fascinated by "ruins that have been standing—as ruins—some of them, for many ages before the beginning of the Christian era." To his son, Fred, Grant described "the ancient Egyptian [as] a cultivated man, but governed—sole [*sic*] and body—by a ruler," because, "[w]ithout a thorough command of all the strength, muscle and mind of the inhabitants such structures [as the pyramids] could never have been built." Ten days later, he was still pondering the nature of ancient Egypt when he wrote on February 4 to Adam Badeau that "[o]ne is kept in constant wonder how any people could have [mo]ved such immense blocks, in such large numbers, for so great a distance as most of them ha[d] to be moved, and put them in their places."[10] The historical paradox both fascinated and repelled Grant: an accomplished civilization ruled by an educated elite that found nothing unusual in its accomplishments being dependent on forced labor and slavery.

Ancient Egypt had ended in ruins, and in the late nineteenth century, both the Ottoman and Chinese Empires were on a ruinous path because of dynasties ill-adapted to their contemporary domestic and foreign-policy challenges, attempting to maintain their historic grandiosity by procuring loans they could not hope to repay. In the same letter to Fred in which he had commented on ancient Egypt, Grant told his son, "I wish Egypt was free from debt and the iron heal [*sic*] of her creditors." Nearly two months later, he was still thinking about the issue when he wrote to General William T. Sherman from Rome on March 21 that "things are different with [Ismail Pasha] from what they were when you were in Egypt [in 1872]." His "debts, public and private, have accumulated to such an extent that the resources of the state cannot possibly meet the interest." The debt was "mostly held in England and the English Govt. have appointed agents—with big salaries paid out of the resources of Egypt—to collect and pay out all the revenues to bond holders. This leaves nothing for the Khedive to use in payment of current expenses of Govt."[11] Eighteen months after Grant's visit, Britain and France deposed Ismail Pasha, installing his brother in his place, and in 1882 Britain occupied Egypt. While still *de jure* part of the Ottoman Empire until its defeat in World War I, the country belonged *de facto* to the British Empire, "subject to military occupation and overall political and economic control."[12]

The former president had begun his visit to Egypt by having "a long conversation upon African matters" with John Russell Young's "renowned friend and colleague" Henry Stanley, "fresh from the African wilderness," who was passing through Cairo en route home to New York. At the end of his stay, Grant transited the Suez Canal, south to north, aboard a "special boat" provided by the khedive from Suez to Port Said, and dined in Ismailia with Ferdinand de Lesseps.[13] Rejoining *Vandalia* at Port Said on February 9, Grant's party spent the next five weeks with the ship as she made port calls in the eastern Mediterranean. From Jaffa, the Grants and some of *Vandalia*'s officers visited Jerusalem and Bethlehem from February 11 to 17, in some of the worst winter weather the area had ever seen, with "snow six inches deep in Jerusalem." They wanted "to go like any other pilgrim to the Holy Land and Jerusalem," but the local Turkish governor and the US consul, Joseph Willson, had arranged a fanfare, a "great show," with the "consuls of all nations . . . with their flags and pennants," and a military escort, "with silver helmets, bearing their flags and mounted on fine horses." Jesse Grant recalled his father saying, "I didn't want to parade into Jerusalem, Julia," but he was required to do so.[14] While there, Grant dined with the local governor and met with a relief committee distributing aid to Jewish American citizens living in the city.

When *Vandalia* rendezvoused in Smyrna on February 22, with USS *Trenton,* flagship of the Mediterranean Squadron, Grant was welcomed by the American consul, E. J. Smithers, who approached the ship "in a lavishly decorated barge that looked less like a real boat than a floating circus band wagon." He wore a "glittering uniform" that Jesse Grant described as "a creation in blue, faced with red and covered with gold braid; on his head was a sort of helmet surmounted by two enormous plumes, and at his side, clanking and jangling against festoons of chain, swung a sword in a golden scabbard." At this sight, Jesse wrote of his father, "I understood by his utter absence of expression that he was as amazed as I." Aboard *Vandalia,* Smithers hastened to explain to Grant that European diplomats and consuls all wore uniforms; he was the only one in Smyrna with no uniform and no decorations. As a result, he was seen as "a person of no importance" and got "scant respect" from Ottoman officials. Knowing that Congress would have no sympathy for his plight, Smithers had designed a uniform for himself "that outshone that of any Eastern potentate," and he began to award himself fictional decorations. From then on he "took first place among the consuls." Jesse remembered that "Father was laughing when the consul reached this part of his explanation." The tale was not finished, though. Whenever Smithers awarded himself a fictional decoration, local officials awarded him a real one, and "he had no choice but to continue. Any diminution of his glitter would arouse suspicion that he had fallen into disfavor with his government." Grant's arrival had posed a particular problem for the consul because "he had no choice but to greet father wearing everything he had. To have done less would have reflected upon father."[15]

For more than two months since boarding *Vandalia*, although he had been hosted by the British governor on Malta and Ismail Pasha in Cairo, and called on local officials with Admiral Le Roy in Smyrna, the former president had principally been a tourist. The Grants had visited the sites of the ancient world that Julia Grant, especially, had long wanted to see: Pompeii, the Nile Valley, Jerusalem and Bethlehem, Ephesus and the Temple of Diana. This respite came to an end in Constantinople where, from March 1 to 6, Grant was the guest of the Ottoman sultan, Abdul Hamid II. "The city," he wrote to Edward Beale, "is very quiet, but in government circles one discovers a deep gloom. The Russians are but a few miles out side of the city and can come in when they please. But as terms have been signed [the March 3 Treaty of San Stefano] and the Russian minister to Turkey is now in this city, they may abstain from coming in altogether." Grant, who knew well the situation of a capital fearing encirclement by an enemy army (Washington from 1861 to 1863) and a capital under siege (Richmond in 1864–65), was interested in the behavior of both officials and the public. He was struck by the phlegmatic reaction of the city's population to the presence of the Russians, writing to his brother-in-law, Michael Cramer, the US charge d'affaires in Copenhagen, that "[a] stranger would not detect from appearances that an enemy was so near." From Athens on March 9 he told Alfred Torbert that Ottoman officials were "very gloomy, but the appearance of a successful foe immediately outside the gates of the city did not seem to effect [*sic*] the population generally." Nevertheless, "the sight is wretched enough." Grant wrote:

> In a small portion of the city is stored away in the Mosques and public buildings probably more than a hundred thousand refugees . . . who have fled to the Capitol before a conquering Army. They are fed entirely by charity and mostly by foreigners. . . . Beside these many tens of thousands have been shipped to places in Asia Minor and turned loose upon the inhabitants.[16]

Grant was still thinking about the future of the Ottoman Empire when he wrote to General Sherman from Rome on March 21, that

> [t]he effects of the war have no doubt materially changed the high official[s] of the Govt. and saddened them very much. But in going through the city you could not discover from the manner of the people that anything unusual had taken place, although there was an invading army within

> eight miles of the city, and nothing to keep them out, and all the Mosques filled with refugees—probably not less than fifty thousand of them—being fed by charity.

Grant's assessment of the Ottoman future was pessimistic and prophetic. He told Sherman that "[t]he state is bankrupt without the costs of a disastrous war being added to former indebtedness. Except they pay in real estate and disappear from the Continent of Europe, the Archipelago (islands of) and some of Asia Minor, or Syria, it seems to me their creditors will go unpaid." And to Daniel Ammen four days later, despite his fascination with ancient Egypt, Grant expressed his negative reaction to the societies he had visited from Alexandria to Constantinople:

> [I]n the East they have a form of government and a civilization that will always repress progress and development. . . . The people would be industrious if they had encouragement, but they are treated as slaves, and all they produce is taken from them for the benefit of the governing classes and to maintain them in a luxurious and licentious life.

He was especially troubled that women were "degraded even beneath a slave. They have no more rights than the brute. In fact, the donkey is their superior in privileges."[17]

Despite his personal views, Grant understood that his diplomatic role was as a guest of the Ottoman government, not a participant in the events absorbing its officials. He had three occasions to play that role during his stay in Constantinople. The first came after a visit to the sultan's stable of Arabian thoroughbreds. Lieutenant Commander Caldwell was with him, and he wrote home that "Grant was more interested than I've ever seen him before—would go back & look again at horses & ask opinions about them—got quite enthusiastic over them." Caldwell noted that "Sultan gave Genl Grant one but I think he will not receive him," and he was right; Grant initially declined to accept the gift of one of Abdul Hamid II's horses, offered through an intermediary. But later, as he wrote to Edward Beale, at a dinner with members of the Ottoman Cabinet, "I was told that the Sultan would think hard of it if I should decline to receive the horse, and that he would be sent to Marseilles for me." Grant relented. He asked Beale, if the stallion should be sent, to take him in charge, reflecting that "it may be of some value to breeders in the United States to get some of this [pure Arabian] blood, and if so I will be amply repaid."[18]

The second occasion involved an exchange between Ottoman military leaders and their American counterparts that was a precursor to the "mil-mil" diplomacy routinely practiced by US armed forces with allied and partner militaries since the mid-twentieth century. In his March 21 letter to Sherman, Grant told him that he had been asked by the sultan's adviser and naval minister, Said Pasha, "to furnish him with a list of the studies at the [US] Military and Naval Academies. I promised him that I would do so, and would send him a complete copy of all the text books." Grant asked Sherman "to ask the Sec. of War and Sec. of the Navy if they will not furnish a complete copy . . . of these books," and if that were not possible, he asked Sherman to buy the books and send the bill to his son Buck in New York City. "I am sorry to put you to this much trouble," he wrote, "but the request was made of me while I was in the palace of the Sultain [*sic*] and I made the promise." Sherman did what Grant asked, writing on April 8 to General John Schofield, superintendent of West Point, enclosing the portion of Grant's letter that requested the books and list of courses for Said Pasha, "a Request that I ask you to comply with." He told Schofield that the books would be paid for with War Department contingency funds and directed him to send them, "carefully and neatly boxed," by express to Said Pasha at the address given in Grant's letter. He also informed Schofield that the secretary of the navy was arranging with Annapolis for shipment of the Naval Academy's curriculum materials and books to Constantinople. On May 29, Said Pasha wrote to Sherman that the materials had arrived, and expressed his "profound gratitude to General Grant for his kindness in requesting you to forward me the above."[19]

Grant's final diplomatic stroke in Constantinople was one of self-denial. The US minister to Turkey, Horace Maynard, reported to Secretary Evarts on March 7 that the former president had been "invited to breakfast with the Grand Duke Nicholas at San Stefano," but had declined the invitation from the Russian commanding general. "I feel a great desire to visit the Russian camp," Grant wrote on March 6 to Edward Beale, "but as the Turks have been very hospitable, and might look upon such a visit with suspicion, I shall refrain." Two weeks later, in a March 22 letter from Rome, he told his son, Fred, that "[t]he Russian army was but eight miles outside and the road entirely open from the city to the Russian camp." Grant had been "anxious to visit their camp, but having received the hospitality of the Turkish officials I doubted the propriety of such a visit and therefore abstained." Julia Grant remembered that, when the invitation came, he said, "I cannot.

It seems so heartless. I have but just now grasped the hand of the Sultan and I cannot step outside the gate and breakfast with his foe." Although the war had ended with the March 3 treaty, and Grant had a legitimate interest in seeing the operational and tactical situation from the Russian perspective, he understood the grand strategic situation and his part in it. He was no military observer, but the former president of the United States, traveling on an American warship and accompanied everywhere by officers of the US Navy. As he had recognized in Britain that he must give speeches, Grant realized in Constantinople that his personal inclination to visit the Russian headquarters must be subordinated to his diplomatic role. Maynard told the secretary of state that "a feeling of delicacy constrained [Grant] to decline" the Russian invitation, and "[t]his forbearance on his part . . . gives great satisfaction to the Ottoman officials."[20]

Vandalia departed Constantinople on March 6 for Piraeus, the port of Athens, where Grant resumed the public diplomacy role he had played in Britain the year before. The young King of the Hellenes, George I (son of the king of Denmark and brother of the future British queen, Alexandra, and Russian tsarina, Maria Feodorovna), had accepted the Greek throne at the age of seventeen in 1863. George's long reign (he was assassinated in 1913) was dominated by the effort to unite ethnic Greeks throughout the Balkans and eastern Mediterranean into one Greek state. Having won its independence from Ottoman rule in 1832 after a decade of fighting, Greece was in high irredentist mode in the late nineteenth century as Constantinople's political and military dominance of the region receded. But despite the king's connections to the British royal family, Greece's grander ambitions were regarded warily by the British government, which did not want the Ottoman Empire weakened to a point where it was no longer a bulwark against Russian expansion into the Mediterranean. Grant arrived in Athens at a critical moment, when the Greeks hoped to profit territorially from the Russian victory over the Ottomans that he had just experienced firsthand. George I and his government took advantage of Grant's visit to wage a public diplomacy campaign designed to impress not only the former president but also American public opinion in order to win support for the country's territorial ambitions, as Greeks in the 1820s had won it for independence. In Athens, as Jesse Grant recalled, the Grants found "the most crowded round of entertainment we had faced in months."[21]

For once, the former president lost the diplomatic equilibrium that otherwise characterized his words and behavior while overseas. Grant came to Athens after two months in a part of the world that fascinated him historically, but the governance of which troubled him deeply. Perhaps for that reason he was susceptible to the efforts of his Greek hosts to win him over as a champion of their political cause. Athens seemed free and open, compared to the "stolidity" of the people and the "sumptuous" lifestyle of the Ottoman leaders he had just left behind in Constantinople. The history of ancient Greece may also have had an effect on Grant. Julia Grant remembered that, for the victor of Appomattox, "[t]he Parthenon and the Acropolis were illuminated . . . a wonderful and beautiful sight." Touring "[t]he great battlefields of Greece . . . including the plain of Marathon," the former first lady and her companions "all consulted our little volumes, the *Iliad* and the *Odyssey*, which had not been read by me since my girl days at the old farm, White Haven."[22] Modern Greece knew how to profit politically from that legacy; the Ottoman Empire had nothing to offer that could compete with the Americans' deeply imbedded cultural "memories" of ancient Greece. It took less than two days for *Vandalia* to clear the Dardanelles and cross the Aegean Sea to Piraeus. The Acropolis was visible from her deck as she lay at anchor, a constant reminder of the western civilization that Grant cherished. To the extent that Greek leaders could convince him that they were the worthy heirs of Pericles, he was predisposed to favor their nation's aspirations.

The government had prepared a "splendid reception" to welcome Grant, as the US charge d'affaires, John Meredith Read, reported to the State Department on March 9: "[L]arge crowds gathered to witness the landing, which took place at the new quay whose marble square was ornamented with arches and banners, while a broad carpet was spread from the water's edge to the spot where the carriages were stationed." Two American vessels greeted *Vandalia*'s arrival, USS *Marion*, based in Piraeus, and Admiral Le Roy's new flagship, USS *Alliance*. As a boat ferried Grant to shore, the three American ships, as well as two Greek vessels, two German ones, an Italian warship, a French one, and a ship of the Royal Navy all "ran up our flag, manned their yards, cheered, and fired a salute of twenty-one guns." The mayor of Piraeus hailed Grant as "a great General and a wise ruler" and expressed the "warmest sentiments of love and gratitude towards the American nation for what it did in behalf of Greece at the time of the struggle for independence in 1821, and for the sympathy which your country has so often and constantly manifested" toward the Greek nation. Before departing for Athens aboard "a special train with a royal carriage attached," Julia Grant was presented, by "the little niece" of the Piraeus station manager, "dressed in the Greek costume," with "a beautiful bouquet composed of violets with thirteen white roses therein referring to the original United States." In Athens, the mayor welcomed Grant with words almost identical to those used in Piraeus, expressing his country's "undying gratitude towards the great American Nation for the aid and sympathy which it copiously granted to her great struggle for independence." John Russell Young wrote wryly that, after his arrival in Greece, "[t]he General is gradually getting over the idea that it is possible for him to travel as a private citizen."[23]

The American charge was enthusiastic about Grant's visit to Greece. Read told the secretary of state that he would "spare no pains to carry out the instructions of the Department by extending every mark of attention and respect in my power to General Grant." The Grants were his houseguests, and Read gave a dinner in Grant's honor, attended by Admiral Le Roy, "a number of navy officers, a large number of Americans, and all the diplomats in Athens." The king and queen hosted "a grand reception" at the palace, and George I, once an officer in the Danish Navy, "lunched with the General and the officers of the *Vandalia*." Read reported to Evarts that "a great crowd is uninterruptedly stationed opposite the Legation in the hopes of catching a glimpse of" the former president. When *Vandalia* departed for Naples on March 14, the arrival scenes of the week before were repeated, including twenty-one gun salutes from "all the ships in the harbor." The king had intended "to accompany General Grant to the railway, but his intentions were frustrated by an accident which fortunately proved to be of no lasting consequence." Instead the foreign minister was at the station where he "took leave of General Grant with words of warmest friendship and respect," to which "General Grant replied in feeling terms." Read described the "constant expressions of respect on the part of the King and the people" shown to the former president: "I have never witnessed a more enthusiastic reception."[24]

Read was a strong partisan of the Greek government's aims. It seems likely that he advised the government on its reception of the former president and influenced Grant's reaction to Greece. In his report to the State Department, Read recommended to Secretary Evarts that "our vigorous country should seek on every occasion to manifest her sympathy for the Hellenic Kingdom," and he obfuscated where his summary of Grant's views ended and his own began. Nevertheless, Read accurately reported that "General Grant was surprised and impressed by the . . . evidence of progress, prosperity, and civilization apparent on all sides. . . . [Grant] felt that . . . the King's slender territories should be increased by important additions, enabling Greece to take the position in the world to which her ancient renown and her modern struggles and triumphs entitle her." The US minister wrote to former secretary of state Fish on March 22 that "General Grant left us last week with great apparent regret for he had formed most agreeable impressions of Greece."[25]

This was true; in public and private, Grant was enthusiastic about the country. The former president wrote to Daniel Ammen from Rome on March 25 that the Greeks "have certainly made wonderful progress. I hope they may have their territory increased as one of the effects of the present [Russo-Turkish] war, so as to give them more Greek population, more space, and a full chance to develop." Fred Grant had visited Greece with General Sherman six years before, and had apparently not been as favorably impressed. Grant wrote to Fred from Rome on March 22, that, "I differ from you in regard to the Greeks. They seem to me to be a very energetic and advancing people. . . . I am inclined to think that if they could regain their former territory, or a good part of it, with the addition of the Greek population this would give them, they would become a very respectable Nation." Grant knew very well who would have to give up this territory. "The Turco-Russian war," he wrote to Fred, "may yet end in this. My visit through the Turkish Empire does not impress me favorably with their power to develope [*sic*] the resources of a country."[26]

Vandalia arrived in Naples on March 18, and the Grants left the ship there. They would not sail on her again, although they were reunited briefly with Commander Henry Robeson and his officers in Gibraltar at the end of the year. Lieutenant Commander Caldwell wrote to his mother from Naples, "I'm sorry Grant is going away. He is chock full of information and good ideas." The feeling was mutual. Grant wrote to Sherman from Rome on March 21 that "[w]ith the Naval Officers of the Vandalia—some of whom accompanied me always when I left the ship—there was no durth [*sic*] of agreeable company at all times." Four days later to Rear Admiral Ammen, he described Lieutenant Commander Caldwell as "a very superior man in education and acquirements, and especially so in all scientific subjects, and professional ones too." *Vandalia*'s "officers, without exception, were agreeable and did all they could to make us feel at home."[27] Grant arrived in Italy a little more than a year after leaving the White House. The "well-deserved rest" to which Secretary Evarts had referred in his May 23,

1877, message had not exactly materialized. There had been very few days, except in the Swiss mountains and along the upper Nile, when the former president had not been required to attend formal dinners, give speeches, and discuss the issues of the day with presidents, prime ministers, queens, kings, khedives, and sultans.

Despite press coverage of his reception in Britain, and the enthusiasm of US diplomats in Paris, Athens, and elsewhere about the positive impact of his visit to their capitals, when Grant disembarked from *Vandalia* in Italy, he arrived in a country where the American minister, George Perkins Marsh, seemed entirely to have missed the point. In part because of Marsh's inability to understand the possibilities inherent in Grant's presence, the Grants' nearly two months in Italy were mainly a family reunion and vacation with their daughter, Nellie. John Russell Young left the former president's party when it arrived in Rome, and Jesse Grant visited the capital with his parents but then left for Paris, rather than travel with them to other Italian cities.[28] After visiting Rome from March 21 to April 14, the Grants and their daughter were in Florence from April 15 to 21, then Venice, Milan, and Turin, before returning to Paris via Dijon on May 7. Although they met Pope Leo XIII and the Italian royal family, it was fortunate that Ulysses and Julia Grant were happy to be with Nellie again and to have time to visit the artistic, historic, and religious sites of Italy, because Marsh had no interest in taking advantage of Grant's diplomatic skills. He regarded the former president as a protocol problem, not a diplomatic asset.

Unlike his American colleagues in the other capitals Grant had visited, who had served under and worked with General and President Grant through more than a decade of war and peace, Marsh had been overseas since 1861. Named by Abraham Lincoln as the United States' first minister to the newly united Kingdom of Italy, he served there until his death in 1882 and was buried in Rome's Protestant cemetery. More than 150 years after his appointment, Marsh's more than two decades as minister to Italy still made him the longest-serving chief of mission at a single diplomatic post in American history. He was the classic example of the pre–Civil War American diplomat, a literary scholar who did not regard it as his job to deal with American merchants, military officers, and citizens abroad—consuls did that—even if one of them was the former president of the United States. Marsh's petulant attitude toward Grant's presence in Italy was a stunning contrast to Pierrepont's efforts to deal with protocol issues before Grant arrived in Britain; to Washburne's recognition of the impact his arrival in Paris would have at a pivotal moment in French history; and to Maynard and Read's understanding of the significance of Grant's visit to, respectively, Constantinople and Athens. Marsh apparently yearned for the good old days when former presidents knew their place.

In a closely written, single-spaced, eight-page dispatch to the secretary of state on April 17, 1878, three days after Grant left Rome for Florence, Marsh gave vent to his feelings. He marked his report "confidential," as he told Evarts in a closing paragraph in his own hand, "in order to avoid the possibility of wounding any susceptibilities." At the same time, "[t]here is however nothing in it which I see cause to conceal."[29] It is hard to imagine that Evarts agreed; the person most likely to be spared embarrassment by keeping the dispatch confidential was the minister himself. In one long sentence that took up the first page of his report, Marsh complained of the situation created, in his opinion, by the man to whom he was writing, with his May 1877 circular letter:

> The peculiar position occupied by General Grant as one who had honorably filled the highest civil and military stations in the service of his country and who now visits Europe under special commendation from the Government of the United States, but who no longer sustains any official relations with that government, nor enjoys any social rank, title or prerogatives beyond such consideration and deference as upon purely moral grounds belong to him, naturally gave rise to questions in regard to the treatment which it was proper he should receive from the representatives of his government in Italy and from the public authorities of the Kingdom during his stay at this capital.

In case Evarts was not sufficiently appreciative of the difficulties he had caused Marsh, the minister intended to tell him:

> Although some of the details into which I must enter may seem too trifling to be made matter of formal communication, I deem it my duty to report, with some fullness, the steps I have taken to comply with the instructions of your circular of May 23, 1877.

And he proceeded to do so in the following seven pages.

In fact, Grant's reception at the Rome railroad station by Marsh, the king's aide de camp, and "several of the principal American citizens resident at Rome" was very much like his reception in other capitals. But Marsh felt he had been put to a good deal of trouble by having to decide how to handle the visit; he had "observed in my despatch No. 743, dated March 5, 1878," that the court was in mourning for the recently deceased king, new embassies were being opened in Rome, and he was involved in "meetings of the diplomatic corps called by the dean of the body for mutual consultation" to discuss "the rights of precedence and other prerogatives of the ambassadors." Marsh told Evarts that

> these discussions were conducted with the utmost courtesy, but it was evident to me that the ex-President's presence in Rome, under the circumstances to which I have above alluded, might give rise to annoying social questions. . . . The embarrassment was increased by the fact that I could cite no precedent for asking for General Grant attentions corresponding to those which he was said to have received in London, for though three ex-Presidents, Mr. Van Buren, Mr. Fillmore, and General Peirce [*sic*] had visited Europe, including Italy, I could not learn that so distinguished honors had been anywhere paid to either [*sic*] of them.

Despite "the character of the attentions paid to the ex-President at London and at Paris," such treatment was not possible in Rome: "The Masters of Ceremonies here were perfectly clear that General Grant could not take precedence of ambassadors, who . . . give place to none but princes of the blood royal, and such princes as, by special order of the Court, are occasionally admitted to the honors of princes of the blood." And "[t]he ambassadors whom I consulted took the same ground." Marsh went on to describe at some length a precedent, "cited as having great weight on this point" by the ambassadors, that involved a visit to St. Petersburg by the German Emperor, Wilhelm I, when he was crown prince of Prussia. But Marsh was not done; there were still more than three pages of complaints remaining in his report.

It is interesting to speculate on the likely astonishment of the secretary of state when Marsh's dispatch arrived in the department on May 4, 1878. For the past year, Evarts had been receiving highly laudatory reports from his diplomats in the other capitals Grant had visited, most recently from Read in Athens. Moreover, John Russell Young's stories in the *New York Herald*, as well as foreign press reports that reached Washington, described the former president's successful diplomatic efforts. Marsh not only failed to understand Grant's meaning to Americans, but he also lacked the imagination and initiative shown by his colleagues in other capitals who took advantage of Grant's presence to expand their legations' contacts with a broader cross-section of local society. Marsh apparently saw his role as dealing solely with the court and with other members of the diplomatic corps, a role disturbed by the arrival of the former president in Rome. His carping comments about Grant's lack of status compared to "princes of the blood royal" were precisely the kind of remarks that led Congress to regard the State Department as an outpost of European aristocracy and to threaten to abolish the entire American diplomatic establishment. Perhaps most astoundingly to Evarts, the minister had approached Grant directly to discuss the protocol issues that troubled him so much. One of them was "the question of precedence at table" if Marsh invited ambassadors to dinner with the former president: "[A]s it was certain that the ambassadors would not yield their claims, I said to General Grant that I must either place ambassadors above him or refrain from asking diplomates [*sic*] of that rank" to dine with him.

If Evarts was surprised to read this, Grant must have been equally amazed to be told such a thing by a man he had had the power to remove from office for eight years. Other US ministers also had to deal with the rigid diplomatic protocol established at Vienna in 1815,[30] but they had the good sense not to reveal to him a greater concern for upholding that protocol than for carrying out the expressed wishes of the American president and secretary of state. Grant's reply to Marsh showed his usual concern for the dignity of the United States: "The ex-President said that personally it was a matter of indifference to him, but perhaps it must be regarded as a matter of principle on which he ought not to compromise, and it was agreed that I should not ask ambassadors to any of the dinners I proposed to give him." Marsh concluded his report by detailing the events he had hosted for Grant during his stay in Rome, as well as other "entertainments" given in Grant's honor, including one hosted by the king and queen "at which the places of honor were given to the General and Mrs. Grant." Marsh did "not know how, under the circumstances, more could have been done for them, and I have reason to believe that our distinguished guests were satisfied with the arrangements made to do them honor."[31]

Unfortunately, Marsh's petulant report to Evarts and his direct discussion with Grant of his lack of protocol precedence were not the only blips on the American diplomatic screen in Italy. US consular officers were as tone deaf as the minister in expressing their easily wounded vanity in inappropriate ways in inappropriate places, and both the former president and Lieutenant Commander Caldwell had depressing encounters with the pomposity and self-absorption of their countrymen. Caldwell's came when *Vandalia* docked in Naples; Grant's was in Florence, a few weeks later. US consul general Charles McMillan was in charge of Grant's visit to Italy, in modern parlance, the former president's "control officer." When McMillan went to Naples to welcome Grant, his appearance resembled that of his consular colleague in Smyrna, but Smithers had had a sense of the absurdity of his dress and self-designed decorations. He laughed at himself, and he had made Grant laugh. McMillan, on the other hand, took himself very seriously, and he put Lieutenant Commander Caldwell in a black mood. "I saw today a sight that makes me doubt we are a republic," Caldwell wrote home to Indiana. The US consul general

> came aboard . . . and at first I really took him for a foreigner . . . on his left breast . . . were nothing but medals . . . for all the world like the medals on the breast of a first coat tail holder to a King—this is but one instance—I've seen many such and can't help doubting the future—we are ripe for a Dictator. I hope it may be as sensible a man as Grant if it must come. I say . . . make it a penal offense to sport a livery, a monogram on a card or carriage or wear anything resembling an "order"—we can't be too careful—there is a growing love for these things in America which will culminate one day in oligarchy.[32]

Grant's reaction to McMillan's appearance was not recorded, but as *Vandalia*'s sailors had commented, the former president also had an aversion to pretentious dress—even if it did not induce in him Caldwell's momentary political pessimism.

Even more ridiculous than the ribbons and medals he wore at Naples, however, was the squabble that erupted a month later between McMillan and the American consul in Florence, J. Schuyler Crosby. On April 15, McMillan accompanied the Grants on the short train ride from Rome, where Crosby and a delegation of Americans resident in Florence welcomed the former president and his family at the railroad station. The consul general felt slighted by the way he was greeted and introduced by Crosby to those present at the station. Crosby, for his part, claimed not to have known that McMillan would be with the Grants, and to have been taken by surprise to see him in Florence. McMillan was furious, and he returned to Rome that evening in a huff, without a word to Crosby, who was at a dinner with the Grants. Before he left the city, McMillan expressed his anger to several of the Americans who had been at the station, including Crosby's vice consul. Taking a cue from Marsh, who had seen nothing wrong in approaching Grant directly to discuss his seating order dilemma, McMillan "also *wrote a note to Gen. Grant* saying [Crosby] had acted so discourteously to him that he could not remain in Florence."[33] The contretemps went on for months, resulting in many pages of accusatory, self-justifying, and exculpatory correspondence among the two consuls, the minister, private American citizens resident in Florence, the State Department, and Ulysses Grant.

In late April, the former president replied from Venice to two letters from Crosby. After thanking him "for your courtesy and attention during our stay in Florence and which contributed so largely to the pleasure and profit of the visit," Grant wrote, "I have written to Col. McMillan saying how much I regretted the unpleasantness created by his reception at the Florence's [*sic*] station, that I was sure from your subsequent manner that you regretted it also, and that nothing of the kind was contemplated, much less meditated." Nearly a year later, Grant was still trying to soothe the ruffled feathers of the two consuls. In the midst of hectic preparations for his trip to Asia, he wrote from Paris to General Sherman on January 12, 1879, that he had "just received a letter" from McMillan "complaining of secret and underhanded efforts that are being made to undermine him." Grant called McMillan "a most capable and faithful officer" and authorized Sherman to pass on that comment to the president and secretary of state, if he wished to do so.[34]

The readiness of both consuls to involve Grant in their disagreement reflected the parochialism and lack of professionalism of the American diplomatic and consular community in Italy. For all their pretensions to aristocratic customs and prerogatives, Marsh, McMillan, and Crosby demonstrated in their treatment of Grant an apparent inability to understand their proper relationship not only to him, but to the president and secretary of state. No diplomat or consul from one of the European powers, even one obtuse enough to feel that his *amour propre* was more important than the reception of a visiting dignitary entrusted to his care, would have conceived of involving that person directly in complaints about a colleague. Embarrassment, if not good sense, forbade such behavior. But clearly neither Marsh nor the two consuls were embarrassed by their treatment of Grant. For his part, the former president wrote virtually nothing about the American minister and consuls in Italy in his letters to family and friends, a silence that contrasted sharply with what he had to say about their counterparts in other countries, and, especially, with his effusive praise of the US naval officers with whom he had spent three months on *Vandalia*.

On May 7, 1878, Grant was back in Paris. He had been overseas for almost a year, and reports of his reception by the leaders of Europe, and by average people throughout Britain, had had an impact on the American public's opinion of him. Since Europeans saw Grant as an international statesman, his countrymen began to do so, too, and his political friends were happy to encourage this development. By the time he left the French capital for the Netherlands in June, it was unclear whether "former president" was an accurate way to describe him. Grant was certainly that, but was he also the next chief executive of the United States? The 1880 presidential election was still more than two years away, but news from home indicated that he was increasingly favored to win the Republican nomination for an unprecedented third term, and, according to many reports, to be elected. Had that news reached Italy before Grant's visit there, perhaps it would have affected the behavior of Marsh, McMillan, and Crosby; it is impossible to know. But in his remaining fifteen months abroad, the predicted third term had a major impact on the reception accorded to Grant by foreign governments and the diplomatic and consular officers of the United States. Their treatment of him became not a matter of courtesy to a military and political leader whose historical moment had passed, but an opportunity to shape the opinions of a man thought likely to reenter the White House.

CHAPTER THREE

A Summer of Summitry from the North Sea to the Neva: 1878

After visiting the Paris Universal Exposition that opened in May,[1] Ulysses and Julia Grant might have been expected to sail home with their son, Jesse, who returned to New York in the summer of 1878 to begin his legal studies. But the former president decided on a different course, to see as much of the European continent as he could before winter set in. From June 14 to September 25, the Grants visited the Netherlands, Germany, Denmark, Norway-Sweden, Finland, Russia, Poland (like Finland, then a part of Russia), Austria-Hungary, and Switzerland. One of their purposes was tourism, but from Amsterdam to St. Petersburg, Grant also conducted public diplomacy and summitry on behalf of the United States. Before the summer was over, he had met with the Russian tsar, Alexander II; the emperor of Austria-Hungary, Franz Josef; the German emperor, Wilhelm I; and all the prime ministers and foreign ministers attending the Congress of Berlin. When he returned to Paris in late September, he had extensive personal knowledge of the leaders of every European country except Spain and Portugal (which he would visit before year's end), and they had formed an opinion not solely of Grant but of what an American president was like. This was an entirely new situation in transatlantic relations. European leaders had met and negotiated with each other for centuries, but with the partial exception of Adams, Jefferson, Monroe, and Quincy Adams, the four founding-father diplomats who became president, the American chief executive was an unknown quantity to Europe's monarchs, prime ministers, and foreign ministers. The first American president they met was Ulysses Grant.

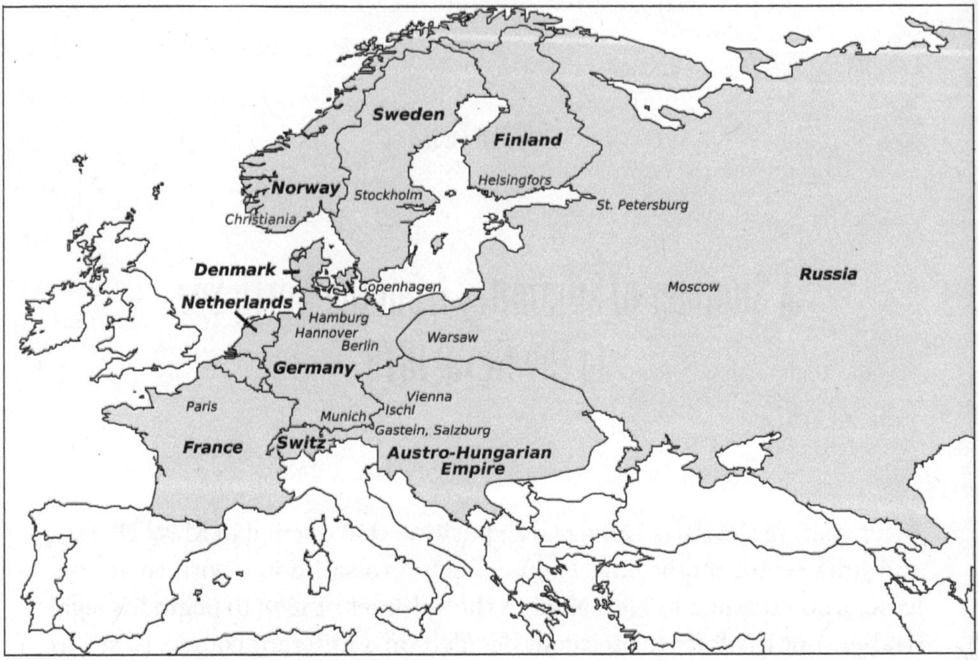

North-central Europe, May 7–September 25, 1878. Grant spent more than a month in Paris before leaving on June 14 for the Netherlands. Over the next three months, he visited Germany, Scandinavia, Russia, and Austria, returning to Paris via Switzerland on September 25.

Grant became president in 1869 at a moment when the number of international actors was expanding, including Japan, Germany, Italy, and the United States itself. By the time he left office, he had dealt with more foreign-policy issues involving more countries than any of his predecessors. While steam power and telegraphy put states and people into closer contact with each other, literacy was on the rise in the western world, increasing the demand for and the influence of newspapers.[2] Early nongovernmental organizations, like the Universal Peace Union (UPU), with which Grant had a close relationship, began to drive government policy and action in ways previously unknown. Thanks to his own intellectual curiosity and eight years of working closely with Secretary of State Fish, Grant was far better prepared to represent the United States overseas than most of his countrymen realized. He brought to his diplomacy the same qualities that had characterized his generalship, especially the ability to see the overall strategic picture and to assess accurately the strengths and weaknesses of the United States relative to those of other countries. He also understood something that many Americans, both in his day and since, have had trouble grasping, that foreign policy decisions, like military ones, were constant and overlapping. No general, diplomat, or president had the luxury of dealing with one finite problem at a time before moving on to the next one. The need to deal with issues simultaneously could be turned into an advantage, however, by someone with an agile mind and strategic *coup d'oeil.* As in a war, each diplomatic front contained its own risks and challenges, but also offered opportunities to resolve other issues. And the lesson Grant had learned in 1861 about the willingness to initiate battle applied to diplomacy; while Washington focused on other countries' resources and capabilities, those countries were equally nervous about what the United States' next move would be.[3]

The strategic environment in which Grant's 1878 conversations with European leaders took place had existed for less than a decade. It was the product of Prussia's victory in three wars, against Austria, Denmark, and France, from 1864 to 1871, and the unification of the German states in 1871. The Grant administration had been intimately involved through its minister in Berlin in the establishment of a united Germany, and its principal foreign policy success, the 1871 Anglo-American Treaty of Washington and the resulting Geneva arbitration, was directly affected by German unification. Before Grant met the architect of that unification, Otto von Bismarck, in Berlin, however, he spent ten days in the Netherlands in June 1878. He found there a concept of citizenship and civic responsibility akin to his own, and was "pleased . . . with what he saw in Holland—with the prosperity, the freedom and the hospitality of the people." The Grants were invited to dine by members of the royal family, and the foreign minister hosted a dinner in Grant's honor. There was a military parade at which "[t]he soldiers and people were much disappointed that [he] did not put on uniform and mount a horse." Grant reviewed the troops in a way more to his liking, in civilian clothes, seated in the American minister's landau, and "rising and taking off his hat" as the officers passed with their commands. Julia Grant remembered how much she and her husband enjoyed seeing the "wealth of pictures" in Dutch collections and visiting "a model farm . . . being mowed by one of Mr. McCormick's mowers brought from Chicago, driven by a skilled driver from Illinois at the good wages of five dollars per day." Grant was also "much interested in a piece of engineering which unites Amsterdam with the North Sea."[4] With the Dutch, he got to do what he liked best—see how a country functioned, how its people worked.

The *New York Times* wrote with approval on July 21 of Grant's skillful public diplomacy in the Netherlands, both his ability to engage with audiences and the content of his remarks. At the dinner given in his honor by the city of Amsterdam, he "made a very happy speech . . . which received enthusiastic applause." The *Times* commented that "the reputation which the General acquired in America for reticence, for a Sphynx-like uncommunicativeness, and for making responses by an eloquent stroke of silence, is rapidly passing away." Grant was beginning to make the same impression in public that he made in private on individuals like Lieutenant Commander Caldwell. "[S]carcely any gentleman can be found who converses more fluently, intelligently, entertainingly, and continuously on all topics of general interest. . . . [H]is remarks were ready, direct, abounding in fact and common sense, liberal and magnanimous to opponents, but positive in his conclusions." After a year abroad, the former president had begun to volunteer his opinions on the international environment. He was, the paper wrote, "thoroughly a man of peace. He has no fondness for conflict, no fondness for the trappings of war. He often expressed his surprise that the Governments of Europe still tolerated the maintenance of such large bodies of troops at the expense of the people."[5]

From the Netherlands, after a brief stay in Hannover where their son, Buck, had studied, the Grants traveled to Berlin on June 26. The US minister to Germany, Bayard Taylor, and John Russell Young boarded the train in Stendhal, sixty miles west of the German capital, to welcome them. Young had been in Berlin "on a personal mission for [*Herald* publisher John Gordon] Bennett," and he stayed on to report on Grant's visit. The former president's expected meeting with Bismarck was of particular interest to Americans. At the time of German unification in 1871, Prussia-Germany enjoyed an overwhelmingly positive reputation in the United States. It owed part of this reputation to first-generation German-Americans who emigrated after 1848, as well as to those who had earlier settled Pennsylvania and the Ohio Valley. Hard-working, pro-Union, and often abolitionist, they had constituted a large part of Ulysses Grant's armies. Although many of the "Forty-Eighters" had left their homeland to escape Prussian oppression, this was largely forgotten in the excitement over Germany's defeat of France and unification in 1871. In his February 7, 1871, message to Congress welcoming establishment of the German empire, President Grant commented that "the large number of citizens and residents in the United States, of German extraction, and the continued flow of emigration thence to this country, have produced an intimacy of personal and political intercourse, approaching if not equal to that with the country from which the founders of our Government derived their origin."[6] In the midst of negotiation of the Treaty of Washington, this was a statement sure to attract attention in London.

The president's attitude toward German unification was also influenced by the American minister to Prussia-Germany from 1867 to 1874, George Bancroft. A well-known historian for decades when Andrew Johnson appointed him to Berlin, Bancroft offered in his dispatches to Washington his comments on Prussia's motives, methods, and goals in "accepting" leadership of Germany in 1871. His analysis of the events he was witnessing in Europe was immensely flattering to the American ego, since he claimed that German unification had been accomplished on the American "model." On January 18, 1871, the day of Wilhelm I's coronation at Versailles, as German armies besieged Paris, Bancroft wrote to Secretary of State Fish that "United America may see in United Germany a reproduction of its own constitution with such modifications as the history and condition of Germany seemed to require." German unification, he declared, was

> the greatest step in favor of political order and freedom that has been made in Europe in the last century or in this. . . . Germany thus united becomes the leading power on the continent of Europe. Its constitution in another respect resembles our own; it imparts exceeding strength for the purposes of self defence & takes from its chief the power of entering upon wars of conquest & ambition.

On November 29, 1870, Bancroft had told Fish that "United Germany [would mean] establishment of the most liberal government on the continent of Europe." There was no reason for Grant to doubt Bancroft's judgment. The minister had first come to Germany as a student in 1817, and he received his doctorate from the University of Göttingen in 1820, two years before Grant was born. His views also fell on willing ears in the White House because they reinforced the president's hostility to Napoleon III, and in his February 7 message Grant called "[t]he union of the States of Germany . . . an event that cannot fail to touch deeply the sympathies of the people of the United States." But by then, the French emperor was long gone. Elihu Washburne wrote to Secretary Fish on February 28 that Grant's message had been "commented upon very generally and very unfavorably by the Paris journals. It is looked upon as being complimentary to the monarchical institutions of

Germany and a 'slap in the face' to the new Republic of France."[7] Grant's pro-German reputation followed him to Europe six years later, and his hosts in Berlin in 1878 no doubt counted on it working in their favor.

The Grants stayed at the Kaiserhof, a glittering new hotel that reflected Berlin's arrival as a major European capital, and residence of the delegates to the congress of the great powers revising the Treaty of San Stefano. It was a sign of the changing times that such a meeting was held in the German capital, rather than Paris or Vienna; but the times had not yet changed that much. The United States was not represented at the Congress of Berlin, nor was any other extra-European country. Those who governed in London, Paris, Berlin, St. Petersburg, and Vienna still made the rules by which the international system functioned. It was another twenty years before the United States played a major role in reshaping that system, at the 1899 Hague Conference, and twenty years after that when an American president traveled to Europe for the first time to participate in a multilateral postwar peace conference to redraw the map of Europe, at Paris in 1919.[8] Grant's visit to the German capital during the Congress of Berlin, however, gave the United States a diplomatic profile among its delegates that it would not otherwise have had. It was indicative of how hard he had worked on behalf of American diplomacy since his arrival in Europe that he had already met all the principal delegates except the Russian foreign minister. While in Berlin, Grant called on Prince Gortchakoff (Gorchakov) and was invited to visit Russia later that summer.

Grant's presence in Berlin during the congress demonstrated the absurdity of the protocol regime that had caused Marsh so much distress in Rome. To circumvent the issue, the US minister gave "no formal official dinner (which would involve no end of trouble, questions of etiquette and expense)"; Taylor instead invited "a select company of about a dozen, all of whom speak English"[9] to dine with the Grants. But if not with ambassadors, Grant could dine with prime ministers and princes. The Grants were hosted by the Bismarcks, and by Friedrich and Victoria, the crown prince and princess. "Vicky" was the eldest and favorite daughter of the British monarch, and she and the prince represented the hopes of Germans who favored the evolution of the Second Reich into a constitutional monarchy committed to good relations with Britain. Their political views did not endear them to Bismarck, but he had good reason to expect that their liberalism would make a positive impression on Grant. Since the emperor was eighty years old in 1878 and recuperating from the second of two assassination attempts that year, it seemed likely that, if Grant were reelected in 1880, Friedrich would succeed to the throne while Grant was in the White House. It was not to be. Not only did the former president not win a third term, but Wilhelm I lived another ten years, dying at age ninety in 1888. When he became emperor, Friedrich III was fifty-six years old and, like the former president he had met a decade before, dying painfully of throat cancer. He was emperor for only ninety-nine days, succeeded by his twenty-eight-year-old son, Wilhelm II, in what became known in German history as the "year of the three emperors."

Bismarck was, in any case, overly optimistic in expecting Grant to be susceptible to a German charm offensive. Certainly, he had once had a deep-seated antipathy toward France because he regarded France and Bonapartism as one and the same. But Grant's time in Paris, especially his meetings with Gambetta and other French Republicans, had planted a seed of skepticism about Germany that Bismarck probably did not anticipate from the statements of President Grant seven years before. Moreover, John Russell Young, whose opinions always mattered to Grant, was no admirer of Prussia. Although he was not with the former president when he traveled through Alsace-Lorraine in 1877, Young devoted many pages of *Around the World with General Grant* to a critique of Germany's annexation of the two provinces.[10] And long before Grant's stay in Europe, a year after his February 1871 message to Congress, two of his most trusted sources had an experience that called into question the allegedly liberal tendencies of Germany's Prussian leaders as described by Bancroft.

At a dinner at the Russian embassy in Constantinople in 1872, General Sherman and Fred Grant met Wilhelm I's nephew, Prince Friedrich Karl. Sherman's comments in his diary were not flattering. The prince's "fame as a general in the late French war was very great," but he "seemed stiff and conceited" and was "every inch a German, and evidently proud of his country and himself." Most irritating to Sherman was the display of royal arrogance when, after dinner, "a grand Turkish pipe was served to the prince, but to nobody else, and though I at first thought it was accidental, I soon saw that it was etiquette, and that even I must look on a prince as hedged around by some divine rights and privileges." Sherman's aide, "Fred Grant, perceiving this personal slight to me, most courteously came and offered me cigars and cigarettes. I took one of the latter, lighted it, and smoked it in unison with the prince general." About Friedrich Karl and his country, Sherman concluded:

> As a general, his fame is established; as a prince, he is not the subject of criticism; as a gentleman, he will rank very low, and thus is one of the delusions of my life vanished. I am told that Prussians are elevated beyond limit by their brilliant successes over the French—a great pity, but one that in due time will bring down on them the judgment of the world, if not disasters such as now the French groan under.[11]

Sherman's diary entry was not published until 1899, but long before Grant came to Berlin he surely would have heard from both his son and his friend about their evening with the Prussian prince.

Unlike Britain and France, the German press showed little interest in the former president; he was not interviewed, and his presence in Berlin was simply noted in the court circular and government calendar.[12] Public opinion as a factor shaping foreign policy did not exist in Germany, and local governments dealt with local issues, not national ones. It was inconceivable that the mayor of a German city would welcome Grant as the mayors of Birmingham, Manchester, and other British cities had done, speaking their own mind on national issues. The country had no influential independent parliamentarians whose voices were heeded at home and abroad; there was no German John Bright for Grant to meet. Foreign policy was in the hands of two men, the emperor and the chancellor, and those they chose to consult. As a result, Grant spent most of his time in Berlin at the summit, getting to know those at the highest levels of the German government and delegates to the congress.

Grant had a largely negative reaction to his week in the German capital. John Russell Young's accounts of the former president's activities suggest the reason for this: the omnipresence of the military in the life and politics of the country. The ambiance of Berlin was far removed from the model Dutch farm Grant had visited only a few days before, but the contrast was also stark between Berlin and all the other capitals of Western Europe. The president of France was a military man, and there was certainly a panoply of uniforms on display in Paris, London, Athens, Rome, and The Hague; but in none of those cities was there a deference to military values and military hierarchy akin to that in Berlin. "Prussia," wrote Young, "is a living paradox. She tries to combine the highest intellectual culture with the greatest physical force. She pushes forward on the chessboard of Europe, side by side, her philosopher and her soldier. Which will win the game no one can say, but one will be sure to absorb the other."[13] Grant himself was too gifted a diplomat and politically too astute to say even one negative word in public about Bismarck and Germany. German-American voters were proud of the "Iron Chancellor," and Germany was becoming an important trading partner of the United States, especially as a market for US agricultural products.[14] Had any negative remarks been published, it would have been a losing proposition for the Republican Party in the run-up to the 1878 Congressional elections.

Grant met Bismarck for the first time on June 30. Young described the former president's five-minute walk from his hotel to the chancellery across "a small square . . . laid out in memory of the great Frederick [and] decorated with statues of his leading generals." Bismarck was "wear[ing] an officer's uniform" when he greeted Grant. The chancellor later paid a call on the Grants at the Kaiserhof, but not by walking across the square; at the hotel entrance he descended from a carriage, dressed "in a full military uniform, a gilded helmet covering his brows." The prime ministers of France and Britain did not wear gilded helmets. Only in Cairo and Constantinople, where rulers answered not to people, press, or parliament, had the tone been similar to the militaristic aristocracy of the German capital, and given his reaction to the Ottoman Empire, that thought cannot have been a comforting one to Grant. Young editorialized "that everything runs to war in Germany . . . the prevailing religion is swordsmanship."[15] At their first meeting, Bismarck insisted on what became Grant's most unpleasant experience in Berlin, a military review on the Tempelhof parade grounds, hosted by the crown prince because of the emperor's incapacity.

The chancellor told Grant that Wilhelm I was "so much of a soldier and so fond of his army that nothing would give him more pleasure than to display it to so great a soldier as yourself." Grant's reply has been much quoted as evidence of his kinship to George Washington, a great general who preferred plowshares to swords: "The truth is I am more of a farmer than a soldier. I take little or no interest in military affairs. . . . I never went into the army without regret and never retired without pleasure." Those words did, indeed, say a lot about Grant, but they were equally significant as an expression of his disapproval of leaders, like both Napoleons, in thrall to "blood and iron" and the use of armed force. By describing himself, rather than commenting on the emperor's fondness for his army, Grant offered a subtle rebuke to his hosts without giving them any overt cause for offense. Perhaps he hoped the review would be canceled if he showed a lack of interest in it; at his request, the French president had abandoned plans for one, despite finding Grant's disinterest "incomprehensible."[16] That was not going to happen in Berlin. The Prussian army was virtually synonymous with the state and royal family, and there was no possibility that the House of Hohenzollern would allow Grant to leave Berlin without showing it off.

Monday, July 1, was a miserable day. As Young described it, "It had rained all night, a heavy, pitching, blowing rain, and when the morning came the prayers . . . for better weather were found to have availed not." Grant "had a severe cold and chill, which had been hanging over him for two days, and when he arose he could scarcely speak. There was a suggestion that the review might be postponed. But the troops were under way . . . and the General would not hear of the suggestion. He only hoped, he said, when the crown prince's officer came to attend him, that the display would be as brief as possible and not severe upon the men." That hope, too, was futile. "The manoeuvres," wrote Young, "went on all the same." There was a sham infantry battle, artillery practice, two march-pasts, "the General reviewing the line with bared head, to which the pitiless rain showed no mercy," and a visit to a military hospital. The day ended with "a quiet mess room lunch" with the crown prince and his officers. Grant thanked his host for the "pains that had been taken to show him this sample of his magnificent army," to which Friedrich replied "that the annals of his regiment would always record the pride they felt in having had at their mess and as their guest so illustrious a leader." Young could not resist noting that "[o]n our way home the skies relented and the sun began to shine."

The most revealing incident of the day, and one of the more astounding experiences in all of Grant's travels, was an argument that he had with the major detailed to attend him over the utility of the bayonet. The former president expressed the opinion that "anything that adds to the burdens carried by the soldier is a weakness to the army" and declared that "the army would be stronger" if the weight of the bayonet were replaced "in food or ammunition." In close combat "the club end of their muskets" was "as much good" to soldiers as a bayonet, and a pistol would serve them better than a saber—"always an awkward thing to carry." The major argued with him. He "did not think the experiences of the Prussian army would sustain the General's view"; there had been "effective work done with the bayonet," and "the Prussians would not abandon it." Grant replied that he did not doubt that there were "instances when the bayonet was effective," but they "were so few" that they did not warrant "the heavy burden imposed upon an army by the carrying of the bayonet." The major, Young reported, "was not convinced by the General's reasoning." This encounter spoke volumes about the lack of respect in Berlin for Ulysses Grant, the United States, and its army. It is impossible to imagine a Prussian field grade officer contradicting the crown prince or Count Moltke, no matter how much he disagreed with them, or for that matter, a general officer from any other European army. But the American in civilian dress was no aristocrat and apparently did not strike the major as worthy of his deference and respect. Characteristically, Grant treated him with respect, engaging in a discussion of tactics, soldier to soldier. But depressingly, this probably only increased the major's disrespect for him; a Prussian general officer would have silenced him immediately.

While Grant was with the crown prince and his army, Bayard Taylor wrote his dispatch to the State Department, summarizing the former president's activities in Berlin. Grant's "last opportunity of receiving special honor in this city" would be "his presence tonight at the soiree given by Lord Odo Russell to the members of the European Congress and the Diplomatic Corps." Taylor emphasized the efforts to which the German government had gone to receive Grant, despite Moltke's absence in Silesia, the incapacity of the emperor, "the presence of the European Congress, and the number of pre-arranged dinners and social assemblages arising therefrom." He described in approving detail the June 28 dinner at the New Palace in Potsdam, at which the Grants were given the places of honor, the former first lady next to the crown prince, and the former president opposite him. He told Secretary Evarts that "I did not consider it consistent with the dignity of the Government I represent to make any stipulation concerning etiquette, in advance, or even to ask any question, and I am consequently all the more gratified to find that it would have been unnecessary."[17]

Taylor had some unusual news to report that showed how worried the German government was about the impact on German-American relations of Grant's successful visits to Britain and France, especially if he again became president. Historically, Berlin's relationship with Washington had been better than London's and Paris's, as the Grant administration's reaction to the Franco-Prussian War had shown. But with the Geneva arbitration and the new French republic, that had been changing. Bismarck knew that the British and French governments were cultivating better relations with the United States, in part through their reception of Grant. The German government used a surprising party, Empress Augusta, to do the same. While the emperor was recuperating, Taylor correctly expected that the empress "would probably feel bound to maintain her privacy in the palace." She did not receive the Grants, but the day after they arrived in Berlin, the US minister was told "that Her Majesty would receive me on Friday afternoon." His description of the audience is worth repeating in detail:

> The Empress took occasion to express to me the Emperor's interest in Genl Grant's history, his desire to meet him personally, and his great regret that this was now impossible. Her words and manner implied an authorization that I should repeat these expressions to Genl Grant. She then spoke very freely and feelingly of the disturbances occasioned by the distress of the laboring classes, declared her belief that a period of peace would be the best remedy, and finally said, "The Emperor knew that I should see you today. He has the peace of the world at heart, and he desires nothing so much as the establishment of friendship between nations. I ask you to make it your task to promote the existing friendship between your country and ours. You cannot do a better work, and we shall most heartily unite with you in doing it. This is the Emperor's message to you, and he asked me to give it to you in his name as well as my own."[18]

Grant's letters make no reference to this message, and it is unclear how much of it Taylor shared with him; but he certainly would have told Grant, as had Bismarck, that Wilhelm I regretted not being able to receive him in Berlin. It is hardly surprising, then, that the former president went out of his way two months later to meet the German emperor at the Austrian spa, Bad Gastein, on September 11.

The Grants left Berlin for Copenhagen on July 2 and for the next nearly three months did a good deal of sightseeing in Scandinavia, Russia, and Austria. But as reports from the United States predicting a third presidential term began arriving in Europe, the summer also became one of summitry with leaders who wanted to meet Grant. His success overseas for the past year was a major factor in the groundswell of discussion among Republicans about the desirability of a third term. They needed a candidate who could be elected, and the admiration of the American people for their ambassador-at-large grew as he traveled. Only a handful of people, former Secretary of State Fish chief among them, had expected Grant to be such a successful representative of the United States. To almost everyone else reading their daily newspaper, his activities in Europe were the diplomatic equivalent of the capture of Forts Henry and Donelson. No one in February 1862 had expected the Union's first great victory of the Civil War to come from an unknown general in the West, and the surprise was nearly as great fifteen years later when Americans discovered that their reputedly taciturn and stolid former president was a gifted diplomat. It took about ten days for stories published in the American press to reach Europe by transatlantic steamer, and the bulk of third-term reports began arriving just as Grant was leaving Berlin. He wrote to Edward Beale from Copenhagen on July 7 that "I note what you say about the prospects for /80, and hear the same thing from other sources—letters and papers. But with the revival of business all this will be forgotten, and I am very sure it will be gratifying to me. I have had all the honors, and would like to avoid the vexations of political life in the future."[19]

Nevertheless, the stories continued. In a July 25 interview with the *Washington Post*, the Confederacy's "grey ghost," John Singleton Mosby, now a political ally and friend of Grant, declared that he had "no doubt of [Grant's] nomination by acclamation" in 1880, and that "he will be overwhelmingly elected." A month later, on August 15, the *Chicago Inter-Ocean* interviewed Rev. John Newman, the Methodist minister who was pastor to Julia Grant. Newman had written to the former president "that everyone was asking me about his sentiments regarding the third term," and Grant had "replied that he had been through the trials and labors of sixteen years of public life and was taking a rest." Nevertheless, Newman told the paper, "[S]hould an emergency arise where the American people demanded his services again, I know he would not refuse." Newman declared:

> The point I wish to make is that General Grant . . . , when he returns, will be the best informed man in America upon the manners, institutions, geography, topography, populations, and, above all, the resources of all the peoples of the globe. This nation has never appreciated the intellectual greatness of the man.

Later in the year, on December 7, the *New York Times* published an interview with Senator Blanche K. Bruce of Mississippi, who had talked with Grant in Paris and "called his attention to the popular feeling looking to his nomination for the presidency in 1880." While Grant "was really happy in the freedom from official care . . . if a general demand for his services should be expressed by the American people," said Bruce, "I have no doubt he would accept the nomination."[20]

Amid all this speculation, Ulysses and Julia Grant continued their travels. The chancelleries and foreign offices of the countries they intended to visit had to decide how to receive them, which meant deciphering the meaning of the reports crossing the Atlantic. People who claimed to know Grant well seemed certain he would be offered and would accept the Republican nomination in 1880. If European governments had any doubts about how seriously to take these stories, they were likely dispelled definitively in late July. What the American papers wrote was one thing, but it was quite another when the *Times* (London) reached the same conclusion in a long report on Grant's prospects published on July 25. "[T]here is nothing more likely than that General Grant will be the candidate," the paper wrote. "This feeling . . . has been gradually growing, until it has assumed among the Republicans a pronounced form, which finds vent in every gathering of the party, and has made General Grant to-day the most popular American, and if the Republican nominating convention for 1880 were now to meet, would give him the nomination in spite of the 'third term' or any other objection that might be urged." Unlike Mosby, the *Times* did not claim that Grant's nomination meant his winning the election: "[I]t is too soon now to predict the success of either" the Democratic or Republican candidate. But emphasizing the importance it accorded to the issue, two days after the initial article, the paper concluded in a July 27 editorial that "Republicans may well turn back upon the thought that they abandoned General Grant without much advantage of any kind either to their party or to their country."[21]

The Grants broke their trip to Copenhagen with a brief stop in Hamburg, where the former president, fresh from the gilded helmets of Berlin, celebrated July 4 with the resident American community. The speech he gave on the fifteenth anniversary of the surrender of Vicksburg was a particularly eloquent and impassioned one that vigorously rejected the idea of an "indispensable man" as having any place in a democratic society:

> I must dissent from one remark of our Consul, to the effect that I saved the country during the recent war. If our country could be saved or ruined by the efforts of any one man we should not have a country, and we should not now be celebrating our Fourth of July. . . . If I had never held command; if I had fallen; if all our generals had fallen, there were ten thousand behind us who would have done our work just as well, who would have followed the contest to the end and never surrendered the Union. Therefore it is

> a mistake and a reflection upon the people to attribute to me, or to any number of us who held high commands, the salvation of the Union. We did our work as well as we could, and so did hundreds of thousands of others.[22]

The Grants visited Copenhagen from July 7 to 12. Until their arrival in St. Petersburg on July 30, in Scandinavia they had the chance to be tourists again. Not exclusively—that was no longer possible; but the balance of public diplomacy, summitry, and sightseeing shifted for a few weeks in favor of the last. They toured Copenhagen and its environs and dined with the Danish king and queen, whose son, George I of Greece, had hosted them in Athens in March. One thing Grant did not do was meet with Louis Napoleon's son, who was in Copenhagen at the same time. "I did not feel inclined to call upon the heir of the Bonapartes," he told a Norwegian reporter:

> I don't like the family. . . . [Napoleon III] abused in a shameful manner the confidence placed in him by the French people when they elected him to be the President of the Republic and he founded the Empire; and later, his unnecessary wars brought shame and ruin on the country.[23]

Scandinavia, like the Netherlands, pleased Grant immensely. In contrast to his silence about Germany, for weeks after his visits to Holland and the Scandinavian countries, he described them enthusiastically to his friends and family.

On July 7, the day he arrived in Copenhagen, Grant wrote to Edward Beale that "[t]he Hollanders are a great people, good looking, industrious, free and rich." In a letter the same day to General Sherman, he praised the US minister in Berlin, Bayard Taylor, but to neither Sherman nor Beale did he say a word about Bismarck or the crown prince. The Netherlands was, he told Sherman, "the most interesting country—and people—that I have yet seen. The people look prosperous, free and happy, and entertain an exalted opinion of our country and countrymen." From St. Petersburg on August 4 Grant wrote to Adam Badeau that his reception in Norway, Sweden, and Finland "was by all the people and as hearty, with as much cheering, as you ever saw in the states or in England." On the same day he reported to his son, Buck, that "[t]hrough the Scandinavian countries—Denmark, Norway, Sweden, and Finland—my reception . . . was much like what you have seen at home soon after the war . . . most enthusiastic, with loud cheering &c." In a long letter to Admiral Ammen from St. Petersburg on August 13, Grant told his old friend that he was "very much pleased with the people of Holland, Denmark, Norway, Sweden, and Finland. They are a free, intelligent, honest, and industrious people." And on August 22 he wrote from Vienna to Hamilton Fish that "there are no finer, more honest and simple people than the Norwegian; in fact, you might include all the Scandinavians." At the end of his swing through north-central Europe, of all the countries he had seen since May 1877, Grant was most impressed by Scandinavia. He wrote to Sherman from Ragaz, Switzerland, on September 21, that his "visit through Norway, Sweden & Finland was delightful. The weather was very fine, the scenery grand and the people I regard as very superior, and very fond of America and Americans."[24]

In 1878, Norway was joined in personal union with the Swedish crown, and its foreign affairs directed from Stockholm, where the diplomatic corps was based. In June, the US minister, John L. Stevens, had "informed His Majesty, verbally, of the proposed visit of General Grant to his Capital, which intelligence he received with marked cordiality."[25] But Grant arrived later than originally expected, in the middle of the summer holiday, and the king and crown prince were in Norway. As a result, the dinner given by the king in Grant's honor was held in Christiania (Oslo), not Stockholm, and was, by European court standards, a relaxed affair. Many years later, the US consul in Christiania, Gerhard Gade, wrote that "[s]trict court etiquette—of which the small Norwegian court needed little—would have seemed to Grant both foreign and tasteless." The former president's arrival in Christiania on Saturday, July 13, was memorable:

> All the Norwegian and several foreign vessels had their colors flying in honor of the General's visit. While going up the fjord toward Christiania, the steamer was met by a great number of fishing-smacks and pleasure-boats, all festively decorated, and a number of them carrying the American flag. These boats were filled with people, whose rousing cheers and hospitable welcome evidently pleased the visitors, as both the General and his wife were continually waving their handkerchiefs in token of appreciation. . . . [A]t the wharf in Christiania . . . the numerous ships in the harbor also had their colors flying, likewise all the public buildings and a number of private residences. The steamboat landing was crowded with people, who cheered lustily when the steamer hove to.[26]

The Grants were not aboard an American warship, as they had been in Alexandria and Athens, but that made it even clearer that the welcome reflected the genuine feelings of the Norwegian people, rather than an officially decreed demonstration.

A Norwegian newspaper, whose account was published in the August 11, 1878, *Chicago Tribune*, wrote that the people of Christiania expected that Grant "would appear in a fine uniform, decked with plumes and 'fixings,' like European Kings and Princes, and having a whole army of uniformed adjutants and waiters along, as well as a set of monkey-like coachmen and 'hind-riders,' clad in cloth of glowing colors." Instead

> the first man in that great and mighty Republic, that renowned warrior, walked ashore, his wife leaning on his arm, just like the other passengers. . . . It was not until he entered the carriage of the Consul . . . that the people recognized the man . . . and then the multitude broke out in rousing cheers. The General arose in the carriage, gracefully lifted his hat, bowed and smiled.

The crowd waiting at the hotel missed Grant entirely because of behavior they did not expect from a general and head of state: "The carriage stopped, the occupants alighted, and the General remained outside quite awhile looking after his baggage. It was not until he had entered the hotel that the people were made aware of the fact that he whom they were so anxious to see had been among them, but they knew him not."[27] The Grants spent ten days in Norway touring the countryside and relaxing at Frogner, the home of Gade and his American-born wife. They left for Stockholm on the overnight train on July 22.

The former president and first lady spent only five days in Sweden, and their time was largely filled with public engagements. On July 24, the American minister hosted a dinner for the Grants at his residence, attended by members of the Swedish cabinet and the diplomatic corps, and a larger reception for "the Chief Government officials and their ladies . . . some of them coming from their summer residences at a distance in the country to pay their respects to the distinguished American citizen." The king offered the royal yacht, "in command of an officer of the Swedish Navy," for the Grants' use, and they took two day trips aboard her, to Ulricsdol and Drottningholm. As he had in Britain, in Stockholm Grant received "a large association of mechanics and laboring men" who came to his hotel to pay their respects on July 25. Stevens reported to Secretary Evarts that "[t]heir numbers were increased by other Swedish citizens to four or five thousand persons, who gathered" at the hotel and "behaved with great decorum." The Grants left Stockholm on Saturday, July 27, "a clear and most beautiful day," by steamer for St. Petersburg after having "been received with earnest, orderly, and most respectful enthusiasm" in Sweden and Norway. Stevens reported that "the vessels in harbor were crowded with national flags from deck to topmost spar, and the front of [the Grants'] hotel and an extensive space on the quay were packed with the thousands" of Swedes who had come to honor the departing American. In the US minister's view, they did so because Grant's "life and services for fifteen years had been so closely identified with the history of a great people in the other hemisphere—a land which many Scandinavians have found a land of promise and to which thousands of others look with eager hope."[28]

After a brief stop in Helsingfors (Helsinki) en route to the Russian capital, Grant was definitively back in the world of great power politics and summitry in St. Petersburg, and he knew it. So did former secretary of state Fish, who wrote to him on July 12. At the time, Fish did not yet know about Grant's meeting with Gortchakoff in Berlin, so he asked if he might

> venture to express the hope that you will not go to Russia, unless *specially* invited, in the name of the Emperor. Gortchakoff, has not forgiven the dismissal of his pet, that scamp Catacazy, & he persuades the Emperor to believe, that you did not sufficiently appreciate the visit, of the Grand Duke Alexis, & will not lose the opportunity of doing something disagreeable, either by omission or commission, if you go within his jurisdiction.

During Grant's presidency, he and Fish had had to deal with the inappropriate activities of the Russian minister in Washington, Constantine Catacazy, who was eventually declared persona non grata by the American government. By the time Grant received Fish's letter, he was already in St. Petersburg; he replied from Vienna on August 22 that he had "enjoyed a visit of about two weeks [in Russia] very much" and explained that the invitation had come personally from the foreign minister. "While in Berlin Gortchacoff expressed a great desire to see me, but his physical condition was such at the time—from goute [*sic*]—that he could not walk. I went therefore to see him, and had a long pleasant talk. He asked me about my proposed visit to Russia, and . . . said I would meet with a most hearty reception."[29]

Grant understood that the changing strategic situation in Europe explained why Fish's fears had proved unfounded, "although we both had serious apprehensions that the case would be quite different." Russian armies had been at the gates of Constantinople earlier in the year, but the Congress of Berlin modified the Treaty of San Stefano and deprived St. Petersburg of much that it had won on the battlefield. "Whether felt or not the reception was mos[t] cordial in appearance," Grant told Fish. "Our Ministe[r] was requested days before my arrival to notify the Prime Minister the very moment I got there. He did so an[d] in two hours . . . an answer was sent fixing the time for an audience with t[he] Emperor. When I called the Emper[or] approached me and taking me by the hand led me to a seat after which we had a talk of some twen[ty] minutes or more." As Grant told his secretary of state,

> There is no doubt but that the United States stands very high in the estimation of the Russians, from the Emperor down. They fully expect some day to have [American] aid in the settlement of European matters, which they think further from a satisfactory and peace inspiring solution than before the Berlin Congress met.

"European matters," not surprisingly, were on the former president's mind, since he was writing to Fish from Vienna after visiting St. Petersburg, Moscow, and Warsaw. Grant wrote on the same day to his son, Fred, that "I do not like to write about European politics, particularly as I have been received so well everywhere":

> But it looks to me as if the Berlin Congress has by no means settled affairs even for a short time. I hope I am mistaken, but I feel that there is more danger now of a general war than there was at any time during the conflict between Russia and Turkey.

"Do not," he concluded his letter to Fred, "express this as my view."[30]

Despite the Catacazy affair, Grant was inclined to think favorably of the Russian government and Alexander II. St. Petersburg had not dallied with the Confederacy; it had abolished serfdom; and in 1867, with the sale of Alaska, it ceased to claim territory in North America. Grant's antipathy toward the Ottoman Empire also likely influenced his attitude toward Russia, as it did his opinion of Greece. In contrast to his silence about Bismarck and the German crown prince, he wrote to Adam Badeau from St. Petersburg on August 4 that "[h]ere, to my surprise somewhat, I have been received by the officials not only with courticy [*sic*] but with warmth." He had "had a conversation in the most familiar style of near half an hour" with Alexander II," and indeed, "Everything has been most agreeable."

Grant wrote on the same day to his son, Buck, that "[t]he Emperor makes the impression of being a very superior man, and one who will look to the best interests of his people." He told Daniel Ammen on August 13 that "[h]ere, in Russia, I have been surprised at the cordiality; though there has always existed a traditional friendship between the two countries."[31]

Grant was still pleased by his reception in Russia when he looked back on it three years later. On March 13, 1881, Alexander II was assassinated. Interviewed on the same day by the *New York Times*, the former president described his visit to the Summer Palace, the tsar conversing in English and French, the latter interpreted by Gortchakoff, whose "English was as perfect as that of any American, and was without the slightest foreign accent." Alexander II "was somewhat nervous," Grant said, "as one would naturally be after so many attempts had been made upon his life. My visit to him was an agreeable one." Grant, the *Times* reporter commented, "could not see what the people of Russia would gain by [the assassination]. . . . The Czar had been greatly harassed by his subjects, and had indeed led a miserable life. Yet he seemed to have an interest in his people, as was evidenced by his freeing the serfs." Grant also spoke favorably of the crown prince, now Alexander III, and his wife, Maria Feodorovna, daughter of the king of Denmark and sister to the Princess of Wales and the king of Greece. "They entertained Mrs. Grant and myself in the most agreeable manner. It was more like meeting with Americans, and our visit was all the more enjoyable on that account."[32]

After more than a week in St. Petersburg, the Grants visited Moscow for five days, August 8–13, with the American minister to Russia, Edwin Stoughton, and his wife. They returned briefly to St. Petersburg and then toured Warsaw for two days before continuing to Vienna,[33] arriving in the Austrian capital on August 18. The Grants were guests of the American minister, John Adams Kasson, for eight days. Although Kasson was a protégé of the US minister in Rome, he did not share Marsh's annoyance at having to deal with Grant's travels. Kasson reported to the State Department that the former president "did me the honor to accept the invitation to be my guest during his sojourn in this Capital" and told Evarts that he had, "with much pleasure . . . endeavored to fulfil [*sic*] on my part the instructions contained in your Circular of the 23rd of May 1877." Perhaps the reports of a likely third term had an impact on Kasson's attitude toward Grant, but more likely, he was simply not as out of touch as Marsh was with his own country. A native Vermonter who had emigrated west as a young man, Kasson was a leading Iowa Republican who had been a member of the House of Representatives during Grant's second term and, after his diplomatic service in Vienna and Berlin, he was reelected to Congress in the 1880s.[34]

On the Grants' thirtieth wedding anniversary, August 22, Grant wrote to his son, Fred, that his "reception by the Authorities has been very cordial." Vienna was "one of the most beautiful cities in Europe if not the most beautiful," and "[t]he people too compare, in appearance, very favorably with any others." But like Constantinople and Cairo, Berlin and St. Petersburg, and unlike Britain, the Netherlands, and Scandinavia, there were no press interviews or meetings with average Austrians; visits from foreign dignitaries were the business of the court and government. The US consul general, the secretary of the US legation, and Kasson all hosted lunches and dinners in honor of the former president, including a "special dinner" with guests "from the higher Austrian official and military ranks, and from the diplomatic corps." However, as Kasson reported to Evarts, "Here, as elsewhere on the continent, the Ambassadors were unwilling to yield precedence to an Ex-President of the United States—a fact which, at a dinner given in his honor . . . , necessarily deprived both himself and them of the pleasure of meeting on that occasion." Franz Josef received Grant on August 20 and hosted him at dinner the following evening. Grant's letters contain no comments about his conversations with the Austrian emperor, but Kasson informed the secretary of state that Grant had been seated at dinner "at the right-hand of the Emperor," who had "detailed an aide-de-camp to be at the General's disposal during his sojourn at the Capital."[35]

At the end of August, the Grants left Vienna to spend two weeks as tourists in Bad Ischl and Salzburg. There was one meeting left in the former president's summer summitry. Julia Grant remained in Salzburg when her husband, accompanied by Kasson, traveled from there to Bad Gastein on September 10 to meet Wilhelm I and Bismarck the next day. Unfortunately, as with Franz Josef, Grant wrote nothing about his meeting with the German emperor.[36] En route back to Paris, the Grants visited Munich, Germany, before spending a week in Ragaz, Switzerland. In Munich, they encountered a Marsh-like consul, G. Henry Horstmann, who in his 1886 memoirs still bristled at Evarts's May 23 circular—"I think it would have been more graceful on the part of the Department to have left its consuls and ministers to follow their own instincts"—and found everything associated with the visit burdensome. The Grants arrived a day earlier than expected, but the train was late; no one but "a hired fellow" was available to accompany Horstmann to the station; and while they waited, "it was raining in torrents, and the wind blowing a gale as if it would lift the roof from the building and carry it away." The former president disappointed. Inexplicably, Horstmann "was picturing to [himself] something like General Scott," but Grant "looked like a meek Pennsylvania *Friend* from the country in his First-day clothes." And "what took me still more aback was the smallness of his voice. Could those thin, piping tones, I thought, be the ones that were heard above the roar of artillery, the rattle of musketry, the clashing of swords—shouting commands to his aides?"[37]

The consul's attitude did not matter much, however; the Grants' stay in Munich was short and involved only sightseeing. They went on to Ragaz, and then paused briefly in Zurich for a September 23 dinner in the former president's honor. On September 25 Ulysses and Julia Grant returned to the French capital. For the second time in 1878, the US minister, Edward Noyes, John Russell Young, and other American residents of the city welcomed them "home" to Paris.[38]

Hamilton Fish (1808–93), former New York governor and senator, was President Grant's secretary of state from 1869 to 1877. By the time Grant left office, Fish had become a personal friend who saw the Grants off from Philadelphia in May 1877 and arranged for their special passports. Fish corresponded regularly with the former president during Grant's first eighteen months abroad. Author's collection; scan courtesy of John Wilkes, The *Vanity Fair* Print Company, www.vanity-fair-prints.com.

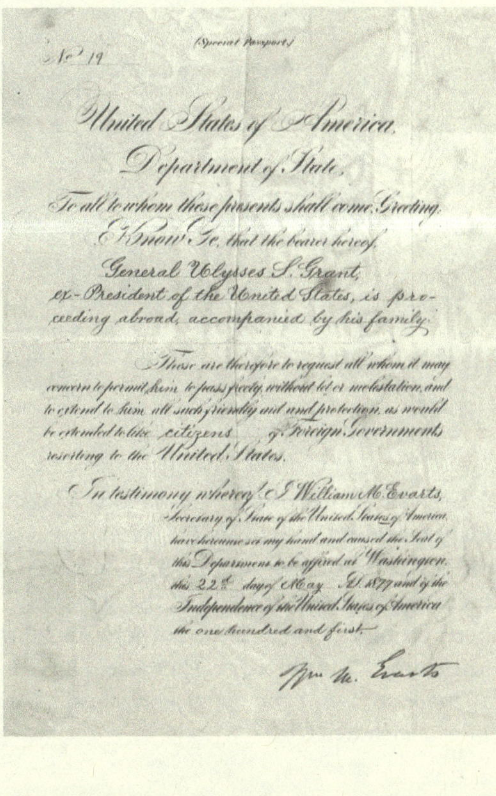

(Special Passport)

No. 19

United States of America,

Department of State,

To all to whom these presents shall come, Greeting.

Know Ye, that the bearer hereof, General Ulysses S. Grant, ex-President of the United States, is proceeding abroad, accompanied by his family.

These are therefore to request all whom it may concern to permit him to pass freely, without let or molestation, and to extend to him all such friendly aid and protection, as would be extended to like citizens of Foreign Governments resorting to the United States.

In testimony whereof, I William M. Evarts, Secretary of State of the United States of America, have hereunto set my hand and caused the Seal of this Department to be affixed at Washington, this 22d day of May A.D. 1877 and of the Independence of the United States of America the one hundred and first.

Wm. M. Evarts

The Grant family's passport was issued by the State Department on May 22, 1877. It was forwarded by Secretary of State William Evarts to the former president in London, along with a copy of Evarts's May 23 circular letter to all US diplomatic and consular posts, requesting that they assist Grant in his travels overseas. Evarts also issued individual passports to Ulysses, Julia, and Jesse Grant. Ulysses S. Grant Association's Ulysses S. Grant Presidential Library, Mississippi State University.

Edward, Prince of Wales (1841–1910), was instrumental in seeing that Grant was received by the British government with many of the courtesies due a head of state, in accord with the wishes of the US minister, Edwards Pierrepont. Author's collection; scan courtesy of John Wilkes, The *Vanity Fair* Print Company, www.vanity-fair-prints.com.

In the summer of 1877 Grant took a break from public diplomacy and summitry, traveling with his wife and youngest son up the Rhine to the Black Forest and the lakes of Switzerland and northern Italy. He was especially interested in visiting Geneva, the site of the successful CSS *Alabama* arbitration. While there, on July 27, he laid the cornerstone of the building that remains in use by Emmanuel Church today. Photo from *The American Church in Geneva: A Century of Service, 1873–1973*, Emmanuel Episcopal Church, Geneva, Switzerland, http://www.emmanuelchurch.ch/.

Joseph Chamberlain (1836–1914), as a member of Parliament (MP) for Birmingham and the city's former mayor, welcomed Grant on his visit in October 1877. Grant thanked the people of Birmingham for their steadfast support of the Union from 1861 to 1865, and gave an important speech to the Midlands International Arbitration Union in which he supported the peaceful settlement of international disputes and eventual creation of a "league of nations." Author's collection; scan courtesy of John Wilkes, The *Vanity Fair* Print Company, www.vanity-fair-prints.com.

John Bright (1811–89), a native of Birmingham and an MP from 1858 until his death, was known as "the foremost British champion" of the Union cause. He was not at home when Grant visited his city, but he met Grant in London. Grant told Bright's constituents that their MP's name was "as familiar in my own country as in his own home." Author's collection; scan courtesy of John Wilkes, The *Vanity Fair* Print Company, www.vanity-fair-prints.com.

French president Patrick MacMahon (1808–93) provoked the "16 Mai crisis" that delayed Grant's visit to Paris by several months in 1877. When Grant finally arrived in the capital in October, he was warmly welcomed across the French political spectrum. The city became the Grants' home base in Europe. Before they left Paris for their journey east of Suez, MacMahon gave a final dinner in the former president's honor. He resigned two weeks later, on January 30, 1879. Author's collection; scan courtesy of John Wilkes, The *Vanity Fair* Print Company, www.vanity-fair-prints.com.

Grant met Leon Gambetta (1838–82) in Paris in November 1877, and the French republican leader "impressed [him] as one of the foremost minds in Europe." After nearly two months in the French capital, the former president left for Egypt in December 1877 with a radically different, far more positive opinion of France and its people than he had before staying in Paris. Author's collection; scan courtesy of John Wilkes, The *Vanity Fair* Print Company, www.vanity-fair-prints.com.

Ismail Pasha (1830–95) lavishly entertained the Grants, putting at their disposal his private railcar and boats to travel from Alexandria to Cairo, visit the Nile valley, and traverse the Suez Canal during their January–February 1878 visit to Egypt. The khedive's wars, building projects, and lifestyle indebted the country to European creditors, and he was deposed in 1879 by Britain and France. Grant warned the leaders of China and Japan to avoid the khedive's fate by steering clear of foreign loans. Author's collection; scan courtesy of John Wilkes, The *Vanity Fair* Print Company, www.vanity-fair-prints.com.

George I (1845–1913), the son of Christian IX of Denmark, was placed on the throne of Greece in 1863 with the support of the European great powers. His country's March 1878 reception of Grant was an enthusiastic expression of Greek nationalism and "undying gratitude" to Americans for their support of Greek independence fifty years before. The Grants encountered George's family throughout Europe: they dined with his parents in Copenhagen, with his sister, Dagmar, the crown princess of Russia, in St. Petersburg, and with his brother-in-law, the Prince of Wales, in London. Author's collection; scan courtesy of John Wilkes, The *Vanity Fair* Print Company, www.vanity-fair-prints.com.

George Perkins Marsh (1801–82), the US minister to Italy from 1861 until his death, found Grant's March–April 1878 visit to Rome to be a protocol burden he did not want to bear. While Marsh's attitude allowed Ulysses and Julia Grant to enjoy the city as tourists after intensive summitry and public diplomacy in Constantinople and Athens, his inability to see the diplomatic possibilities inherent in Grant's visit showed the inadequacies of American representation abroad.

Otto von Bismarck (1815–98), chancellor of Prussia and Germany, met with Grant several times during the former president's visit to Berlin in June–July 1878. During the 1870–71 Franco-Prussian War, President Grant, while insistent on maintaining US neutrality, had a reputation as being pro-German; but his attitude had changed by the time he visited Berlin. The former president was not favorably impressed by the militaristic aristocracy of the German capital. Author's collection; scan courtesy of John Wilkes, The *Vanity Fair* Print Company, www.vanity-fair-prints.com.

Friedrich (1831–88), the crown prince of Germany, and his wife, Queen Victoria's eldest daughter "Vicky," hosted the Grants at a dinner at the New Palace in Potsdam in June 1878. Often at odds with Bismarck's policies, the royal couple was the hope of those Germans who wanted their country to evolve into a constitutional monarchy on the British model. But Friedrich reigned for only three months in 1888 before dying painfully of throat cancer, as Ulysses Grant had done three years earlier. Author's collection; scan courtesy of John Wilkes, The *Vanity Fair* Print Company, www.vanity-fair-prints.com.

Eugene (1856–79), the prince imperial of France, fled with his mother, Eugenie, to Britain after his father, Napoleon III, abdicated the imperial throne of France in 1870, and became head of the House of Bonaparte with his father's death in 1873. He and Grant were in Copenhagen at the same time in July 1878, but the former president made a point of not meeting the prince imperial because, as he told a reporter, "I don't like the family." Author's collection; scan courtesy of John Wilkes, The *Vanity Fair* Print Company, www.vanity-fair-prints.com.

Alexander II (1818–81), the tsar of Russia, warmly received Grant in August 1878 at his palace outside St. Petersburg. Hamilton Fish had warned Grant to be wary of visiting Russia because Foreign Minister Gorchakov "has not forgiven the dismissal of his pet," Russian minister to the United States Catacazy, declared persona non grata by the Grant administration in 1871. But the former president enjoyed his time in Russia. In March 1881, when Alexander II was assassinated, Grant told the *New York Times* that he did not see how the tsar's death would help the Russian people. Author's collection; scan courtesy of John Wilkes, The *Vanity Fair* Print Company, www.vanity-fair-prints.com.

Franz Josef (1830–1916), the emperor of Austria-Hungary, hosted Grant at a dinner and assigned him a military aide-de-camp during his stay in the Austrian capital, but as in Berlin and St. Petersburg, the former president's visit attracted little public or press attention. Ulysses and Julia Grant celebrated their thirtieth wedding anniversary on August 22, 1878, in Vienna, which Grant found perhaps "the most beautiful" city in Europe. Author's collection; scan courtesy of John Wilkes, The *Vanity Fair* Print Company, www.vanity-fair-prints.com.

CHAPTER FOUR

A Decisive Letter from Washington: 1878–79

In late summer 1878 Ulysses Grant still seemed unlikely to turn his European travels into a world tour. He and the former first lady intended to "go to Spain and Portugal after which nothing will be left but to spend a quiet Winter and go home in the Spring," as Grant wrote to Fred on August 22. A week later he told Buck that "we will make our winter stay in Paris." Grant liked Paris because "one sees more Americans there than any place else in Europe, and I find it pleasant abroad exactly in proportion to the number of Americans one finds to talk to." Anticipating Hemingway and Fitzgerald, he declared that "no American would stay in Paris if he found himself the only one of his countrymen there" and added wryly, "Washington City ought to superscede [*sic*] Paris as a resort for our people who think they must go away from home." John Russell Young wanted the former president to circumnavigate the globe, but Grant insisted it was not to be. He wrote to Young from Bad Ischl on September 3 that

> [i]f I should go home by the east I should be delighted to have you with me. Will always be glad to have you along, when it is convenient to you, in my travels. But I shall not go home by the east, this winter at least. There is so much water communication and so little to see that I am rather deterred from making the journey.

Three weeks later, on September 21 Grant told General Sherman, "I have no idea of going round the world. If I was alone I might, but there is to [*sic*] much sea travel and to [*sic*] little to see Without [*sic*] hardships to [*sic*] great for a lady."[1] Sherman did not agree and he wrote to say so, but the Grants, accompanied by Young, left Paris for Spain and Portugal on October 12, and did not receive Sherman's letter until December.

Iberia, France, and Ireland, September 25, 1878–January 23, 1879. On October 12, 1878, Grant left Paris for a two-month visit to Spain, Portugal, and the British Crown Colony of Gibraltar, returning to Paris via Pau, in the southwest of France, on December 12. After a brief visit, via London, to Ireland early in 1879, Grant returned for the last time to the French capital. He departed Paris for Marseilles on January 21.

Grant's visit to Spain brought him to the only country with which the United States had come close to going to war during his presidency. After Russia's sale of Alaska and the withdrawal of French forces from Mexico, only two European countries still controlled territory in the Western Hemisphere of strategic significance to American interests: Britain and Spain. President Grant's October 12, 1870, neutrality proclamation prohibiting Fenian activity on American territory, the Geneva arbitration, and the administration's efforts (even if not fully successful) to mitigate the effects on Canada of US Army operations against the Sioux effectively eliminated the major points of friction between London and Washington.[2] The British government was a responsible and stable negotiating partner, with excellent lines of communication, fully in control of its armed forces in North America. Spain's situation was far more precarious. Throughout Grant's years in office, Madrid sought to quell an insurrection in Cuba, the Ten Years' War, while Spain itself was in turmoil. After Isabella II fled the country in 1868 and then abdicated, from 1870 to 1874 Spain experienced an elected monarch (Amadeo of Savoy) who renounced the throne after twenty-six months; a republic, whose principal leader was Emilio Castelar, that survived from February 1873 to December 1874; and finally, restoration of the Bourbon line under Isabella's son, Alfonso XII. Given the instability in Madrid and Spain's tenuous control of its forces in Cuba, the United States could not assume that what happened on the island was sanctioned by the Spanish government. At the same time, it was harder for Washington to control the misuse of American territory to mount anti-Spanish activities in Cuba than it was to deal with incursions into Canada, and there were more Americans willing, for mercenary and other reasons, to support the Cuban insurrection.[3]

This situation culminated in 1873–75 in the *Virginius* crisis. The vessel, built as a Confederate blockade-runner, had been purchased (illegally, under Grant's neutrality proclamation) in the United States to run arms to Cuban rebels. Captained by a former Confederate naval officer and manned by a crew including US and British nationals, she was seized on the high seas, carrying weapons and mercenaries, by a Spanish naval vessel in October 1873 and taken to Santiago, Cuba. The captain, mercenaries, and many of the crew were executed as pirates before a British warship arrived from Jamaica and obtained a halt to the executions. When news of this reached the United States there was an outcry for war similar to that created by the sinking of USS *Maine* twenty-five years later. President Grant and Secretary of State Fish, with the cooperation of Castelar in Madrid and working through the Spanish minister in Washington, prevented the situation from escalating into war. The final settlement, which included Spain's paying reparations to the United States for the families of the executed American nationals, was not reached until early 1875, after restoration of the monarchy. Even before the *Virginius* affair, Grant, like the majority of his countrymen, saw Spanish withdrawal from the island as inevitable; the only question was whether its departure would involve US military action.[4] His visit to Spain allowed him to assess the capabilities of the armed forces, the cohesion and stability of the government, and the nation's infrastructure. When Alfonso XII invited the former president to meet him in Vitoria, just south of the French border, in October 1878 to observe Spanish army maneuvers, it was not only courtesy that caused Grant to accept the invitation.

But Grant was also interested in both Iberian countries and the British colony of Gibraltar for other reasons. For one thing, he was a tourist. No matter what else he was doing on behalf of the United States, the former president remained the curious individual he had always been, and he wanted to see the sights. The sights to be seen in Spain and Portugal had a lot to do with the history of the Americas. The issues that had once dominated Anglo-Spanish rivalry in the hemisphere now preoccupied the United States, especially the desire for a maritime link between the Atlantic and Pacific oceans. Grant had been thinking about this since he was a young officer who crossed the Nicaraguan isthmus en route to California in 1852, and he spent much of his time after 1880 organizing support for a transisthmian canal.[5] Grant's interest in Mexico also led him to be interested in its mother country, Spain. Although Spain and Portugal were no longer the global powers they had been in their sixteenth- and seventeenth-century heyday, they still had important colonies in Africa and the Far East and played a role in the European commercial and territorial rivalries that dominated the international system. For the foreseeable future, colonial empires were a fact of life that Americans needed to understand if they were to pursue their own interests successfully around the world.

The Grants spent nearly two months touring Spain, Portugal, and Gibraltar. After the army maneuvers in Vitoria, they were in Madrid for a week, October 18–25. John Russell Young's *New York Herald* articles were normally filled with details of Grant's activities, but the stories he filed from Madrid were an exception. As in France the year before, "Spanish politics [were] full of torpedoes," and the domestic political situation forced the former president to tread carefully. Young reported in generalities: "There were arsenals to be inspected and picture galleries, the royal palace and the royal stables. There were long walks about Madrid and long talks with [American minister James Russell] Lowell, whom General Grant had never met before, but for whom he conceived a sincere attachment and esteem."

Grant wanted to host a dinner for the republican leader, Castelar, who "had been so friendly to the North in our war" and had made possible the peaceful settlement of the *Virginius* affair. But the former president "was in some sort a guest of the nation, and it was feared that the dinner might be construed into a republican demonstration—an interference in other people's affairs—and it was abandoned." Castelar called on Grant, however, as did Joaquin Jovellar, who had been sent to Havana as captain general in November 1873 to maintain control of the situation there while Madrid and Washington negotiated. Jovellar and Grant "had satisfying talks about Cuba."[6] The king gave a state dinner in honor of the former president, and Lowell reported to Secretary of State Evarts that he had received "[e]very possible attention and courtesy . . . the Minister for Foreign Affairs took occasion to tell me that these civilities were intended not only to show respect and good will to General Grant, but to the Government and people of the United States."[7]

The former president left Madrid on Friday, October 25, and arrived in Lisbon the morning of October 27. Later that day, he wrote ruefully to Adam Badeau that "Spain may contain much of interest to see, but the accomodations [*sic*] for travel are horrible."[8] In the Portuguese capital Young was back in his usual form, reporting that Grant had several conversations with King Luis during his week there, especially about expanding Portuguese-American trade. Young described lyrically Grant's day trip to Cintra, where "[y]ou see the Tagus spreading out to the sea, forcing its way through forests and hills and valleys until it falls into the ocean's arms. . . . There was a fascination in this view that made us loth [*sic*] to leave it, and for a long time we lingered." In this environment, Grant's mind was on maritime commerce. "It was over that sea that Vasco de Gama [*sic*] sailed, and from this lofty summit King Manuel . . . saw him come, bringing tribute and empire from the Indies." Young wrote in his diary on October 28 that he had made "several valuable notes," after a conversation with the former president, "about the Southern isthmus canal."[9]

Grant's visit to Spain and Portugal was about summitry and tourism, not public diplomacy; there was no public or parliamentary opinion to be influenced. "In Spain," Young remarked, "there are no newspapers." This was not literally true; he meant there was no independent journalism. In contrast to Britain, France, Scandinavia, and the Netherlands, "Spanish journals seemed not to have heard of [Grant's] presence" in Madrid. The situation was better in Lisbon, where "every morning we had columns of choice info in the good old-fashioned homely style." But even so, Portuguese journalists "did not interview the General as to what he thought of the world." Like Berlin, St. Petersburg, and Vienna, only a handful of men made the decisions that mattered, and Grant concentrated on meeting them. Still, Young felt, comparing Spain to Portugal, "the breezes that come from the Mediterranean are enervating compared with what come from the Atlantic."[10]

The former president traveled extensively in Spain, visiting historic and cultural sites and, as he always did, observing the daily life going on around him to see what he could learn about the likely future of the country. From Lisbon, Grant went overland to Cordoba, Seville, and Cadiz, and then by water (with land excursions as necessary) to Gibraltar, Malaga, Grenada, Cartagena, and Barcelona. Despite the efforts of the Spanish monarch and government to impress him, Grant was not optimistic about their future. From Gibraltar on November 14 he wrote to Fred that "Spain gives some evidence of recent improvement, but there is great room for more. There seems to be no satisfaction with existing affairs and I would not be surprised to hear of a revolution breaking out at any time. A republic is inevitable at no distant day." The next day, he told Daniel Ammen that "[t]he [Spanish] people are good enough if . . . they could see any return for their labor. But . . . there seems to be no integrity among the ruling class. . . . The revenue-officers are so abundant that there is no chance of escaping any tax except by bribery, which is resorted to, to the extent of depriving the government of a very large percentage of its revenues." As a result of this corruption, "There is the greatest discontent, and the least thing would start a revolution. I have no idea that the existing state of affairs can last long. It will not be long before the experiment of a republic will be tried again, and probably with more success than the last time."[11]

Grant had been traveling for almost eighteen months when he reached Gibraltar on November 12, and although there had been press stories that he intended to go around the world and friends urging him to do so, that was still not his plan when he arrived in the British colony. He told Fred in his November 14 letter that "[a]s we have seen every thing there is to be seen, without going through the east to San Francisco, I am becoming very homesick." And to Ammen the next day, he wrote that "[f]rom [Barcelona] we will in all probability make our way to Paris, and remain quiet until about six weeks before the time to sail for home. I want to spend about a month with Nellie before going back, and want to make a run through Ireland."[12] But the phrase "in all probability" indicated that

Grant's returning home to the United States from Europe was, in fact, less probable than it had been just a few days before. What finally changed his mind came together at Gibraltar in November 1878: the presence of John Russell Young, the influence of the governor of Gibraltar, a reunion with the officers of USS *Vandalia*, and the arrival of a letter from Secretary of the Navy Richard Thompson.

Grant valued Young's judgment and opinions. The two men had been together almost constantly for a month when they arrived in Gibraltar on November 12, and Young had had ample opportunity to make his case for going around the world. Born in 1840, he was the friend of, and in some respects older son to, Grant that Adam Badeau aspired, and failed spectacularly, to become. As a young *Philadelphia Press* reporter during the Civil War, Young had recognized the breadth and depth of Grant's intellect, and he wholeheartedly supported Grant's aims, initially preservation of the Union and emancipation, then, when Grant became president, Anglo-American rapprochement, the peaceful settlement of international disputes, and universal access to economic and educational opportunity. Briefly, in the early 1870s, Young had his own newspaper, the *New York Standard*. He wrote to President Grant on November 5, 1870, that he wanted the paper to be "a decorous,—able,—moderate Republican journal, giving direct and affirmative support to your administration." For himself, Young told the president that he wished "to do the work set down for me in my own way,—to give your administration what no other newspaper here does,—a generous, hearty, fighting support."[13]

In 1871, with President Grant's approval, Young went to London to influence British public and elite opinion to support arbitration of the CSS *Alabama* claims. In an April 18, 1871, letter to the *Times* (London), he wrote:

> I am anxious . . . that England should do justice to the president of the United States. His administration means peace. Like your own Wellington—to whom, in fact, his character bears many points of resemblance—he has seen enough of war not to view with horror and deep concern any question that might lead to war. All that military renown can give him he has gained. His further renown must come from victories of peace.[14]

President Grant appreciated Young's commitment to the administration's foreign-policy goals, and he admired his journalistic integrity, which Young combined—quite easily, in fact, although Grant's detractors doubted it—with his personal admiration for the president. By the time they began their travels together, Young had been Grant's trusted confidante for nearly a decade. He had to return to Paris before the Grants did. Leaving them in Malaga on November 23, Young confided to his diary, "Am sorry to leave the General with whom I have been much this year and whom I esteem as a high-minded & peace-minded man."[15] Young wanted to visit Asia, and he wanted to do so with Grant, but he especially wanted Asian leaders to meet the former president.

In Gibraltar Grant was also encouraged to travel east of Suez by Baron Napier of Magdala, who had become governor of the colony in 1876 after six years as commander in chief, India. Born in Ceylon in 1810, Napier's entire military career had been spent in Asia and East Africa, including service in the two Anglo-Sikh Wars of the 1840s, the Indian Mutiny, the Second Anglo-Chinese war, and Abyssinia in 1867, where he earned his baronetcy. Napier had a young family, and the Grants spent a good deal of time in their company while in Gibraltar. The governor's stories of his own experiences in Asia, particularly India, would have reinforced Young's encouragement to travel there. In January 1879, as Grant prepared to leave Europe behind, Napier wrote the former president that he was "glad you have decided to visit India. You will Enjoy [*sic*] your visit." He hoped that the Grants would "find it convenient to go as far as Jullalabad or at least to the Khybur."[16]

Fortuitously, the Grants found themselves in Gibraltar at the same time as USS *Vandalia*, en route home, and remembered how much they had enjoyed traveling with the US Navy. Julia Grant recalled that "Captain Robeson sent his gig to the steamer to take us ashore. Just as it arrived, one came from the Governor of Gibraltar, Lord Napier, to perform the same friendly duty. The General took our American gig which had performed the same service for him so often before and so well." In Gibraltar, the Grants "were the guests of the American Consul, who gave several enjoyable parties to the General and the officers of the *Vandalia*"; the former president and first lady were with their old shipmates "quite often" during their stay. At precisely the right moment, Grant was reminded of those officers' Christmas dinner in honor of Julia Grant; visiting Malta, the Holy Land, and Constantinople with them; and his evenings playing "Boston" with Lieutenant Commander Caldwell.[17] The American flag flying from *Vandalia* in Gibraltar harbor would have reminded him that his travels aboard her had not only been pleasant, but had served the foreign-policy interests of the United States.

As important as Young, Napier, and *Vandalia*'s officers were in Grant's decision to go around the world, however, it was a letter from Secretary of the Navy Richard Thompson offering the former president passage on another US naval vessel that proved decisive. Grant received Thompson's October 23 letter when he arrived in Gibraltar on November 12. The offer was confirmation that the United States government had been pleased with Grant's diplomatic activities in Europe and the Near East, and Thompson asked him to duplicate and enlarge on those achievements in the months to come. The Hayes administration in May 1877 had had a general idea that Grant's presence overseas would be a diplomatic asset, as evidenced by the secretary of state's circular letter to US diplomats and consuls, and Thompson's initial offer of passage on US naval vessels that had led to Grant's three months on *Vandalia*. Eighteen months later, Thompson's second letter showed that the government now had an even clearer conception of Grant's foreign-policy role. This time, the secretary had a specific mission on a specific vessel in mind.

"The U.S. Steamer Richmond, designed as the Flag ship of the Asiatic Naval Station," Thompson wrote, "will probably leave the United States about the 10th of December, en route for Singapore, and may be expected to reach Point de Galle in the Island of Ceylon by the middle of January next. If it is your purpose to visit British India, China, and Japan, it is probable that this vessel, being a flag ship, will afford you more facilities and conveniences of travel than you will be likely to obtain by any other method of conveyance." Thompson told Grant that if he wished "to join her at any point en route to her station [Yokohama, Japan], upon notification of that fact the department will immediately issue the necessary instructions to carry out your wishes." The secretary outlined the route that *Richmond* would likely take, which would "undoubtedly furnish to you many opportunities of interesting observations and research." But the United States government had a greater purpose in mind. "[A]part from the personal gratification to yourself of observing the tastes, customs, and wants of the inhabitants of the countries visited," he told Grant, "the department feels assured that . . . your intercourse with them would lead to more extended and intimate commercial relations between them and the United States." Commercial opportunities were only part of what the administration envisioned, however:

> [Y]our presence on board a Man-of-war, in the ports to be visited by the Richmond, will so arrest public attention as to bring prominently into view, not merely the character and extent of our commerce, but the nature and value of our institutions.

Should Grant decide to travel aboard *Richmond*, "orders will be issued to Captain Benham, who will command her, and to Rear Admiral Patterson, commanding the Asiatic Station, of similar import to the instructions to the Commanders in Chief of Naval Stations in reference to yourself, and of which you have been heretofore advised."[18]

This was a remarkable statement of the US government's understanding of the importance of public and commercial diplomacy. It was part of a concerted State-Navy Department effort, conceived by Thompson and Secretary Evarts, to find new markets for American goods as a way of overcoming the lingering depression that followed the economic Panic of 1873. The mission Thompson proposed to Grant was one prong of a two-pronged approach involving USS *Richmond* and USS *Ticonderoga*. At the same time he was writing to Grant, the navy secretary was also ordering *Ticonderoga*, under the command of Commodore Robert Shufeldt, on a mission to extend American commerce into Africa and Asia, "to visit the 'unfrequented ports . . . where there are at present no American Commercial representatives with a view to the encouragement and extension of American Commerce.'" *Ticonderoga* departed Hampton Roads on December 7, 1878, and returned to Mare Island, California, on November 9, 1880, having logged over thirty-six thousand miles from West Africa around the Cape of Good Hope to the Persian Gulf and East Asia. *Richmond*'s mission, on the other hand, was not to visit the "unfrequented ports" of the world en route to Yokohama, but to extend American influence in those ports that were most frequented, by having on board the former president of the United States. She departed Norfolk on January 11, 1879, a month later than the date given in Thompson's letter to Grant.[19]

The former president's initial reaction to the secretary's offer was to decline it. He did not mention it at all in his November 14 letter to Fred, but instead wrote on the same day to Thompson that "I would cable you my determination not to go east,—certainly not this winter—only that I previously communicated the fact to Adml Ammen who I presume has informed the Department before this." Still, Grant admitted to Thompson, "It is a splendid opportunity however and I feel much tempted to accept. If I should change my mind I will cable you at the earlyest [*sic*] moment after having done so." The next day, Grant wrote to Ammen that he had received "the very kind letter of the Secretary of the Navy tendering to me the use of the Richmond for an Eastern tour." He told his old friend that he had written Thompson, "that I had determined on not going home by way of China and Japan, at least for this winter, and that no doubt you had communicated the message." Grant commented that "[i]t seems a long journey to go from here to San Francisco by water for as little as there is to see along the coast. If I was alone, or with a party of gentlemen that could penetrate the interior of countries passed through, I should not hesitate."[20] Grant's elliptical prose (most unusual for him) in his letters to Ammen and Thompson mirrored his indecision; he was surrounded by people, including Julia Grant, who thought he should "go east," and now he had a letter from the secretary of the navy telling him that his doing so would serve the foreign-policy interests of the United States.

Grant made his decision to accept Thompson's offer on December 5, when he arrived in Pau, France, and found Sherman's letter, and a letter from Ammen, both urging him to go around the world. Ammen's opinion carried special weight with Grant because, as a career naval officer until his retirement earlier in 1878, he knew the countries that Grant had not yet visited. Ammen later recalled that he advised Grant to "reconsider his determination to come home without having gone around the world. . . . [H]is visit to China and Japan would have an excellent result, in placing our people and our government in excellent relations with them . . . I happened to meet General Sherman within a few days and mentioned the above to him. He said he had received a similar letter from General Grant, and had written him almost in the same terms." Sherman had two reasons for favoring the trip; he thought it was a good idea for Grant to visit Asia, but he was particularly interested in his returning home via the West Coast. Sherman had written to Philip Sheridan on October 13 that Californians "counted on his 'coming that way' and will be much disappointed [if he doesn't]. I wrote him as much, and if he Contemplates [*sic*] another tour of the White House, I am sure it would be to his interest to Come [*sic*] back by that route." Sheridan agreed, telling Sherman on October 29 that "I think as you do, that general [*sic*] Grant should go to California." West Coast residents "were greatly disappointed at his not going out there when he was at Salt Lake some three years ago—and he ought to make himself good." Sheridan was also interested in a third term for the former president: "He has grown wonderfuly [*sic*] in public confidence as an able and strong man, and it would not surprise me a bit, if he was called upon to again go to the White House. There would certainly be no doubt about it, if the election was to take place this fall."[21]

After receiving Ammen's and Sherman's letters, Grant cabled the secretary of the navy the next morning: "Accept passage on the Richmond for Self and family." President Hayes was informed immediately of Grant's acceptance, as the *Philadelphia Press* reported on December 7, with a dateline of December 6: "The ex-President's cablegram was read to the Cabinet today." Grant wrote to Ammen that he had accepted the US government's offer, and to Edward Beale, telling him that the former first lady would travel with him: "Mrs. Grant would not give up the trip for the world. In fact, she has been urging me to go that way ever since I first announced my determination to return by the Atlantic." On December 8 Grant replied to Sherman. He had "found a very large mail" waiting for him in Pau, and "[a] number of these letters—like yours—insisted that I ought to go back by the way of India, China & Japan." Like Beale, Sherman had suggested that the trip might be too much for Julia Grant, and he got the same reply, expressed in a more intimate and teasing tone: "Mrs. Grant . . . says for me to saus you for even suggesting the idea of her going back by the Atlantic." Grant wrote on the same day to John Russell Young that he had "determined to make the trip eastward," and told him that "I shall be delighted to have you go as Mrs. Grant is also."[22]

The Grants left Pau for Paris on December 11 to spend their few remaining weeks in Europe. There was one final European country, Ireland, for Grant to visit if he could manage it, and arrangements were to be made for his travels east. These included putting together the members of the party that would accompany him to Asia, a question that made its way into the American press. The *New York Times* reported on December 22 that, according to the secretary of the navy, only members of Grant's immediate family currently with him in Europe could accompany him on USS *Richmond*. Since Jesse Grant had returned to the United States some months before, and such a stipulation would, of course, have excluded John Russell Young, this would have left Ulysses and Julia Grant without traveling companions. It is unlikely they would have boarded *Richmond* under such conditions, but the matter was quickly clarified. On December 24 the *Washington Post* confirmed that, at no expense to the US government, Grant would be able to invite "one or two friends" to travel with him. In addition to Young, the Grants were joined by their eldest son, Lieutenant Colonel Frederick Grant, who received permission from Secretary of War George McCrary to make the trip; Grant's good friend and first secretary of the navy, Adolph Borie; and Borie's young physician, Dr. John Keating.[23]

The trip to Ireland also fell into place. Grant left Paris on January 2, 1879, accompanied by the US minister to France, Edward Noyes, while

Julia Grant remained in the French capital.[24] John Russell Young and Adam Badeau joined Grant and Noyes in London, and the four arrived in Dublin on January 3. Grant also visited Londonderry, Coleraine, and Belfast, departing Ireland on January 8. There was little tourism and only one event that came close to summitry, since Ireland was governed from London. On the day of his arrival, the former president was invited to lunch by the Lord Lieutenant of Ireland, the Duke of Marlborough, John Winston Spencer Churchill (grandfather of the future prime minister), at his residence in Dublin. There was a greater-than-usual partisan political tinge to Grant's public diplomacy in Ireland, since the Republican Party was at risk of losing (and eventually did lose) the competition for Irish-American votes to the Democrats. A vocal segment of Irish immigrants to the United States regarded both the former president and his party as insufficiently supportive of Irish nationalism. Grant's pursuit of Anglo-American rapprochement, his administration's efforts to prevent Fenian incursions into Canada, and his firm opposition to using public funds to support parochial schools all made his presence in Ireland controversial. Badeau worried in a December 30, 1878, letter to Orville Babcock about the visit: "[T]he consul at Dublin writes me that the Fenians are very hostile to him, because he refused to receive their deputation when he was President. There must be a demonstration, the Consu[l] says, and there may be trouble."[25] There was, but it was not as serious as it might have been.

Grant was warmly welcomed by the Lord Mayor of Dublin, John Barrington, in a speech that linked him to Abraham Lincoln: "Ireland mourned for his loss when she heard the news that the great disciple of freedom had been struck down. A truly great general took his place and carried out the work that had been begun . . . the shackles of the negro and slavery disappeared from America, every part of which is now free." But as Grant was being welcomed in Dublin, the corporation of the city of Cork, which (mistakenly) believed that he planned a visit there, was discussing whether or not he would be welcome. One official denounced him as anti-Catholic and said he had "insulted the Irish people in America," while another claimed that Grant "went out of his way to insult their religion." The discussion was reported in newspapers in the United States, and General Sherman (married to a Catholic, with a son about to become a priest) was called upon to defend Grant. He told a reporter on January 10 that the former president was not anti-Catholic, but a defender of "the freedom of our public schools from sectarian influence"; and that "the ceaseless clamor for set religious exercises in the public schools [came] not from Catholics, but from Protestant denominations." Grant himself, in a November 4, 1879, interview, after his return home, about the "Cork affair," declared that "[i]f any Methodist friends should ever undertake to divert public funds to the support of sectarian schools, they and I would be at outs."[26]

Nevertheless, it was fortunate that the visit to Ireland had become a footnote to Grant's travels east of Suez. In addition to the hostility of Cork's municipal leaders, the former president had an encounter with workers at the Londonderry train station on January 6; they faulted him for not receiving a Fenian leader who had visited the United States during his presidency. The incidents were not numerous, but if they had occurred at the beginning of Grant's travels in 1877, they would have set an entirely different tone than that established in Manchester and at the London Guildhall. Had they been his final experiences on foreign soil—as they would have been, had Grant returned home from Europe—they would doubtless have overshadowed the warm public welcome that he had received elsewhere for the previous year and a half. Instead, the visit reflected the effort that Grant made, in the dead of winter, to travel from France to Ireland, because, as he said in Londonderry, "I could not think of having seen so much of the Old World, and pass by your little island without putting my foot on your soil." America, he declared, offered "a home for all who find themselves limited on this side of the water. We will make you all welcome when you come there to see us—and more than that, we will make you all citizens . . . and give you an equal voice with ourselves in saying who shall make the laws, and what laws should be made."[27] These were not the words of a man who wanted to keep Irish Catholics out of the United States.

Grant saw London for the last time on January 9, 1879, en route back to Paris from Belfast. The new American minister, John Welsh, hosted him that evening, and the former president finally learned while in the British capital that USS *Richmond* had not yet departed the United States. It remains unclear why this information was not cabled to him several weeks earlier. Her delay was no secret. The *Philadelphia Press* reported on December 10 that repairs would keep *Richmond* from sailing on schedule and that "General Grant has been informed of the change of time and will regulate his movements accordingly," but this was simply untrue. The secretary of the navy had written that *Richmond* would "probably leave the United States about the 10th of December," and a full month's delay could hardly be construed as being "about" December 10, even with the caveat of "probably." It does not seem to have occurred to anyone in Washington that a cable might be necessary; nor did Grant apparently request that anyone inquire by telegraph, at least not until just before he left Paris for Ireland. Meanwhile, telegrams about other subjects were going back and forth. Young noted in his diary on December 18 that Grant had "sent a cable to his son F.D. to come and go to India"; on December 28 the former president told Adam Badeau that "a cablegram informs me" of Fred's and Borie's sailing dates. Young himself had cable connections between the *Herald*'s New York and European offices; the paper published a section called "Telegraphic News from All Parts of the World." And while the US legation in Paris and the State Department generally avoided sending transatlantic telegrams because of the cost, they knew that Grant was waiting for news.[28]

Sherman knew of the delay, at the latest by December 22, when he wrote—a letter, not a cable—to Grant telling him that *Richmond* had not sailed. He proposed a course of action to Grant that he described in detail in a December 30 letter to Sheridan:

> I wrote him fully to the effect that the U.S. Frigate Richmond . . . had not yet started; that this was a large Comfortable ship, though slow—that instead of reaching Nice by January 12, it could not possibly be there before the middle of February &c &c. I advised him to start on his own time . . . leaving word for the Richmond to follow . . . I think this plan much better than to wait the Slow Movement of the Richmond at Paris.

Grant received Sherman's letter on January 10 when he got back to Paris from Ireland and replied on January 12 that he "had learned in London, with great disappointment, of the delay of the Richmond, and determined to do the very thing you advise; take a regular steamer and make my visit to India before joining a Govt. steamer." Grant was not happy; he told Sherman (somewhat petulantly, given the Navy's role in his Civil War victories, and his recent travels with *Vandalia*) that "[i]t does seem to me the Navy was never up to time, except in war, and then only with some of the Commanders." Still, he had good reason to be annoyed. In addition to the delay itself, the secretary of the navy failed to mention any problem in a letter he wrote to Grant on, of all days, December 10. Thompson's letter was informative about everything except the key question. He wished Grant "a pleasant voyage and can see no reason why you may not [have one], as the Richmond is in excellent condition and a good sailer." Grant replied on Christmas Day with "my thanks for the courticy [*sic*] thus extended" and assured Thompson that "my accepting it will neither result in cost to the Department nor delay or prejudice to the public service." He asked the secretary to "[p]lease present my compliments to the President and your associates in the Cabinet, wish them all, for me, a merry Christmas, a happy New Year, and many returns."[29]

The delay in *Richmond*'s departure, the lack of communication with Washington, and the resulting confusion and frustration did not seem to be an auspicious start to Grant's trip to Asia. He had expected to board *Richmond* on or about January 20, and with or without her, he was determined to leave Europe on that schedule. It was not that difficult to book passage on a commercial steamer to Egypt. The former president had a January 16 dinner invitation from President MacMahon, Grant's final host in Paris, as he had been his first in October 1877. "As the dinner is given to me," Grant wrote to Sherman, "I cannot well withdraw my acceptance so as to start at an earlyer [*sic*] day." But he intended to "find out the date, and places of departure, of steamers from Mediterranean ports and start by the earlyest [*sic*] after the 16th."[30] He did just that. Grant's journey east of Suez began on January 23, 1879, when he and his party departed Marseilles for Alexandria aboard the French steamer *Labourdonnais*.

CHAPTER FIVE

The "Distinguished Foreigner" East of Suez: 1879

When the P&O steamer *Venetia* departed Suez on January 31, 1879, bound for Bombay (Mumbai) with the former president of the United States on board, Ulysses Grant was about to enter not only a different geographic region of the globe, but the twentieth century. His trip came at the moment when the European international system had begun its transition to a global system, although the actors involved, both European and non-European, with rare exceptions, did not yet see it that way. The Europeans believed, with good reason, given the evidence of the previous half century, that they determined the rules of the game. Asians believed, also with good evidence, that there were two sets of rules, one that applied to European powers, based on negotiation among (theoretically) equal states, and another dictated to Asians by Europeans alternately wielding loans, Bibles, and Gatling guns. By 1879 the best informed leaders of Asia had given up the hope that they could keep Europeans at bay, confining them to trading ports or not dealing with them at all; what to do about them was an existential question.

Grant's arrival in Asia was a sign of the emerging global political system. When the American colonies had sought allies in their war against Britain a century before, those allies could be found only in Europe; the countries of Asia existed in a separate political system. By 1850 the projection of European economic and military power had had a significant impact on the political and military balance of power in Asia, but that impact was still a one-way street. During the Civil War the aim of both Union and Confederate diplomacy remained that of the thirteen colonies, to influence the policies of the European powers.[1] But by the time Grant became president in 1869, independent countries outside Europe, including the

United States itself, were beginning to affect the political-military balance of power, not only in their own regions, but in Europe itself. The Juarez government's military resistance to Napoleon III and Maximilian, and the political opposition of the United States to their Mexican adventure, were significant because for the first time the attempt of a European power to establish its presence on another continent was defeated, not by another European power, but by forces indigenous to that continent.

Mexicans not only thwarted Napoleon III's ambitions in the Western Hemisphere but they also weakened the Second Empire at home by defeating him there. Two years later, that empire suffered its ultimate defeat in the Franco-Prussian War. When that war came, Prussia and the other German states requested that the United States serve as protecting power of German interests in France. On July 20, 1870, five days after war was declared, Elihu Washburne wrote to President Grant from Paris:

> The Prussian archives came to our Legation to-day and the Saxons have asked us for our protection. Dont [*sic*] this show that times have changed, so far as our country is concerned, in a few years. Ten years ago what great power in Europe would have asked the U.S. to protect their subjects?

Less than two months later, after Napoleon III had been defeated and captured at Sedan, Washburne told the president on September 12, 1870, that "[o]ur Country has never before stood out so prominently as now. Our prompt recognition of the Republic thrilled the whole country, and 'vive l'Amerique' is on all lips. . . . I dont [*sic*] believe in departing from our traditional policy of non-intervention in European affairs, but if our good offices could do any good they perhaps might be sort of unofficially extended. If you could be instrumental in making a peace, never could a man have so much gratitude."[2] In less than a decade the position of the United States had become that of France in 1861. The Confederacy, like the thirteen colonies eighty years before, had wanted French recognition; now the new government of France wanted American recognition and good offices to end its war with Germany.

In Grant's first term as president, another country emerged from its own civil war determined to be an independent actor on the international stage: Japan. No two countries were more different, historically, culturally, and politically, but by the 1870s, the United States and Japan had one big thing in common. They were the first countries outside Europe with the potential to challenge the dominant European international system. From

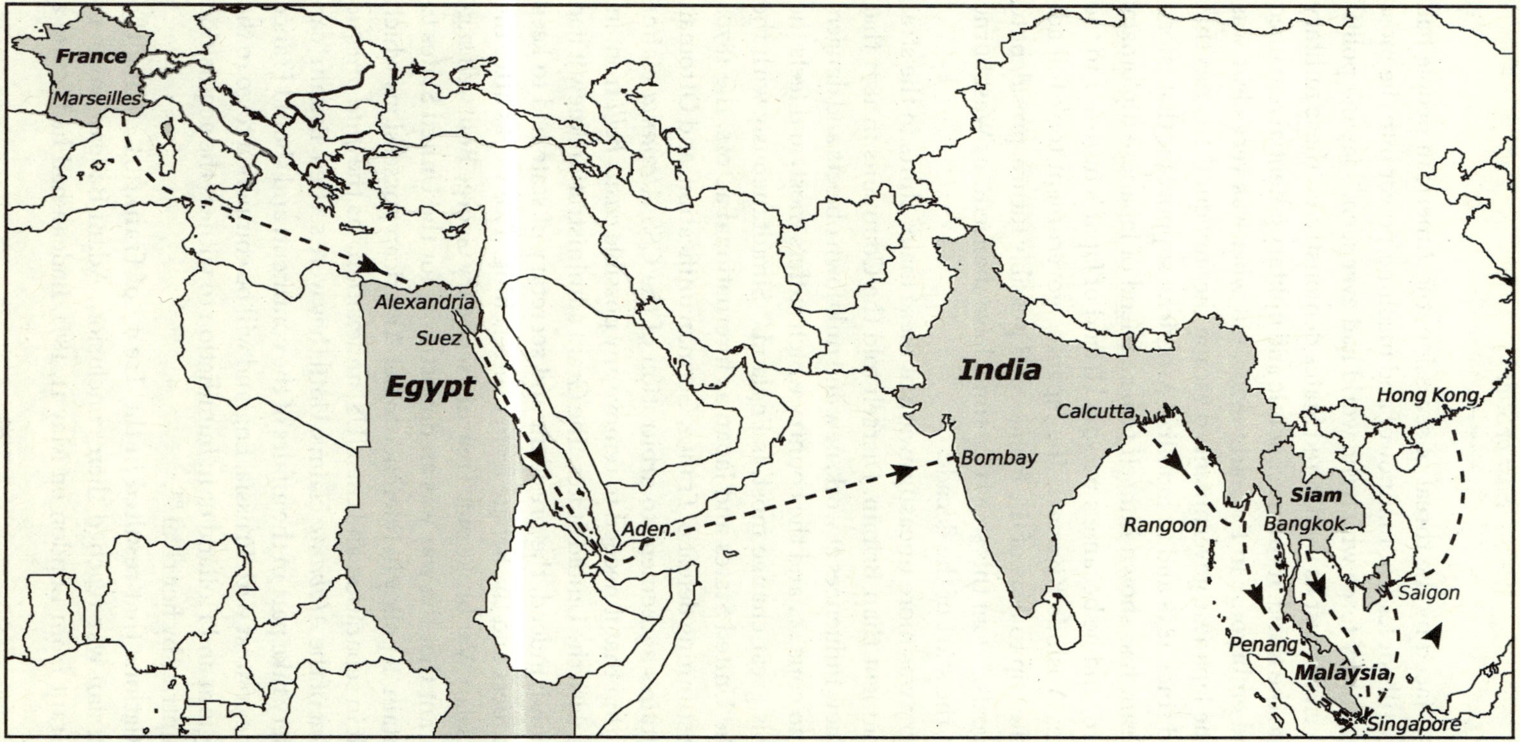

India and Southeast Asia, January 23–April 30, 1879. Grant embarked on his journey east of Suez on January 23 aboard the steamer *Labourdonnais*, bound for Alexandria, Egypt. He traveled overland (not via the Suez Canal) to Suez, where he boarded the steamer *Venetia* for Bombay, India, via Aden. For the next three months, Grant visited India, Burma, Penang, Singapore, and Thailand. Leaving Singapore aboard the steamer *Irrawaddy* on April 23, Grant arrived a week later in Hong Kong, via the French colony of Saigon.

1861 to 1865, "faced by the threat of secession, the American people had forged their still adolescent manpower and machine-power into the most formidable military force which the world had ever seen."[3] Japan's political isolation ended just as the United States demonstrated these military capabilities to the world. Its own economic and military potential remained inchoate and embryonic in the early 1870s, but what was very clear was the will of the Japanese government to escape the "unequal" treaties that it had signed since 1858 and to mobilize American support for that effort. President Grant had shown himself to be a friend of Japanese diplomacy in that regard, and he became a personal friend of Japan's minister to the United States, Yoshida Kiyonari. The Japanese government took full advantage of the trip to Asia of the former, and possibly future, president to advance its goals. "Dont this show that times have changed?" as Washburne had put it at the start of the decade.

No country was more uneasily aware of these major shifts in the strategic environment than Britain. Disraeli told the Commons in 1871 that there were "new influences at work, new and unknown objects and dangers with which to cope . . . and the country which suffers most, and feels the effects of this great change most, is England."[4] Simultaneously with the advent of the United States and Japan as international actors, the 1870s brought the stunning defeat of France, German unification, and Ottoman decline. Britain's agreement to arbitration of the CSS *Alabama* claims was recognition that it needed to remove any possible *casus belli* from its relationship with the United States. The Grant administration knew it had the upper hand; indeed, the president and secretary of state had to keep cabinet members and the Senate from overreaching. Two weeks after the Franco-Prussian War broke out, Treasury secretary George Boutwell suggested to Grant that the war was an opportunity for the United States to press on Britain "a policy in reference to her American possessions which would result in separation and then [US] annexation," as the *quid pro quo* for settlement of the *Alabama* claims. Until they were settled, Britain "can not with safety take part in the affairs of the continent; and should France prevail in the contest with Prussia, England will be compelled to go to the relief of Belgium and Holland or in humiliation to witness the acquisition of those countries by her rival."[5]

As negotiations that resulted in the Treaty of Frankfurt ending the Franco-Prussian war reached their conclusion, Adam Badeau wrote to President Grant from London on May 11, 1871. Badeau had had "quite a long and interesting conversation" with Prime Minister Gladstone about the Treaty of Washington, which the president had submitted to the Senate for its advice and consent the day before. Gladstone "was apparently very anxious that it should be ratified by the Senate, and spoke with great earnestness of his desire for complete accord with America." The British government, Badeau told Grant, "will yield even more than they have done, rather than let the treaty fall through. They cannot afford another defeat from any quarter, *just now*."[6] Badeau was right, and six years later, Britain showed its appreciation of Grant's judicious approach to settling the *Alabama* claims. But welcoming Anglo-American rapprochement did not mean that British elites welcomed a growing American presence around the world. Had Grant returned home directly from Europe, he might never have realized how ambiguous they were about competition from the United States for markets and political influence; but that soon became apparent when he headed east of Suez.

The ambiguity cut both ways. The British government, victim of its own "English mother, American daughter" rhetoric, seemed not to realize, at least initially, how ambiguous Grant was about British power. At times the British Empire seemed to him both ably administered and concerned for the people under its control. He said in Belfast on January 7, 1879, that "it would only be an enemy of the two countries who would raise a hand to cause a difference between" Britain and America, "two nations peculiarly adapted for impressing our customs upon other nations, and inducing them to become the consumers of our produce, and to labour to make the most of whatever their own soil or climate can produce."[7] But at other times, and increasingly so once he reached China and Japan, British policy seemed to him arrogant and racist and determined to thwart those governments' efforts to develop new economic and political infrastructures. Grant's arrival in India brought him for the first time into close and extended contact with the practice of British colonialism.

Venetia arrived in Bombay on February 13, two weeks out of Suez, with a brief stop in Aden midway through the journey. Grant did not transit the Suez Canal on *Venetia*. When *Labourdonnais* docked in Alexandria at dawn on Thursday, January 30, he and his party immediately took a train to Suez, expecting to depart for India that evening. But *Venetia* was delayed a day in her transit of the canal, so Grant and Adolph Borie toured "the old city of Suez riding through on the diminutive donkeys of the country." The next evening, Grant's party was en route to India, and Grant was learning that there were advantages in USS *Richmond*'s delay. Except for brief ferry passages in Scandinavia and the Baltic, and across the Channel and Irish Sea, the former president had not traveled with normal commercial passengers since his transatlantic crossing nearly two years before. Deciding not to wait for *Richmond* in Europe, but to book passage instead on commercial steamers, meant that for long stretches at sea he was in the company of Europeans heading east to do the daily business of empire. From Suez to Bombay, as Grant noted in his travel diary, his fellow passengers were "[g]enerally . . . connected with the government service—Civil or Military—of India, or are the families of such." He took great pleasure in getting to know them, writing as he arrived in Bombay that "[t]he voyage has been most delightful and the passengers most agreeable. . . . I almost regret that the voyage is so near at an end." The Grants saw several of their shipboard companions again, including "a distinguished young officer" in Allahabad, and a judge in Lucknow who extended "a pressing invitation to visit him."[8]

Grant's party spent over a month in India, visiting Bombay, Jabalpur, Allahabad, Agra, Ulwur, Delhi, Benares, Lucknow, and Calcutta (Kolkata). Grant approached India with the same desire to learn about a country and its people that he had brought to his travels in Europe. He was not interested in exotica, but in observing how Indians lived and worked and how British colonial government functioned. Of Bombay he recorded in his diary that "[e]very Nationality of the East is represented here. . . . Bombay differs from all the other Eastern cities I have yet seen in this regard; I have seen no beggars here yet." Grant was pleased to find that the city was "well gridironed with the Yankee Horse rail-road," and to meet members of the miniscule "American Colony . . . seven gentlemen in all, enough however to show that wherever trade & traffic goes the universal Yankee may be found." The Grants were houseguests of the regional British governor, "receiving the most bounteous hospitality." The former president wrote to Adolph Borie's wife, Elizabeth, from Singapore on April 3, that "[w]e have been most hospitably treated every place we have yet been where British rule prevails. . . . Every night since we reached Bombay has been either a dinner party—often a reception following—or we have been traveling." Very little of this hospitality involved Indians, however, except for a few "Parsee merchants and the better to do Hindoo natives."[9] Grant's public diplomacy and summitry throughout the British Empire in Asia were focused on the British elites who ruled in India, Burma (Myanmar), the Straits Settlements (Malaysia and Singapore), and Hong Kong.

The former president's welcome in Bombay, although certainly hospitable on the part of the individual officials involved, was lacking one thing that had always been rendered to him in Europe: a twenty-one-gun salute from ships of the Royal Navy. London had instructed its representatives east of Suez that Grant was a private citizen, not entitled to the royal salute, and they were ordered not to pay him that honor. The order came from the colonial secretary, Michael Hicks-Beach. Perhaps the Foreign Office did not have the influence to block it, but more likely it had its own reasons to downplay the significance of Grant's presence in Asia before he got to Siam, China, and Japan. The British government apparently assumed that those countries would extend those courtesies to Grant that Britain had extended and withhold those courtesies that Britain had withheld, but this was a serious miscalculation. The three independent Asian countries intended to match or outdo any courtesy proffered by London, but they had no intention of being guided by British practice when it came to withholding such honors. The discourtesy shown by denying Grant a twenty-one-gun salute played into their hands, and into France's. The French naval and colonial minister had informed "the Governors of our colonies, as well as the Rear Admirals, commandants in chief of our Naval Divisions" of Grant's "return to America by way of the Indian and Chinese seas," and "requested them to welcome the General with the most assiduous attention, to put themselves at his disposition, and to renter [*sic*] to him on board our vessels the same honors which he would receive on American vessels."[10]

The absence of the twenty-one-gun salute in Bombay did not go unnoticed. On February 15, two days after Grant's arrival, the *Bombay Gazette* published a lengthy editorial in which it suggested that the British Indian government was simply unfamiliar with American practice: "[T]he general opinion is that a President of the United States, after retiring from office, becomes a simple citizen once more, and is never recognized officially in private ceremonies." But the editors were "informed that this is a misapprehension," and that a former president "on board an American man-of-war . . . is received with all the honours paid to the President for the time being, the only difference being that his flag is hoisted at the fore instead of the main. The yards are manned for him, and he is saluted with 21 guns and four rounds of the drums." While "hav[ing] no doubt that General Grant himself takes no thought about what number of guns are fired in his honour, or if any salute is paid him at all," the paper suggested that the decision not to salute Grant should be revisited for a variety of reasons.

Chief among them was the fact that "the United States Government has given to his tour round the world a national character by placing at his disposal the man-of-war Richmond, which has sailed from Gibraltar to meet him at Calcutta."[11] The editorial was wrong on both counts: the lack of the twenty-one-gun salute was not a local mistake, and Grant did care about its absence. He knew the order had come from London and, at the latest when he arrived in Singapore, he also knew of British attempts to pressure Asian countries into denying him, and therefore the United States, the honors he had been accorded in Europe.

But before then the former president was again practicing the diplomacy of Anglo-American rapprochement that he had perfected in Britain in 1877. On Saturday, February 15, he spoke at a dinner in his honor at Government House in Bombay, and "there was no mistaking the evident sincerity of the good feeling he expressed towards England and the English people." Noting that Grant had "preferred arbitration to war in the Alabama dispute," the *Gazette* commented that he "seems to make it a personal matter to cement this good feeling by invariably speaking with admiration of British institutions and British rule, and the impression he makes on all Englishmen who become acquainted with him is a very pleasant one." The paper described Grant admiringly as a man "habitually reserved and thoughtful, of a very genial disposition," who "talks freely enough with people he knows about almost any subject except war." Two weeks later Grant made the same impression at a February 28 dinner in Agra. The *Statesman and Friend of India* (Calcutta) reported on March 4 that "though he is not an orator," he spoke "unaffectedly and to the purpose" about a subject important to him, "the peaceful arbitration of differences between nations, exemplified by England and America since the close of the Civil War."[12] This was effective public diplomacy on behalf of the United States—Grant knew that his speeches would be well-reported in the English-language press in Asia, read by British elites—but his words were sincere.

In fact, as he traveled through India, Burma, and the Straits Settlements, Grant initially developed a more positive impression of the British Empire than he had expected to have. He told Elihu Washburne in an April 3 letter from Singapore that he had now "seen much of the world new to me, and but little visited by our countrymen," and found "[t]he reality is different from my anticipations . . . that English rule in this part of the globe [w]as purely selfish, all for the benefit of 'Old England' and pampered sons sent here to execute laws enacted at home, and nothing for the benefit of the governed."

His hosts were "a most discrete, able, and well chosen set of officials," and "Englishmen are wise enough to know that the more prosperous they can make the subject the greater consumer he will become, and the greater will be the commerce and trade between the home government and the colony, and greater the contentment of the governed." Grant was pessimistic, and prophetic, about the bloodshed likely to follow the end of British colonial rule, predicting "that if the English should withdraw from I[n]dia, and the East, they would scarsely [*sic*] get off the so[il] before the work of rapine and murder and wars between native chiefs would begin." In his diary, Grant was critically reflective about the impact of the West on other societies. After seeing Hindus at worship on the Ganges, he observed, "There can be no doubt about their sincerity. It is a grave question whether they should be disturbed in their faith. It teaches no cruelty to beast or man, and sets up a good system of morals for the guidence [*sic*] of its followers."[13]

Grant's last stop in India was Calcutta. He described it, somewhat contradictorily, in his diary as "a disappointing city" without "many objects of special interest to the traveler," despite the fact that "[t]he English part of the city is well & substantially built and beautifully laid out . . . and the public gardens & parks are very attractive." The real disappointment was not the city, but that *Richmond* was nowhere to be seen. When Grant arrived in Calcutta on March 10, he learned that she had "not yet passed Aden." If he had known where *Richmond* was, he would have given up all hope of seeing her soon; but as in December, there was an inexplicable lack of communication between those who had that information and those waiting to learn it. On Sunday, March 2, seven weeks out of Norfolk, she had only reached Naples. Her captain, Andrew Benham, replied by letter to a telegram from the US dispatch agent in London that "the ship will leave this point, as soon as some repairs, that are now in progress, are completed . . . when I shall make all possible despatch to India." He expected to reach Point de Galle, Ceylon, by April 20, and he told London, "Should I fail to meet Genl G. at Pt de Galle or to hear from him I shall proceed to Singapore and await him there."[14] In fact, Grant arrived and departed Singapore twice before *Richmond* arrived.

Grant's party spent six days in Calcutta. For the first four days of their stay they were houseguests of the viceroy, Lord Lytton, who had served at the British legation in Washington in the 1850s.[15] The viceroy was even more skilled than his government with words that he knew would appear in the American press. At a "grand dinner" on the day the Grants arrived he declared that the former president, "like his classic namesake, has seen men and cities in almost every part of the world, enlarging the genius of the statesman and the soldier by the experience of the traveller." Lytton expressed the "hope that when he returns to the Great Empire of the West, which he has once rescued and twice ruled, he will at least take with him a kindly recollection of his brief sojourn in this Empire of the East, where his visit will long be remembered with gratification by many sincere friends and well-wishers." Implying equality of the two "empires" of the East and West was more flattering to Americans than a reminder that the United States was daughter of an English mother. Lytton left Calcutta for Simla on March 14, but Grant's party stayed on for two days as guests of the regional governor, Sir Ashley Eden, in the vain hope that *Richmond* would arrive. When she did not, Grant wrote to Adam Badeau on March 15 that "[w]e leave here to-morrow morning for Singapore, by a regular steamer."[16]

Departing Calcutta on Sunday, March 16, for the next two weeks, Grant's party was en route to Singapore aboard the steamer *Simla*, with stops in Rangoon (Yangon), Moulmein (Mawlamyine), Penang, and Malacca. They arrived in Rangoon on March 19 and again enjoyed "the hospitality that has been extended throughout India" as houseguests of the governor. In his diary, Grant compared the Burmese to Indians and concluded that "[t]he contrast is all in favor of the Burmese." He noted approvingly that the Burmese "have no Caste and all can compete to better their condition. Females are not shut up but visit and receive visits. . . . The Burmese are not bigoted and do not object to the intermarriage of their race or religion with people of any other race or religion." Grant observed "the greater prosperity of the Burmese, and their much better personal appearance. They like to dress—in gay colors—and all do wear clothing. The Indian covers but little of his person and cares but little about what portion is covered." Burma had a favorable trade balance, and the first railroad to the interior had been completed the year before, with another under construction. Grant expected that "Rangoon will outstrip either Calcutta or Bombay, in wealth, in ten years and in population in twenty-five." After three days in Rangoon, *Simla* departed on Saturday, March 22, for Moulmein, where Grant observed with interest, and described at some length in his diary, the use of elephants in the logging industry.[17]

Simla departed Moulmein on March 25, arriving in Penang the evening of Friday, March 28. Grant was still in the British Empire, and would be, with the exception of his week in Siam, until he left Hong Kong, but between

Burma and Penang he had crossed an invisible line. The American presence in India and Burma, including the ill-funded consular service,[18] was limited, but this began to change in Penang, where there was a large community of overseas Chinese. As John Russell Young told a reporter after his return home, "You begin to see the influence of the Chinese race from the time you reach Penang. They control all the business and industry of the country from the Straits of Malacca on until you reach the cities of Japan."[19] Since Grant's arrival in Bombay six weeks before, his diplomacy in Asia had focused on Anglo-American relations; after Penang, its emphasis shifted to the United States' relationship with China and, eventually, Japan. This shift was captured in the events of one day, Saturday, March 29. Grant was first welcomed to the city by the Penang (British) chamber of commerce, then welcomed a second time by the Chinese merchants and residents of the city. The two groups addressed very different issues and required very different replies. With the chamber, Grant drew together all the strands of Anglo-American relations that he had been discussing for almost two years. With the Chinese community, he addressed congressional legislation banning Chinese immigration to the United States, a bill passed since he had left the country and with which he was unfamiliar. His speech was responsive to the concerns expressed to him, without in any way committing the American government to a specific policy or course of action.

Grant was welcomed to Penang as the future president of the United States. "Should you, by God's Providence, again assume the reins of Government," said Walter Scott, chairman of the chamber of commerce, "we feel convinced that . . . the Bond of friendship now existing between your nation and [Britain] will be cemented if possible more strongly than ever." Scott praised "the steps [Grant] took, when President, to increase the trade existing between America and Britain," and, alluding to the *Alabama* arbitration, described "the most successful results" of his "efforts to bring Great Britain and America into the closest relationship, . . . for, at no previous period had England and America been more closely connected than at the time of your retirement from office." Grant replied "that the welfare of the Anglo-Saxon race—he might say of the world depended . . . upon the harmony and good feeling of this one people—one people in race and civilization, although two nations." With the Geneva arbitration he was "simply carrying out a conviction which he had entertained long before he held any office, that the first thing to be considered in [US] relations with other nations was a good understanding with England," and his "first duty" as president was "to urge . . . the removal of all festering sores between the two countries." He "wished every effort of the English success because the advancement of the common civilization of the two countries meant the happiness, the prosperity and the peace of the world."[20] In fact, in the weeks to come in China and Japan, Grant would realize that he did not wish success to "every effort of the English," but he never ceased to believe that the shared Anglo-American focus on individual liberty would eventually benefit average people around the world.

The Chinese residents of Penang who welcomed Grant had, they said, heard of his years as president, "so administering your Government and enacting good laws, as to induce people of all nations to make America their home." They took advantage of his presence in Penang "to bring to your Excellency's notice that . . . restrictions have been imposed [on Chinese immigration to the United States], and [to] solicit your Excellency's powerful influence on our behalf to advocate [their] removal . . . and thus restore the intercourse between the two nations to its former footing." In Grant's nearly two years abroad, this was the first time he had been asked, at least in public, to influence the outcome of a specific issue being dealt with by the American government, and it was a major one. The right of unrestricted Chinese immigration to the United States was a foreign-policy issue; it had been recognized in the 1868 Seward-Burlingame Treaty, and prohibiting it would contravene that treaty. But Chinese immigration was also a highly charged domestic issue involving the federal government and the states, specifically California, as well as an electoral issue. Denis Kearney, San Francisco's "sand-lot orator," was whipping up Irish-American voters, already out of sorts with Grant and the Republicans, to support exclusion of Chinese immigrants.[21]

There were innumerable ways in which a reply to the Chinese merchants' request could create difficulties for the Hayes administration. The safe course would have been to acknowledge, but not reply to it. Grant did just the opposite. He addressed the concerns of his hosts thoughtfully and at greater length than usual; the summary of his remarks in the *Straits Times* was twice the column length of his earlier comments to the chamber of commerce. It was "a special pleasure to receive the address," he said, because "[h]e was about to visit China,—having received a warm invitation to do so, and he was very anxious to see with his own eyes the institutions and people of that country." With regard to the legislation, Grant "had been absent from the United States for some time, and was imperfectly informed of the public sentiment which had supported the Bill." But despite that, he had something important to say, and his words were meant for many audiences beyond the Chinese community of Penang: for the governments of China, Japan, and Siam, concerned with establishing the principle of racial equality in global intercourse; for any European immigrants to the United States who did not want Asians to receive the same welcome they expected for themselves; and for Americans in general, whether or not immediately affected by Chinese immigration. "In all questions like this," Grant said, "there were demagogues who would pander to prejudices against race or nationality, and favor any measure of oppression that might advance their interests. A good deal of the feeling against people of other races in the United States,—was demagoguery, and did not represent the better feeling of the country."[22]

The former president took the opportunity to state unequivocally that the Civil War had been about ending slavery: "It was in order to free one race from slavery, to put an end to a condition of things that was degrading to both races,—black and white,—that we fought a long war, losing a great number of lives, with an enormous waste of treasure. This was a terrible sacrifice,—he questioned if any nation ever made a greater one. It was to suppress slavery. Having made these sacrifices to free the negro, it would not be expected that the Americans would consent to the revival of another victim of slavery in which the Chinaman and not the negro was the form."[23] If "the Chinese [came] as dependants, slaves of companies, who brought them as merchandize, held them in practical bondage, and enjoyed the fruits of their labor," then "the gentlemen who had signed this petition . . . would agree with him, that emigration to the United States, under those circumstances was not an advantage to us, and was a wrong to the people who were sent as emigrants." Other than objecting to the nature of these conditions, Grant said, his countrymen "had none but the kindest feelings towards the Chinese people and nation," and Americans "would extend to them if they chose to make their home with us, the same welcome they extended to all the rest of the world."[24]

In tone as well as content, Grant's remarks were masterful diplomacy. He spoke conversationally, asking his hosts to understand recent American history and to seek a remedy fair to both Chinese and Americans, rather than treating their petition as a supplication. "He was only a citizen of the United States," he said, "without authority in the councils or the government of the country, [but] he looked with pleasure to his visit to China as enabling him to look into [the question], and make up his mind." He reiterated that his remarks had no "bearing on the Bill to which allusion had been made in the address, because of the Bill he knew nothing, but as giving in a general way the feelings of the American people to the Chinese."[25]

The April 5 *Straits Times* (Singapore) pronounced both of Grant's Penang speeches "excellent and characteristic." His "kindly remarks on the heartiness of his reception in Great Britain and India are only in keeping with the generous regard which he invariably expresses for Englishmen and British institutions, throughout the world, a feeling which is reciprocated for the eminent soldier and ruler—who has done so much for the advancement of liberty by every member of the Anglo-Saxon race." But "the reply to the Chinese especially demands attention" and "must be commended because of the broad and liberal views which dictated it":

> It is evidently a thoughtful exposition of the important question of the policy of affording Chinese unrestricted liberty in the matter of emigration and immigration, and granting them in the United States the same privileges as are accorded to other races. General Grant's views will be read with much interest not only in his own country where the question is now much discussed, but also in Great Britain, and more especially in Australia, and the speech is all the more significant from the fact that its distinguished author usually observes a discreet reticence except when he has had opportunity, of carefully weighing his subject.

The *China Mail* (Hong Kong) agreed, editorializing on April 16 that "General Grant's utterances at Penang . . . cannot fail to do good in China. . . . The sensible and noble sentiments emanating from the General do him the highest honour, an honour which is reflected on the great country to which he belongs." On March 31, on the eve of Grant's arrival in Singapore and before news of the Penang speeches had reached the city, the *Straits Times* published an editorial about the former president's significance, not only to his own country, but to the world. He was, "to foreigners at least, the most conspicuous and most respected figure among American public men. Whether he will be elected for the third term or not, certain it is that his election would be hailed with confidence and trust by other nations."[26]

Leaving Penang Saturday evening and making a brief port call in Malacca on Monday, *Simla* arrived off Singapore at dawn on Tuesday, April 1. Like Penang, Singapore was a city where recently acquired British political control overlapped with centuries of Chinese commercial activity and cultural hegemony. Grant's arrival gave the American consul, Adolphus Studer, the opportunity to promote American interests with both communities. Waiting at the pier, over which "waved the Stars and Stripes and Union Jack in friendly unison," were "the Consuls-General and most of the Consuls, many of the officials, and a representative gathering of the European residents," as well as "officers of H.M.S. *Modeste* in full dress uniform" and "a large company of police." The welcome ceremony was an attempt by the acting governor, Archibald Anson, to follow the letter but thwart the intent of the orders he had received from London. Studer reported to the State Department that Anson had intended to "receive [Grant] with great honors, a salute and guard of honor, . . . but . . . two days before the General's arrival . . . he received instructions from the Secretary of State for the Colonies not to receive the General with official honors, but to show him the honor and courtesy due a distinguished foreigner." Studer "hastened on board" *Simla* before Grant disembarked and found "a quiet moment, within which I could inform the General, that he would not receive an official reception and only such as would be due to a 'distinguished foreigner,' etc., but his equanimity did not seem in the least disturbed."[27]

Perhaps not; but neither Grant nor Studer was pleased with the news. Grant commented that "everywhere" in India he had had "a guard of honor," and Studer reported to Secretary Evarts that Anson was "greatly grieved" by the order. The governor "extend[ed] to [the Grants] the hospitalities of Government House in a most liberal and courteous manner, . . . and . . . Mrs. Anson, noted for her kindness and geniality, was certainly untiring in her efforts to make the party feel at home during their stay." Studer believed "that, notwithstanding the instructions from England . . . to receive the General as a distinguished foreigner, if Col Anson . . . had given him a guard of honor, he would not likely have met with any censure from Downing Street."[28] Forty years later Anson recalled in his memoirs that he had received "a dispatch from the Secretary of State for the Colonies, instructing me that in accordance, I understood, with the wishes of the American Government, these honours were not to be accorded to the General."[29] If Anson's recollection was accurate, his government's attempt to attribute its order to the "wishes of the American Government" was on its face absurd. Even if *Richmond* was nowhere to be seen, it was well-known that Grant was traveling on behalf of the United States, and the US government's wishes would not have been conveyed by a British cabinet minister but by the American consul in Singapore, who was clearly dismayed.

During the welcome ceremony, Grant demonstrated the flair for Sino-American diplomacy he had shown in Penang and would fully develop in China. The *Straits Times* reported that the former president offered "a kindly salute" to all the officials, officers, and consuls present, but at "the name of our deservedly respected townsman, the Hon. H.A.K. Whampoa [Hoo Ah-kay]," he "shook hands with more than ordinary cordiality" and said "that he had heard much of Mr. Whampoa and Mr. Whampoa's kindness to all American citizens."[30] The backstory to this diplomatic moment says a good deal about Grant's willingness to be "briefed"; his ability immediately to assess a situation; and his by now practiced talent for choosing the right word and gesture to respond to his host, whether a Dutch farmer or the German chancellor. Aboard *Simla*, Studer had not only told Grant about the order from London, but had asked him "to give Mr. Whampoa during his stay at Singapore an opportunity to tender hospitality to him," since "no one deserved more to be honored than" Whampoa, a "member of the Colonial legislature, Consul for China and Vice Consul for Russia," who, "has always shown kindness, courtesy, and generous hospitality, in the most disinterested manner, to our Navy officers and American travellers . . . demonstrating on any and all occasions that he is truly our friend." Grant did accept Whampoa's hospitality, visiting his home and gardens, but he also decided to show the United States' gratitude in a very public way. As Studer reported to the State Department, Grant "broke through all the reserve when Mr. Whampoa was introduced, by shaking hands warmly with him and saying: 'Mr. Whampoa, I am glad to meet you. I have heard of you before and how kindly you have always treated my countrymen.' That was a distinction for which the good old gentleman could hardly find an expression of gratitude and pride, as he himself assured me."[31]

The Grants spent a week in Singapore, visiting the city and its environs and attending dinners, picnics, and receptions hosted by Anson, Whampoa, and the maharajah of Johore, of whom Studer was dismissive. He told the State Department that the maharajah "took great pains . . . to show great friendliness to the General and party (the sincerity of which I doubt greatly)"; and he used quotation marks around the word "maharajah," calling it "a title received from the British, not from the Malays."[32] Studer hosted a small luncheon at the consulate on Saturday, April 5, and wrote that "[i]t will be a matter of great pride and satisfaction for the rest of my days" that Grant was his guest: "Having served under General Grant in the old Army of the Tennessee and subsequently received my appointment from President Grant as Consul at this port I can find no words for the gratification this afforded me."[33]

The great disappointment in Singapore was, yet again, as Julia Grant wrote in her memoirs, "We expected *Richmond* daily, but she still loitered." Grant wrote to Daniel Ammen on April 2, "I have been thinking if I have been in any way remiss in not informing the Secretary of the Navy of my determination to proceed in advance of the Richmond. In thinking the matter over, I have come to the conclusion that if there has been any neglect to complain of I am the one to complain." Given *Richmond*'s absence, the former president decided to accept the July 14, 1878, invitation of the king of Siam, Chulalongkorn, who had promised him "a grand reception" if he would visit Bangkok.[34]

Grant received the invitation in September 1878 when he returned to Paris from his summer summitry, but even after deciding to return home via Asia, he was uncertain whether to accept, not knowing if *Richmond* would call at Bangkok. The king reiterated his invitation on February 4, 1879, as Grant was en route to India, and in Singapore the former president found another letter from Chulalongkorn, hand-carried by the US consul in Siam, David Sickels, confirming it. Sickels had arranged passage for Grant's party on the steamer *Kongsee* from Singapore "to Paknam . . . where the King's steam yacht will await your arrival." But John Russell Young reported that there was still hesitation:

> [T]here is a feeling of homesickness among some of the party, which finds relief in looking at the map and drawing the shortest lines of travel between Singapore and San Francisco, and any suggestion of departure from these lines is unwelcome. But in Singapore we met many merchants and prominent authorities who had been in Siam, and the universal testimony was that a visit around the world would be incomplete unless it included that most interesting country.[35]

These recommendations, the letter hand-carried by Sickels, and news from *Richmond*'s captain that she would be in Ceylon by April 12 settled the matter, since it seemed likely that the warship would arrive in Singapore "about the time that we returned from Siam." Grant's party left Singapore aboard *Kongsee* on Wednesday, April 9, in monsoonal rains that also plagued their arrival in Siam. Approaching Bangkok on April 12, *Kongsee* twice ran aground on the bar, the second time "far out of the channel," and was forced to remain there overnight waiting for "extreme high tide."

At midday, Sunday, April 13, the king's guests were finally retrieved by the royal yacht, *Rising Sun*, and brought upriver to the landing at Bangkok. Despite the weather, Grant's reception was all that Chulalongkorn had promised, including a twenty-one-gun salute that "announced to the population of the city, that America's distinguished General and Ex-President had arrived and was being honored, as the Government's guest."[36]

In Bangkok, Grant began the last phase of his travels. It had been three months since he was hosted by a head of state, at President MacMahon's farewell dinner in Paris on January 16. Grant left Europe behind a week later, and since transiting Egypt, he had not set foot in a country that governed itself. From Aden to Singapore, all that he had seen of Asia was ruled by British viceroys, governors, and administrators. Nor had he sailed on a vessel that was not owned by Europeans. The remainder of his time in Asia would be different. After April 13, with the exception of a week in Hong Kong and brief visits to Saigon and Macao, Grant spent nearly five months as the guest of three independent, if hard-pressed, countries: Siam, China, and Japan. While, on the surface, his visits to those countries resembled the year and a half he had spent in Europe as the guest of monarchs, presidents, and prime ministers, there was a qualitative difference between the welcome of even the most hospitable Europeans and the one Grant received as he headed northeast from Singapore. The three Asian countries all wanted something they were not receiving from the European-dominated international system, and they saw the United States as their ally in getting it. For those in power in Bangkok, Peking, and Tokyo, hosting a past, and perhaps future, American president was by no means a waste of their time. They were eager to welcome Ulysses Grant.

This was obvious from the moment Grant arrived in Bangkok. The Grants were offered the palace of Chulalongkorn's younger brother, "so that it would be possible for H.M. personally to visit his distinguished guests without violating the rules of Siamese Royal etiquette." The *North China Daily News*, in its effusive style, told its readers that "[m]ore magnificent, and at the same time more comfortable quarters are rarely seen in this world, whatever may be provided for the righteous in the next." Julia Grant recalled in her memoirs that the king's brother and "a brilliant suite of young Siamese noblemen" greeted them on arrival, and "His Highness gave me his arm and escorted the party to the salon." The prince personally "conducted the General and me to our apartments." Grant was accorded all the accoutrements and entertainments, both Siamese and western, that belonged to a royal reception, including ballroom dancing that paired the former first lady and the other American and European women present with princes of the royal house. One "magnificent spectacle" took place on April 15 when the former president and his party visited the king's uncle, the Grand Master of the Elephants, and "[t]he entire troupe of war elephants, decked in all the trappings and housings of war, and glittering with gold and steel, passed in review before them."[37]

Entertainments aside, Grant had serious discussions with the king, the ex-regent, Si Suriyawongse (Chulalongkorn ascended the throne at age fifteen in 1868, and ruled with a regent for five years), and other members of the government. Grant described the king in his travel diary as "a young man, 25 years of age, quite impressive in appearance and intelligent; speaks english [*sic*] farely [*sic*] well and understands perfectly." As for Siam, "[T]he country is out of debt and the people apparently happy. There is [*sic*] no beggars or deformed people to be seen, and no indication of poverty or distress." Siam and the United States had signed a Treaty of Amity and Commerce in 1833; Chulalongkorn called it a "treaty alliance" at an April 16 dinner in Grant's honor. Siam had "derived great advantages from America, whose citizens have introduced to my kingdom many arts and sciences, much medical knowledge and many valuable books." Siam valued this relationship, and "[t]herefore it is natural that we should be exceedingly gratified by the visit paid to us by a President of the United States," a visit that would "inaugurate friendly relations . . . of a still closer nature than before, and of the most enduring character."[38]

Grant and Chulalongkorn had private conversations on April 14 and 15.[39] The king told the former president that Siam's "policy in foreign relations had been a simple one—peace with foreign Powers and steady development of the country." He understood that "[t]his sometimes led to [Siam] appearing to consent or to submit to some things which, under other circumstances and by other and greater nations, would not be endured." But there was, "on the whole, no reason for regret. In the main, these relations had been for the good of the Siamese people." The ex-regent in a separate conversation told Grant much the same. His country "existed by the friendship of the great Powers. His policy had always been to cultivate that friendship, to do nothing to offend any foreign Power, to avoid controversy or pretexts for intervention by making every concession. This might look like timidity, but it was policy." Siam "valued her independence and her institutions," and "outside nations" should not "be impatient with her for not adopting their ideas rapidly enough." The ex-regent "was himself conservative on the subject. What he valued in the relations of Siam with America was the unvarying sense of justice on the part of America, and as the hopes of Siam rested wholly on the good will of foreign Powers she was especially drawn to America."[40]

This dovetailed well with what Grant told the king, that American policy "was non-intervention in everything that concerned the internal affairs of other nations." The United States "needed all the energies of its own people for its development, and its only interest in the East was to do what it could to benefit the [American] people, especially in opening markets for American manufactures." His countrymen wanted trade, and Grant hoped "to see Siam sharing in this trade. Beyond this there was no desire on the part of the American government to seek an influence in the East."[41] Taken literally, this statement of American commercial interests resulting in a policy of nonintervention was demonstrably false. Commodore Perry had forcibly intervened in Japan's internal affairs a quarter century before in order to open markets; and as Grant spoke, *Ticonderoga* was on her mission to find trading opportunities in western Africa, the Persian Gulf, and the "hermit kingdom" of Korea, in whose internal affairs the United States intervened in the 1880s. But this was not what Grant meant by nonintervention, as Chulalongkorn understood. He meant that the United States had no interest in acquiring colonies in the Far East, so its trading interests posed no threat to the independence of countries like Siam. Indeed, the opposite was true. The policy that Grant described would eventually be called, with regard to China, the Open Door. Grant thought of it as an extension to Asia of the Monroe Doctrine's goal of assuring that markets and investment opportunities remained open to Americans. From Washington's perspective, American support of the independent states of Asia might be commercial policy, but for Bangkok, maintaining Siam's independence was a vital national interest. American antimercantilism and Asian anticolonialism were two sides of the same coin.

Grant's visit to Bangkok coincided with a personal and political crisis involving the British consul, Thomas George Knox. Knox had served in Bangkok since 1857, and his wife was Siamese. In March 1879, just before Grant's arrival, one of their daughters married a member of the royal family, illegally, because the groom did not have the king's permission to marry. The Siamese government, already chafing at what it regarded as Knox's meddling in its internal affairs, saw this as an attempt to gain even more sway over the court and government policy, and Bangkok sent an emissary to London to ask for Knox's recall. There was nothing secret about the Knox affair. Young never referred to it directly, but he commented sarcastically in his June 22 *New York Herald* story (written in Bangkok on April 17): "Why it should be in any way the business of the British as to which sovereign ruled Siam, or why a consular representative should become an aggressive power in the internal affairs of a state to which he is accredited, are questions which, under ordinary circumstances would be puzzling; but in travelling through India and the British possessions in Asia you learn a great many things about how to govern Oriental nations." Knox boycotted all diplomatic events. The May 8 *North China Daily News* described a reception for Grant at which "all Bangkok was present . . . except H.B.M.'s Consul, who not only did not attend, but would not allow any of the employes [*sic*] of the Consulate to be present nor to call on General Grant during his stay in Bangkok. The reason generally assigned for this is that he is not at present on good terms with the Siamese government."[42]

The denouement came several months later, after Grant was home. Sickels, the US consul in Bangkok, wrote to Young on October 8, 1879, that "[t]he Knox difficulty reached its climax last week. [He] was ordered to proceed to London without delay and explain his despotic course in Siam. The mission of [the Siamese emissary to London] was completely successful." Six weeks later, Sickels again wrote to Young, this time about his own ongoing issues with the State Department; his consulate, like many in the Far East, was under investigation for financial irregularities. Sickels blamed Knox for some of his troubles: "Knox was bitterly opposed to me because I refused to support him in his antagonism to the Siamese government—for which he was removed." With apparent schadenfreude at Knox's downfall, Sickels reported that "[the groom] has been beheaded for his crime and the entire family has been arrested for complicity. Fanny Knox (his widow) fled to the British Consulate for protection and is now *a mother*—seven months after her marriage."[43]

Although he must have found it distasteful to speak about a member of the British consul's family, especially a woman, with his hosts, it is clear that Grant did discuss the crisis with the king. Chulalongkorn wrote to Grant on October 8, 1879. He thanked him for his visit and "for the expression of your conviction of what is certainly true, that Asiatics have much to complain of in the treatment they received from other nationalities." He was "very glad to be able to inform you that the diplomatic troubles which was [*sic*] vexing us at the time of your visit is now at an end." Britain had "acknowledged the right of Siam as an independent Kingdom to deal with its own people according to its own laws" and removed Knox. "I know," the king told Grant, "that you who saw and knew our trouble will be very glad to hear that we are now clear of all difficulty."[44] Despite the brevity of his stay in Bangkok, the former president received in Siam an immersion in the personal and political complexities of diplomacy in a part of the world where the lines of communication were thin and the qualities of one individual diplomat, for better or for worse, often had more impact on local events than instructions from foreign offices far away. This experience served him well in China and Japan.

Young observed something else in Bangkok that served Grant well in the conduct of diplomacy in Asia. The former president's reflective manner, his insistence on remaining silent until he had something he thought worth saying, his aversion to flowery speech-making, had all been regarded as a disadvantage, even a disability, in the verbose world of Anglo-American politics. But Grant's demeanor was a distinct advantage in the Far East. Young described his conversation with the ex-regent:

> An audience with an Eastern prince is a serious and a solemn matter. It reminded me somewhat of the Friends' meetings I used to attend in Philadelphia years and years ago, when the brethren were in meditation and waiting for the influence of the Holy Spirit. The Siamese is a grave person. He shows you honor by speaking slowly, saying little and making pauses between his speeches. He eschews rapid and flippant speech, and a gay, easy talker would give offence. I need not say that this custom placed the General in an advantageous position.

Throughout the Far East, the need for translation also contributed to an atmosphere that brought out the best in the former president. Young described "the slow deliberate way" in which Grant's speech was translated, the interpreter "standing in front of the Regent and intoning it almost as though it were a lesson from the morning service."[45] In a part of the world where westerners were known for pompous bluster, Grant's willingness to listen, rather than to talk, and to converse at the pace of his hosts, was a buster of stereotypes that worked in his favor.

By mid-April, Grant's party found the heat of the tropics enervating, and Grant feared not having enough time in China and Japan to "do up" the two countries properly. He was also concerned about Adolph Borie's health. His friend had been persuaded to join Grant in Paris with the assurance of comfortable accommodations aboard *Richmond* from France to Yokohama. Instead, the sixty-nine-year-old Borie had had an adventurous three months, sleeping on deck, dodging tropical rain storms, disembarking from steamers in pitching seas, in addition to the challenges of land travel through India. Borie had invited Dr. John Keating to accompany him, and his traveling companions were attentive to his needs, but the trip had necessarily been far more strenuous for all of them than it would have been aboard *Richmond*. Although Grant never expressed it in so many words, part of his anger at her delay had to be due to his well-founded fears that the trip had been too strenuous for Borie.[46] Although Sickels had booked passage for Grant's party on a steamer departing Bangkok directly for Hong Kong on Sunday, April 20, Grant chose instead to return to Singapore on Friday, April 18, aboard the steamer *Bangkok*, arranged for him by the Siamese government.[47] He wanted to board the American warship as soon as possible.

The former president expected to find *Richmond* waiting for him in Singapore, but arriving late in the afternoon of Tuesday, April 22, was "very much disappointed and disgusted" to find that she was not. Approaching Hong Kong a week later aboard the steamer *Irrawaddy*, Grant wrote to his daughter, Nellie, that he had "confidantly [*sic*] expected the Richmond. But learning that she was at Ceylon and would not reach Singapore for a week I determined to leave by the first steamer going my way. Fortunately one was in port, bound for Hong-Kong, and to sail at seven the next morning. We took it—a very fine steamer of the Messajerie line—and are now here not expecting ever to see the vessel which was fitted out for us until we get to Yokohama, Japan, and then it will be too late to use her." The tone of the letter was calm, but John Russell Young wrote in his diary on April 23 that Grant was "very angry" with the US Navy "at apparent trifling with him." Grant's party had had less than ten hours from their arrival in Singapore to transfer themselves and their baggage "through a most violent tropical rain storm" to *Irrawaddy*, but on Wednesday, April 23, 1879, Ulysses Grant was finally headed north to China.[48]

CHAPTER SIX

The "King of America" and the Viceroys of China: 1879

In his anger over *Richmond*'s absence, Ulysses Grant did not yet know that fate had been more than kind to him. Because *Irrawaddy* had waited in Singapore for the connecting steamer from Java, Grant's party was able to board her and spend the next week in the company of Robert Hart, inspector general of the Imperial Chinese Maritime Customs Service. Hart, as Dr. Keating wrote, was known "world-wide, having a position in Pekin[g] which gives him enormous power in China's government." John Russell Young understated Hart's role in, eventually, over a half century of Chinese history when he described the inspector general as "one of the best-informed Europeans living as to the resources of the Chinese Empire, and the manner and customs of the Chinese people." En route to Hong Kong "there were many conversations between General Grant and Mr. Hart, and we could not but be grateful for the advantage that befell us in the experience and ability of our friend and companion."[1] The most important factor in preparing Grant for his visit to China was the completely serendipitous opportunity to spend a week with "the I. G." The former president took from his conversations with Hart information about the country's leaders and its political and social climate that he could not have learned from anyone else.

But Hart, sitting opposite Grant at *Irrawaddy*'s dinner table, was not the only source of information aboard. The male passengers "were almost all engaged in work in China, either in the government consular service or as merchants." There was also an Italian duke who had been shooting tigers in India and elephants in Ceylon, an Austrian countess, and a Japanese prince returning from a study mission of the French educational system. According to the prince, "Japan was making great preparations to receive

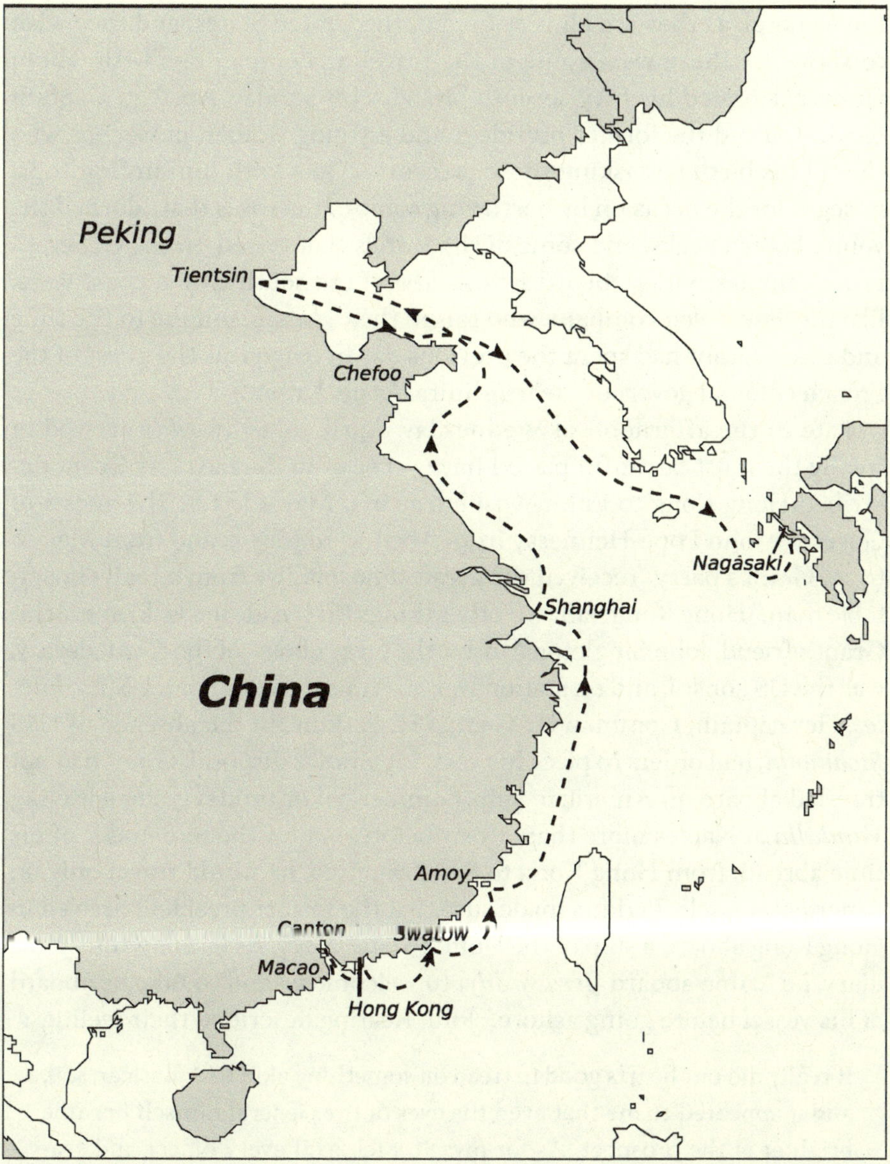

China, April 30–June 21, 1879. Arriving in Hong Kong on April 30, for the next six weeks, Grant traveled along the China coast aboard USS *Ashuelot*, visiting Canton, the Portuguese colony of Macao, Swatow, Amoy, Shanghai, and Tientsin, from which he visited Peking in early June. On June 15, USS *Richmond* met Grant off the China coast to take him, via Chefoo, to Japan.

the General, as they are all very fond of the United States, and they wish to show it." These were some of the traveling companions with whom Grant celebrated his fifty-seventh birthday on Sunday, April 27. Captain Govin toasted the former president and a young woman passenger who shared his birthday, asking those present to "join with him in forming a nosegay for the occasion by borrowing some of the roses that adorned the young lady's cheeks, and some of the laurels that rested on the General's brow." The festivities aboard *Irrawaddy* off the south China coast were, like the assembled company who raised their glasses, unique to the time and place. Grant had spent the previous day in Saigon, as the guest of the French colonial governor, Rear Admiral Louis Lafont.[2]

Late in the afternoon of Wednesday, April 30, *Irrawaddy* arrived in "really the most beautiful place I have yet seen in the East," as Grant described Hong Kong to Elihu Washburne in a May 4 letter. The guests of Governor John Pope-Hennessy from April 30 to May 5, and from May 10 to 12, Grant's party "received the greatest hospitality from a really hospitable man." Hong Kong had two other things that made it a welcome sight: Grant's friend, John Singleton Mosby, the "gray ghost" of the Confederacy, was the US consul, and on station was an American gunboat, USS *Ashuelot*. Her captain, Commander George H. Perkins, in the absence of USS *Richmond*, had orders to place his vessel at Grant's disposal. Grant had not traveled aboard an American ship, commercial or military, since leaving *Vandalia* at Naples more than a year before, but for the remainder of his time abroad, from Hong Kong to San Francisco, he would travel only on American vessels. Perkins made sure that the former president arrived in Hong Kong aboard a ship of the United States Navy. As Grant wrote in his diary, he "came aboard [*Irrawaddy*] to welcome us and to take us aboard of his vessel before going ashore." John Keating described their feelings:

> It really did our hearts good to tread on something akin to American soil, and it appeared to me that even the eyes of the General himself became brighter at the prospect. As for myself, I felt as if every officer and seaman on that ship were my most cherished friend, and the dear old flag above us a glimpse of home itself. And, truth to say, it was gratifying also to feel that an American man-of-war is a reality after all, and not a mere phantom, as some would have us believe.

Ashuelot fired a twenty-one-gun salute as Grant boarded her, and a second twenty-one-gun salute as he disembarked thirty minutes later, "the marines presenting arms, and the seamen manning the yards." Grant noticed that "[n]o salute was fired from the English side, said to be in obedience to orders received from the Colonial Govt." If the Royal Navy did not salute, however, the Imperial Japanese Navy did. Japan had dispatched a warship, *Nisshin*, "sent in anticipation of my arrival in Hong Kong to extend an invitation to that country." The Japanese consul in Hong Kong, Ando Taro, had instructions to convey the "gratification" of Emperor Meiji "at the approaching visit of the gallant General to Japan."[3]

The major event of Grant's stay in Hong Kong was a May 3 state dinner at which Pope-Hennessy did his best to mitigate any snub implied in the "distinguished foreigner" order from London, while stressing the former president's statesmanship in the Geneva arbitration and the intimacy of Anglo-American relations. Although royal princes had visited Hong Kong, the governor said they "would be themselves among the first to say that the man whose health I am now about to propose, is the most illustrious guest that ever sat at this table," not because of Grant's military career, but because of "the toleration, resolute strength, and love of justice of the statesman, when the sword of the soldier was laid aside." Pope-Hennessy cited Prime Minister Disraeli, who "truly said that the future of civilization is indissolubly bound up in the future of the United States," and included a personal note in his welcome. A telegram had just arrived "from London, announcing the birth of a grand-child" to Ulysses and Julia Grant. The timing of Nellie Sartoris's delivery was politically impeccable; Vivien May Sartoris was "another little link to unite the two countries together." Grant replied to the toast with his by now usual, but no less sincere, words of thanks for the "courtesy, hospitality, and good-will to myself and my country" that he had found "wherever . . . I have met Englishmen." He asked the governor's guests "to unite in this sentiment: The perpetual friendship and alliance of the two great English-speaking nations of the world—England and America."[4]

Grant had his last dinner with Robert Hart on May 1 at Government House. Hart left the next day for Shanghai and Peking. Mosby hosted a reception at the US consulate on May 2, where the former president met several Chinese merchants who traded with California. He told them "he had not seen so many vessels flying the stars and stripes together since he had left England."[5] On Monday, May 5, Grant's party left Hong Kong aboard *Ashuelot* to visit Canton and Macao. The trip upriver to Canton brought Grant for the first time to a Chinese city governed by Chinese. Before his arrival, the US consul, Charles P. Lincoln, and Viceroy Liu Kun-i had discussed "a suitable programme to be carried out on the occasion." Liu had been told by "the British Consul . . . that General Grant was not entitled, more than any private Citizen, to any recognition or reception at the hands of the Native Authorities," but nevertheless "received him with courtesies never before extended to any Foreigner." Grant was aware of British pressure on the viceroy. He noted in his diary on May 5 while "assending [*sic*] the river to Canton" that Chinese gunboats were accompanying *Ashuelot* "to do honor to the occasion"; but there were rumors of "British interference—on the part of an officious Consul I suppose—to their making the demonstration they had intended. We will see."[6]

Canton encapsulated the situation of Asian countries confronted by forces outside their cultural and historical experience that they could neither defeat nor ignore. Grant's growing awareness of this was reflected in a diary entry he made while there:

> I am satisfied that the Chinese are badly treated at home by europeans [*sic*] as well as when they emigrate. I blame them for submitting to such dictation. I should not blame them if they were to drive out all europeans [*sic*]—Americans include[d]—and make new treaties in which they would claim equal rights.[7]

Ashuelot arrived in the city after dark on May 5 because of "Tide, and delays in receiving persons who [had] come aboard by way of compliment." Those "assembled for hours to see so many yankees [*sic*]" had given up and gone home. The welcome ceremony took place the next morning. *Ashuelot* "saluted the Chinese flag and the port of Canton. To this the [Chinese] gunboat answered," and then fired "a salute of twenty-one guns . . . in honor of the General, to which our vessel answered." Young reported that this was "the first time that the Chinese ever fired twenty-one guns in honor of any one, and it was explained that the government did so as a special compliment to America." That afternoon Grant paid a call on the viceroy at his yamen (ministry; also normally the residence of the office holder), accompanied by his male traveling companions, as well as the acting US minister in Peking, Chester Holcombe; the US consul in Tientsin, Owen Denny (both of whom had joined Grant's party in Hong Kong); Charles Lincoln; and Commander Perkins. From the US consulate it was three miles to the yamen, and Young described Grant's experience along those three miles as the former president was carried in a sedan chair through the streets of Canton.[8]

The viceroy had offered to clear the streets of all people, as was done "[w]hen the Emperor of China went through a city," since "[h]e supposed that General Grant had been accustomed to similar attentions." But Grant replied that he "preferred seeing the people and would be better satisfied if no such orders were given." Concerned, however, for the maintenance of order, Liu had posted throughout the city placards announcing that "the King of America" had come to China "to do the Viceroy honor, and that the people must do him honor." The placards announced the route Grant would take to the yamen, and so

> [f]or an hour or two before the time large numbers of Chinamen gathered under the trees waiting for the procession. . . . [Y]ou had a feeling in time, with those wondering eyes ever upon you, as if you were on a stage acting, and this was the audience—an intensely interested audience, standing in the sun fanning themselves.

The waiting crowd, hoping to glimpse the American "king," got excited "[w]henever an officer of the Ashuelot arrived . . . in full uniform," since "the Oriental mind runs to gold and lace as emblems of rank." In fact, so had the European mind. The Cantonese were only "able to pin [Grant] down because of the chair in which he rode." The procession began, each man in a sedan chair with attendants, moving through "this teeming city, alive with wonder and curiosity," the people given "this one day to see the foreigner, to look in awe upon the face of the American whose coming had been discussed in every bazaar and by every silk loom in Canton." Grant's visit "had created a flutter in the Chinese mind. No foreign barbarian of so high a rank had ever visited the Celestial Kingdom."

As a journalist, Young wrote, he had "seen some extraordinary sights . . . which are the crowning memories of a lifetime. Among these I place the spectacle of General Grant's entrance into Canton." For "over an hour . . . we journeyed through a sea of faces, a hushed and silent sea, that swept around us, covering windows, doors, streets, roof tops, wherever there was room for a pair of feet or hands. Some of the party estimated that there were 200,000 people . . . [b]ut no massing together of figures, although you ascend into the hundreds of thousands, will give you an idea of the multitude." American and British crowds "become picturesque and animated. In Canton the mob might have been statues . . . A rush, a scramble, a cheer, would have been a relief, but all was silence and repose." In the midst of this silence, their procession was "a show of unusual novelty that had been brought at great expense from over the sea." Canton that day was much like "a country town at home" welcoming "Mr. Barnum." The young men in the crowd regarded the foreigners "with a supercilious and contemptuous expression, very much as men of the same class would regard Sitting Bull or Red Cloud from a club window as the Indian chiefs went in procession along Fifth avenue." Indeed, Young reflected:

> I suppose they looked upon General Grant and his party as some of us would regard Red Cloud and his braves. We were foreigners, outside barbarians, and if we came at all to a viceregal palace—if we were received with music and the firing of cannon and the beating of drums—it was because the Viceroy was in a gracious mood and deigned to give the barbarian a sight of imperial Chinese splendor. We are not the only people in the world who are proud of our country.

Young noticed that some "workmen were at their labors painting silk or lacquer work, or beating silver into odd shapes" and "would not look at us, but went on with their brush and hammer as if the barbarian was not even now going in state past their doors and all Canton was out to see him." He "rather respected" their unwillingness to "be dragged to the sidewalk, to grace the barbarian's holiday."

The procession arrived at the yamen, and Young described the ceremonies and refreshments that followed. Liu Kun-i was "a Chinaman, and not of the governing Tartar race"; but the local military commander, "Chang Tsein, the Tartar General," was also there to welcome Grant. Young wrote at length about the brewing of tea, the serving of food, his (unsuccessful) attempt "to pay my hosts the compliment of using the chopsticks." He noticed important details: "The Viceroy with his chopsticks helped the General. This is true Chinese courtesy for the host to make himself the servant of his guest." Grant's conversation with Liu was interpreted by "Mr. Holcombe and the Chinese interpreter [Yu C. Cheung] of the Consul, a blue button mandarin, who speaks admirable English." The next day the viceroy, General Chang, and other Chinese officials returned Grant's visit, calling on him for several hours, one after the other, at the American consulate, and that evening the same procession as the day before again made its way from the consulate to the yamen, where Liu hosted a banquet in Grant's honor. This time, US Marines from *Ashuelot* preceded the former president's party.[9]

On Tuesday, May 6, after returning to the consulate from his first visit to the yamen, Grant received a delegation of the American residents of

Canton, including Gideon Nye, who had arrived in China as a nineteen-year-old in 1831 and lived there longer than any other American. They presented Grant with an address welcoming him to "the Southern gate of the most ancient of Empires." Three weeks later the *Celestial Empire* (Shanghai), like most of the English-language press of Asia pro-British in its editorial policy, called the address "twaddle" and compared it to a Chinese address to the governor of Hong Kong (of whom the paper also disapproved because of Pope-Hennessy's inclusion of the city's Chinese residents in its governance). Stylistically, the address did resemble a Chinese one, but it is difficult to see why the newspaper objected to the Americans' message, which emphasized the importance of Anglo-American relations. Grant, his countrymen told him, "conspicuously illustrated the principles embodied in the Treaty of Washington," and his visit to Britain had been "the complement and seal of an act that reflects lasting honor upon your Administration." Living as they did "midway between Europe and our own beloved Country," they appreciated "the felicitous manner in which you have conciliated the good opinion and elicited the expressions of the good-will of the European peoples toward our Country; especially in your intercourse with our nearest Kinsmen of the United Kingdom." Perhaps the Americans' evocation of Sino-American relations irritated the editor. They expressed "the hope that your personal observation among the people of Canton . . . will enable you to correct the misconceptions among our Countrymen of the Pacific States which tend to impair the compact of friendly comity" between the United States and China.[10]

Grant's final events in Canton were a May 8 dinner attended by most of the consular corps and a reception for all of the city's foreign residents hosted by Charles Lincoln. The consul described Grant's visit as "the first time that China had been visited by the sovereign, or one who had been the sovereign, of another country," and alluded to a third presidential term: "America saw in General Grant, not only the example of great deeds, nobly performed, but the hope of even greater deeds whose performance would redound to the lasting honour of the nation." Grant chose not to address his political prospects, replying instead by expressing his belief "that peace could have no better assurance than in the harmony and cordial good feeling of the civilized nations of the world." The consul's remarks were the subject of a May 13 *Daily Press* (Hong Kong) editorial. If reelected, the paper commented, Grant would need "a personal knowledge of the country and people against whom so much feeling has been raised in the States," and he would be able to acquire it as he traveled to Peking in the weeks ahead. Viceroy Liu's reception of Grant in Canton showed "that the Chinese Government are not unaware of the great probability that exists of [his] again assuming the reins of government in the United States, and they will therefore naturally regard him as the representative of his country." In the north, Viceroy Li Hung-chang was "said to be well acquainted with the history of the gallant General, and to entertain a very sincere admiration for his genius and high qualities of head and heart. The great Viceroy . . . intends to pay him such honours at Tientsin as no foreigner has met with from Chinese before."[11]

With an extremely successful three days behind him, Grant departed Canton early Friday morning, May 9. Liu Kun-i "proposed to come down with the Tartar-General to see the General off," but because of the early sailing, Grant asked them not to do so. As *Ashuelot* "desended [*sic*] the river amidst the booming of canon [*sic*] from Chinese gunboats & forts all along the way to the Ancient Portuguese town of Macao," Grant returned briefly to the world of European colonial governors. After one night in Macao, he was back in Hong Kong on Saturday, May 10, for a change of command ceremony aboard *Ashuelot*, a final dinner at Government House, and a Monday, May 12, meeting with a Chinese delegation that praised his administration's "impartiality and fairness" in its treatment of Chinese in America. That afternoon, captained by Commander Mortimer Johnson, *Ashuelot* departed for Shanghai. She made two intermediate stops, at Swatow (Shantou) on May 13 and Amoy (Xiamen) on May 14, in both cases arriving in the morning and sailing the same evening. During his brief stay in Amoy, Grant was again fortunate in his encounters, in this case with scholar and British minister to Peking Sir Thomas Wade, and the two men "had a long conversation about China."[12] *Ashuelot* arrived the morning of Saturday, May 17, at the mouth of the Yangtze River twelve miles below Shanghai, and was welcomed with a twenty-one-gun salute from the Woosung forts.

"As soon as the firing of the Chinese forts ceased the batteries of the Iron Duke, the flag ship of the admiral commanding the British fleet in China, ran up the American flag to the fore and fired twenty-one guns. The Chinese gunboats joined in the chorus, and the Ashuelot returned the salutes." The royal salute from HMS *Iron Duke* may have been an individual decision on the part of her captain, because the courtesy was not repeated by the Royal Navy in Shanghai. But Grant was probably less interested in salutes from the British than he was in the fact that "[a]s the smoke lifted the American man-of-war Monocacy was seen steaming toward us, dressed from stem to stern." After so many months without seeing a vessel of the US Navy, Grant had boarded *Ashuelot* in Hong Kong, and USS *Ranger* had been in port at Amoy, "shrouded with bunting" to receive him. Now, approaching Shanghai two years to the day after leaving Philadelphia, the sight of *Monocacy* was surely welcome. USS *Palos* was also in port. On May 22, Grant visited the American vessels, the French corvette *Champlain*, and HMS *Egeria*. Her reception of him caused "a good Briton" to write to the *North China Daily News* that he was "mortified . . . when I saw the General calling on the *Egeria*, with her sails hanging loose, and no sign of respect except a doubtful flag at her fore, while the French and American ships-of-war fired [salutes]."[13]

On May 17 *Monocacy* had onboard members of the multinational committee established by Shanghai's foreign residents to welcome the former president. They were well aware of the possibility of a third term. Grant had led "that great Republic which holds now so large a place in the world's history"; and "it is not unlikely that on his return to his native land, he will be asked once more to undertake the administration of that great country." The number of westerners in Shanghai was still miniscule, 1,673 in the 1876 census, but the *Celestial Empire* boasted that "[t]here is probably no more cosmopolitan community in the world."[14] If Grant's visit to the British Empire that began in May 1877 ended in Hong Kong, in many respects his 1877–78 travels in continental Europe ended in Shanghai. In 1879, eleven European countries, the United States, and Japan were represented there by consuls. Grant had been the guest of every European government with a presence in the Chinese city: Austria, Belgium, Denmark, France, Germany, the Netherlands, Portugal, Russia, Spain, Sweden-Norway, and, of course, Britain. By the end of 1878, he knew every president, monarch, and prime minister in Europe. In Asia in 1879 he saw on the spot the consequences of decisions made in the palaces and ministries in which they had lavishly entertained him, and he observed the men sent by their governments to implement those decisions, as well as Europeans who came east of Suez on their own. Bismarck did not know what "Germany" looked like on the China coast to those who only experienced its power there. After meeting the merchants, missionaries, and military officers who projected European economic, cultural, political, and military influence around the world, Grant did.

The reception committee organized events to fill every moment of his stay in Shanghai. In their welcoming address, its members told him how they saw themselves and their city. Living in "the easternmost commercial settlement of the continent [where] the lines that unite the old and new worlds meet," they were a "small commercial republic, itself as cosmopolitan as the great country from which you come." They hoped that "after you leave us you will remember with pleasure this little band of self-governed representatives of all States, united in peaceful pursuits and furthering, we believe, not without success, the cause of progress in this country." Grant's reply, as always, was courteous. He had not yet seen Shanghai, of course, and over the next six days he enjoyed the hospitality extended to him; but he was increasingly bothered by the reality of which the address boasted—that he was in China but not being welcomed by Chinese, that these "self-governed" Europeans were not subject to the laws of China. Making that clear, the local Chinese governor (taotai) and "a delegation of mandarins of high rank" were present at the ceremony but not in charge of it. In his by now well-practiced way of saying more than his hosts likely heard, Grant told them that during his "short time in the country of which Shanghai forms so important a part in a commercial way," he had "seen much to interest me and much to instruct me. I wish I had known ten years ago what I have lately learned." He would take home "a report of all I have seen in this part of the world, for it will be of interest and possibly of great use."[15] If Grant's hosts took this as praise of the West's role in China, they were mistaken. The former president's mind as he arrived in Shanghai was on his reception in Canton and on the other independent Asian country he had visited, Siam.

The day before, May 16, aboard *Ashuelot*, Grant had replied to a letter he received from Chulalongkorn just before leaving Hong Kong. The king understood that "[y]ou will now pass on to wealthier cities, and more powerful nations, but I depend on your not forgetting Siam, and from time to time I shall write to you and hope to receive a few words in return." Grant's reply assured him that "I shall always be glad to hear from you and to hear of the prosperity and progress of the beautiful country over which you rule with so much justice and thought for the ruled." The former president wished Chulalongkorn "long life, health, and happiness," and "peace and prosperity to Siam." Grant also replied from *Ashuelot* to a letter from Viceroy Liu, who expressed his and his people's "deepest satisfaction" that "Your Excellency whom we have so long desired to see [was] so good as to come among us." It was "only in obedience to your command" that

Liu had not seen Grant off from Canton. "Should I ever [b]e honored by my Sovereign with a mission abroad, it will be my most devout prayer and earnest desire that I may meet you again." Grant replied that, since leaving Hong Kong, "it has been my good fortune to visit Swatow and Amoy, both, I understand, under Your Excellency's government, and have received at each the same distinguished reception accorded at Canton." He and his party, Grant told Liu, "will carry with us from China the most pleasant recollections of our visit to the country over which you preside and of the hospitalities received at your hands."[16]

Grant's six days in Shanghai were filled with events—a torchlight parade, a ball, banquets, and receptions—at which he was lauded as "the consistent friend of peace with England, when a weaker man might have sought the favour of the less-thinking portion of his electors by insisting arbitrarily on some immoderate satisfaction for the *Alabama*'s depredations." His hosts recognized that "a war between the two great English-speaking nations would have been a calamity for the whole civilised world." In reply, Grant took the opportunity of his presence in Shanghai's multinational community to express his hope "that the same brotherhood which existed between the two English speaking nations would exist between other countries." Amid these festivities and speeches, two events personally important to the former president occurred, and one—the usual one—did not. *Richmond* was reported to have left Hong Kong for Shanghai on Sunday, May 18, and "[i]t was thought she would arrive in time to take the General to the North." But as Grant wrote in his diary, "Expected to meet the Richmond . . . She is not in sight."[17] After months without the comforts of the American warship, on the advice of Dr. Keating, Adolph Borie decided to forego the remainder of the trip. He and Keating departed for Japan and, eventually, San Francisco, by commercial steamer on Wednesday, May 21. Julia and Ulysses Grant saw them off. Keating took home not only "the feelings of admiration with which we started on the long voyage, for the General," but "an addition in the warmth of affection which his quiet, unassuming, yet dignified manner had engendered." After four months of participating in Grant's diplomacy, "We had learned to love and respect him, and always looked forward to each reception in a strange place with feelings akin to pride, as co-sharers in the honor brought to our great country by its distinguished citizen."[18]

The other important event in Shanghai took place at the US consulate general the morning of Tuesday, May 20, when seventeen US Army and Navy veterans of the Civil War called on the former president. "[A] few of your old comrades in arms have drifted to these far off shores," their spokesman said, "seeking here to carve out new fortunes for themselves." Although far from home, their "hearts beat just as responsive to every chord of that music of the Union as they did . . . when we followed you, our cherished leader, in that strife and conflict that settled the perpetuity of our government." The veterans presented Grant with a calligraphic address that expressed their "feelings of highest pride in having the right and privilege to address you as Our General." In reply, Grant wished them "success here in a foreign land" and a "return Home to enjoy the blessing of that Government for whose safety you staked and gave so much." Grant had good reason to expect that this microversion of an encampment of the Grand Army of the Republic would be an all-American affair, but it was instead a moving moment in Sino-American relations. One of the veterans was Wu Hung-nyuh, 50th Pennsylvania Volunteers. The *North China Daily News* reported on May 21 that the Reverend Wu, now "a clergyman of the American Episcopal Mission, Shanghai, was a student in Pennsylvania, and in company with his class generally turned out, and served three months to repel the rebel invasion of that State." Grant asked the Reverend Wu to stay and talk with him after the other veterans left.[19]

In his June 2, 1879, report to the State Department, the US consul general, David Bailey, wrote that Grant's "reception here by the entire community, Foreign and Native, marks an era in the history of Shanghai, as being the grandest ovation ever given to any person since the establishment of Foreign Relations with China." The *North China Herald* editorialized that "[t]he last salute has been fired, the last flag has been waved, the last cheer given, the last fire rocket exploded in honour of the ex-President of the United States, and . . . we cannot do otherwise than congratulate ourselves on the general success of the ovation." Referring to the expected third term, the paper called it "an immense advantage for one who may be again the ruler of a great nation to visit various countries, to form the acquaintance of prominent statesmen, to see the workings of different modes of Government, to study the cities and characters of many men. Shanghai has contributed an episode to the new Odyssey." This was certainly true, if not quite in the way the paper imagined. As he left Shanghai on May 23, Grant continued to reflect on his experiences in Canton and Siam and on the control that foreigners had over China. It was not that he failed to appreciate his "reception by foreigners of all nationalities"; his hosts would surely have been pleased to know that he described their welcome in his diary as "the mos[t] cordial & most enthusiastic we have witnessed since leaving England,"[20] but they would probably not have been as pleased with what he wrote next.

Grant's six days in Shanghai had confirmed his observations of the Chinese, and their interaction with Europeans and Americans, in Penang, Singapore, Hong Kong, and Canton. He found them to be "an industrious frugal people and while slow to adopt new ways are nevertheless progressive. They seem to possess the shrewdnes[s] to realize that their safety consists in holding back in modern civilication [*sic*] & progress until they can educate their own people to take the management in building roads, constr[uct]ing machinery &c. and until it can be done with their own capital." He was optimistic about the future of China, but pessimistic about what the West could then expect from the Chinese:

> My impression is that the day is not very far distant when they will make the most rapid strides towards modern civilization, and become dangerou[s] rivals to all powers interested in the trade of the East. They are patient enduring and of long suffering in their weakness. But once feeling themselves strong they are likely to become cruel overbearing and vindictive.

Grant commented, "They cannot be much blamed if this prediction comes true. At present their rights are scarsely [*sic*] respected in any open port where foreigners are admitted. I am not prepared to justify the treatment the Chinese have recei[ved] at the hands of the foreigner."[21]

With Grant's reduced party onboard, *Ashuelot* arrived in Tientsin on Tuesday, May 27. The conduct of Chinese diplomacy was divided between the capital, Peking, and this northernmost treaty port because as the US consul, Owen Denny, observed, Tientsin was "the home of . . . Viceroy Li, by all degrees of comparison the ablest and most progressive statesman in the Empire, and to whom all foreigners look for the introduction of the ideas of modern civilization destined eventually to break the chains which have so long bound this people to the prejudices of their ancestors."[22] On their way up the Peiho from the Taku forts, John Russell Young wrote, "Wherever we passed a fort twenty-one guns were fired. All the junks and vessels were dressed in bunting. A fleet of Chinese gunboats formed in line, and each vessel manned yards." The viceroy's yacht steamed alongside *Ashuelot* as she approached the landing, and Grant and Li Hung-chang met for the first time. "General Grant stood at the gangway, accompanied by the officers of the ship, and as the Viceroy stepped over the side of the Ashuelot the yards were manned and a salute was fired. Judge Denny, advancing, met the Viceroy and presented him to General Grant as the great soldier and statesman of China." Young described Li for his readers, noting especially "his stature, which would be unusual in a European and was especially notable among his Chinese attendants, over whom he towered." (Li was 6 feet, 2 inches tall.) The viceroy "studied [Grant's] face curiously and seemed to show great pleasure, not merely the pleasure expressed in mere courtesy, but sincere gratification." Since Grant's arrival in India, Li had "had all the narratives of the journey translated." Denny had "conveyed a welcome from the Viceroy" to Grant in Hong Kong, and Li had ordered that "no honor should be wanting to the General, and that he himself should be the first Chinaman to greet him in Tientsin and welcome him to the chief province of the Empire." Aboard *Ashuelot* Li told Grant "that he did not care merely to look at [him] or even to make his acquaintance, but to know him well and talk with him."[23]

Over the next three weeks, when not traveling between the two cities, Grant was engaged in summitry with Li in Tientsin and with Prince Kung, regent to the seven-year-old emperor, Kuang-hsu, in Peking. Grant had three full days in Tientsin between his arrival on May 27 and departure for Peking on Saturday, May 31, and two more days with Li after his return from the capital on June 12. In Peking from June 3 to 10, he met with Prince Kung, had public engagements, and, to the extent permitted by the truly awful weather, spent some time as a tourist; the temperature hovered at around 100 degrees Fahrenheit during the entire week, reaching 104 one day. In Tientsin on May 30 Li hosted a dinner in Grant's honor, attended by members of the consular corps. "This," Grant wrote in his diary, "I believe is not an unusual thing, but the Viceroy accepted, & attended, a dinner given by the Consular corps to me and has invited Mrs. Grant to meet Madam Lee [*sic*] on our return from Peking." Li's presence at the May 29 dinner hosted by the French consul was, indeed, unusual, in large part because it was not an all-male affair. Contrary to western etiquette, Grant and Li went in together to dinner, and the former first lady and wives of the consuls sat across the table from the host and guest of honor; Li was certainly unable, and probably unwilling, to go as far as the court had in Siam, where royal princes had offered Julia Grant their arm and danced with her. But it was still an unprecedented moment, as was the invitation to the former first lady, accompanied by the wife and daughter of Owen Denny, the French consul's wife and daughter, and "a missionary lady who interpreted for us," to visit Madame Li in her private apartments on June

14, the Grants' last full day in Tientsin. Julia Grant recalled the invitation as "a great honor and a *very* unusual one."[24] The viceroy's hospitality during Grant's first days in Tientsin set the stage for a successful visit to Peking.

It was slow and arduous going for the men pulling Grant's flotilla of houseboats 150 miles up the Peiho at about two miles an hour. John Russell Young had "seen some curious rivers, but none so curious as the Peiho. It is a narrow, muddy stream, running through a low alluvial country, bordering with crumbling clay banks that break and fall into the water like the banks of the Upper Missouri." The river was navigable by steamship only from the Taku forts to Tientsin; above that city to Peking, "the boats go up and down the river as in the days of Confucius." Young described "the thousands who live on the river, whose home is on the boats, who labor on the water from infancy to old age, who have tracked and splashed and waded through the shallow Peiho, as their fathers did before them." At Tungchow the water voyage ended, but the speed of travel did not increase. The twelve-mile overland journey to the capital took five hours, Grant riding "ahead in a chair carried by eight bearers . . . an honor paid only to the highest persons in China." The courtesies extended to the former president, Young wrote, "confirmed the remark made to me in Tientsin by one of the clearest headed men I have seen in China, that General Grant's visit had done more than anything else to break down the great wall between China and the outer world."[25]

China's need for modern transportation infrastructure was a topic that Grant discussed at length with Prince Kung when they met on June 5. Born on the banks of the Ohio, Grant had in peace and war spent his life almost always in sight of one of the great rivers of the United States: the Hudson at West Point; the Mississippi at White Haven, Galena, and Vicksburg; the Tennessee and the Cumberland; the Potomac, the Rapidan, and the James. He knew them as arteries of commerce, not barriers to it. And as he told Prince Kung, he was "old enough—almost old enough—to remember when the first railway was built in the United States." In Grant's lifetime railroad construction had changed patterns of trade and settlement in states like Illinois, making Chicago a great metropolis at the expense of the once-booming river towns of Cairo and Galena. Even as he spoke to his hosts in China, the construction of new transcontinental rail lines through the Dakotas and Montana was opening settlements beyond the range of Missouri River steamboats. With railroads, the former president told Prince Kung,

> [w]e cannot be sieged, broken up and destroyed in detail, as has happened to other large nations. That, however, is not the greatest advantage. The wealth and industry of the country are utilized. A man's industry in interior States becomes valuable because it can reach a market. Otherwise . . . [h]e would not enjoy the benefits enjoyed by his more favored fellow citizens on the ocean or on the large rivers in communication with the markets of the world. This adds to the revenue of the country.

Li Hung-chang had told Grant that China had "large coal fields as yet undeveloped." If so, "the wealth of such a deposit is incalculable and would be so especially in the East," Grant said to Prince Kung, "[b]ut your coal will be of no use unless you can bring it to a market, and that will require railroads."[26]

The problem for China was the paradox that foreign political influence could best be resisted by adopting the technologies, educational methods, and languages of the foreigners themselves; Grant's counsel was to embrace the paradox. While in Peking he visited an institution that was doing that, Tungwen College, invited by its American president, Presbyterian minister and international legal scholar, Dr. William A. P. Martin. The college, which became part of the new Imperial University (later Peking University) at the turn of the twentieth century, focused on foreign-language education, particularly English. Grant told its students on June 5 that he had "been struck with nothing so much in my tour around the world as with the fact that the progress of civilization—of our modern civilization—is marked by the progress of the English tongue. I rejoice in that fact, and I rejoice in your efforts to attain a knowledge of English speech and all that such a knowledge must convey." The students expressed their "sincere hope that another term of Presidency may come to you, not only that your own nation may be benefitted, but that our countrymen resident in America may also enjoy the blessings of your protection."[27]

Dr. Martin and a delegation of Americans resident in Peking had welcomed Grant to the capital with a call at the US legation on June 3. Like the Chinese in Penang, they were concerned by the treatment of Chinese in the United States and the exclusionary efforts that "threaten[ed] to react so disastrously on American interests in China." They knew that their countrymen at home were closely following Grant's travels:

> Your presence here to-day directs the attention of this venerable Empire to the great Republic from which you come. It will also have the effect

> of turning the eyes of our countrymen toward the teeming millions of Eastern Asia; and fervently do we trust that it will help to impress them with the obligations of justice and humanity in their dealings with the people of China. Your antecedents, sir, leave us no doubt as to the policy that would meet your approval.

The former president's travels, his countrymen told him, "possess[ed] an international character of which it is impossible to divest them." Recognized abroad for his support for abolition, universal male suffrage, equality of opportunity, and the peaceful settlement of international disputes, Grant was "everywhere welcomed as the citizen of a wider commonwealth than that of our native country." He was "the highest representative of our country who has ever gone beyond her borders, and America is the more respected for having given birth to such a son."[28]

A month after he first saw Canton, Grant wrote on June 6 from Peking to Daniel Ammen that he had "found China and the Chinese much as you have often described it and them." It was "not a country nor a people calculated to invite the traveller to make a second visit," but the Chinese "are a people of wonderful shrewdness and industry, and are rapidly monopolizing the trade as carriers, merchants, mechanics, market-gardeners, and servants, from Bombay eastward." He was impressed by the realism of Viceroy Li and Prince Kung, especially their "thorough appreciation of the necessity for internal improvement, such as railroads," and their "horror of introducing them with foreign capital and under foreign control." Grant was pleased that they wished "to make their improvements with their own men and means," and he was optimistic: "My belief is that in less time from now than the half-century since you and I first went to J.D. White's school in Georgetown elapses, Europe will be complaining of the too rapid advance of China." He made many of the same observations in a June 7 letter to Edward Beale. Expanding on what he had written in his diary on May 23 and to Ammen the day before, Grant told Beale that he had "visited the country under the most favorable circumstances to see and study the people, institutions &c. and have drawn rather a favorable view of their future from all I have seen." Although China was "not a military power and could not defend [itself] against even a small European power," Grant thought this would change: "[T]hey have the material for a strong independent nation and may, before many years roll around, assert their power." He "would not be surprised to hear within the next twenty years, if

I should live so long, more complaint of Chinese absorption of the trade and commerse [*sic*] of the world than we hear now of their backward position."[29]

As Grant was writing to Ammen and Beale, a friendly and informal June 3 letter from Owen Denny to John Russell Young arrived in Peking. "How did you like navigating the Peiho?" Denny asked. He had some news for the former president about the event that seemed never likely to happen: "The 'Richmond' arrived off Taku on Sunday evening [June 1]." Most importantly, Denny reported that "[t]he Viceroy is greatly delighted with the General and his visit." The consul knew the summer heat in Peking, and he made no secret of the fact that he would be pleased if Grant abandoned his original plans to visit the Summer Palace and the Great Wall outside the capital so that he could return earlier to Tientsin. He told Young, "[T]hat will give him one or two days more here, which will do *much good* in the 'Friendly Relation' line." Grant agreed. He changed his sightseeing plans, writing in his diary that "I concluded to give them up. I did not feel like encountering this heat & a ride of 114 miles in a mule litter for the pleasure to be derived." Calling at the US legation on June 8, Prince Kung was disappointed to learn that Grant felt "compelled to abandon many of the excursions" he initially had in mind, but understood that "in this season Pekin[g] is always trying." His government had hoped that Grant would stay longer "because China has never been honored before with the presence of so illustrious a guest, and . . . we wish to show our kind feelings to the people of America in honoring one who has been the head of America. China has always been treated well by your country, and never more so than under your administration."[30]

But it was not only courtesy that brought Prince Kung to the legation. He and Li Hung-chang were well-informed about the Treaty of Washington and the Geneva arbitration, and they hoped to involve Grant in peacefully settling China's dispute with Japan over the status of the Loo Choo (Ryukyu) islands. China's principal problem was that Tokyo, having created a *fait accompli* in seizing the islands, would not even discuss the matter with Peking. But Grant was going to Japan at the personal invitation of the emperor, Meiji; if he wished to discuss the Loo Choos, it would be discourteous of the Japanese government not to do so. Prince Kung told the former president that he would "have opportunities of presenting our views to the Emperor of Japan and of showing him that we have no policy but justice. . . . That affords us the opportunity that we cannot overlook." Although Grant told him several times that "my position here and my position at home are not such as to give any assurance that my good offices would be of any value," the prince expressed confidence in the possibilities of Grant's diplomacy:

> [R]eal affairs, great affairs are more frequently transacted informally, when persons meet, as we are meeting now, over a table of entertainment for social and friendly conversation, than in solemn business sessions at the Yamen. I value the opportunities of this conversation, even in a business sense, more than I could any conversation with ambassadors.

Grant agreed to do what he could to help the two countries avoid the "great misfortune" of a war between China and Japan.[31]

Grant's party left Peking on Tuesday, June 10, retraced their route to Tungchow, and boarded boats for Tientsin. They made better time descending the Peiho, and arrived in the viceroy's city on Thursday, June 12. Li "seemed anxious to be as much as possible with the General" until his departure, and for two days the two men discussed virtually every topic related to the prosperity, security, and independence of China. In addition to the dispute over the Loo Choo islands, these included the status of Chinese immigrants in the United States; American federalism as it related to California's attempt to exclude them from the state; the reintegration of Civil War veterans into American civilian life; the work of the US Navy in developing a torpedo service "as a defence for a long coast"; the possibility of accepting Chinese students at West Point and for training on US naval vessels; the Chinese government's desire for an American military adviser; and the utility of railroads in ending the famines that always plagued one part of China or another. Li was frank about the difficulties of introducing foreign ideas to the Chinese, given "the peculiar conditions of the Empire, the vast population, and the existence of traditions and customs that had grown for centuries." He was also frank in expressing his hope that "the kind words spoken by the General about China . . . would not be forgotten when the General became president again." Li "hoped this would be, and that when President the General would remember him and write to him."[32]

Li was reluctant to see Grant leave China. "Heretofore," Young wrote, the "distinguished men who had visited China came either as seekers for the curious and quaint or as ambassadors of rival and not always friendly Powers." But "General Grant represented a nation whose relations to China had always been friendly and sympathetic," and the United States "had no policy in the East inconsistent with the independence of the country." Li valued Grant's views because "the political condition of China, not alone in its relations to the outside world, but in the development of home affairs is such as to make its statesmen anxious for wisdom and information and sympathy." Young seemed concerned that his readers might not appreciate that Li's "reception of General Grant was as notable an event in the utter setting aside of precedents and traditions as can be found in the recent history of China." It had "passed out of the range of hospitality and [become] a question of international politics." China's future was "the gravest problem of the age," and one "which peculiarly concerns the United States." Young had "no doubt that the destinies of China and the policy of her government will show the influence and wisdom of the General."[33]

Late in the evening of Saturday, June 14, following Julia Grant's visit to Madame Li and the former president's last dinner with the viceroy, Grant's party boarded *Ashuelot*. "We left our mooring at three in the morning and were awakened by the thunder of the guns from the forts," wrote Young. "Orders had been given that the forts should fire salutes as the General passed, that the troops should parade and the vessels dress with flags." At the Taku forts, a Chinese fleet awaited them:

> The Viceroy had sent word that he would not take his leave of General Grant until we were on the border of his dominions and out at sea. He had gone ahead on his yacht, and with a fleet of gunboats, and would await us at the mouth of the river and accompany the General on board of the Richmond.

"The river widened," wrote Young, "as we came to the sea, and about eleven o'clock we came to the viceregal fleet at anchor. . . . As we passed every vessel manned yards, and all their guns and all the guns from the forts thundered a farewell." An American warship was also there. Almost exactly seventeen years before, on June 18, 1862, USS *Richmond* had run the guns at Vicksburg for the first time. Now she waited off the China coast for Ulysses Grant:

> Two or three miles out we saw the tapering masts of the Richmond, which, after so long a chase, had at last found General Grant. . . . The sailors rushed up the sides and we swung around amid the thunder of her guns. . . . The Chinese fleet came to an anchor, and at noon precisely General Grant passed over the side of the Ashuelot. On reaching the Richmond the General was received by another salute, all the officers being on deck

> in full uniform. The American ensign was run up at the fore and another salute was fired, the Chinese vessels joining in.[34]

A few minutes later, Grant welcomed Li Hung-chang on board.

The former president and his guest had tea, and the viceroy toured the ship. By midafternoon it was time to leave, but Li was "loath to go, and remained in conversation for some time." The two men revisited all the topics they had discussed in Tientsin, and "General Grant . . . repeated his hope that the statesmen of China would persevere in a policy which brought them nearer to our civilization—a policy that would give new greatness to China . . . and secure the nation's independence." Li "was friendly, almost affectionate. . . . He spoke of the friendship of the United States as dear to China, and again commended to the General and the American people the Chinese who had gone to America." He reiterated China's request that Grant "speak to the Japanese Emperor, and in securing justice remove a cloud from Asia which threw an ominous shadow over the East." The viceroy finally departed "amid the roar of our cannon and the manning of the yards," and Grant's party, at last aboard *Richmond*, set sail for Japan. Although "it was not without a regret that we saw General Grant's flag hauled down" from *Ashuelot*, they were not parting company with Commander Johnson and his crew; the gunboat had been ordered to accompany *Richmond* to Japanese waters.[35]

En route to Nagasaki, Grant's party made two stops, the first to visit the Great Wall where it met the sea, and the second at Chefoo (Yantai), where westerners had built a resort town for the foreign residents of Shanghai and Tientsin. "[T]o come to China and not see the Great Wall," wrote Young, "would have subjected us to adverse criticism for the remainder of our lives." Having abandoned the idea of an excursion to it from Peking because of the heat and uncomfortable travel conditions, "there was a relief to our susceptibilities" when the former president learned that they would have another opportunity after leaving Tientsin. At noon on Monday, June 16, *Richmond* "anchored off the sea end of the great Chines[e] wall at less than a mile distance from shore," and Grant's party landed "on a serf [*sic*] beach where no artificial means have been resorted to make a landing place." Officers and men, "as many as could be spared," accompanied them on the excursion, including "an especial sailor with a pot of white paint to inscribe the fact that the Richmond had visited the Great Wall." They toured the Wall for about an hour and left some graffiti behind before departing for

Chefoo. *Richmond* reached that city the next morning, June 17, and Grant spent the day enjoying the hospitality of the local Chinese officials and foreign residents, returning at midnight to the American warship.[36]

This was China's last opportunity to fire a twenty-one-gun salute for Ulysses Grant, and the gunboats at Chefoo had been ordered to do so when his launch passed them. This posed a problem for *Richmond*'s captain, Young wrote, since no salutes were to be fired after sundown, "[a]ccording to the regulations of the American navy." But Captain Benham, recognizing that "[o]ur mission . . . was one of peace and courtesy and good will, . . . decided that the [Chinese] courtesy should be honored and [*Richmond*] answered gun for gun . . . the midnight salute fired at Chefoo in honor of General Grant." Young waxed lyrical in his final story about Grant's weeks as a guest of the Chinese Empire. "So it came to pass that at midnight, in fire and flame . . . we said farewell to China," he wrote.

> Ancient, vast, unyielding, impenetrable, China sits enthroned in the solitude of Asia, remembering that she was in her splendor before the Roman Empire was born, and that her power has survived the mutations of every age.[37]

Richmond left Chinese waters at 4:00 A.M., on Wednesday, June 18, 1879.

As Grant left China, the US consulate general in Shanghai sent to the State Department a compilation of press clippings about his visit. They included a *North China Daily News* editorial that congratulated its readers on the welcome that Grant had received from the "civilized peoples" represented in the foreign community in China, which "do not confine themselves, like the Orientals, to the histories of their own countries to find objects for their admiration." There was, the paper asserted, a "unity of thought and sentiment that binds civilized nations together," but China, "for a score of centuries, has been concerned only with herself or her children, and the offsprings of other climes have had until lately no sympathetic attention." As a result "[t]he position of foreigners in this country is such that their interests are chiefly identical—not as English, French, Germans or Americans, but rather in the way they all stand, without distinction as to nationality, in the eyes of the Chinese—as 'foreigners,' as 'people from without.'" Based on this assertion, the paper concluded that "the attentions shown by the Chinese themselves to the General must be considered as offered not so much to an American as to a distinguished foreigner, who might have been a German or a Frenchman without making any change in their feelings or sentiments as to nationality."[38]

The suspicious phrase "distinguished foreigner" suggests the editorial may have been part of the British attempt to downplay the significance of Grant's visit to Asia. But whether or not this was the case, the paper was simply wrong in claiming that Grant's nationality was irrelevant to his Chinese hosts. Culturally, China may have regarded all foreigners as outsiders; but politically, where the country's interests were concerned, its leaders knew very well what the "distinction as to nationality" among them meant to China. Understanding those distinctions, and the rivalries of the powers in the rapidly collapsing Concert of Europe, was an existential question for Peking, the difference between extinction and national survival. China's reception of Grant reflected its search for an ally among the western nations that would support its territorial integrity and, eventually, the end of extraterritoriality and the unequal treaties.[39] Li Hung-chang and Prince Kung rightly saw in the United States their only possible hope for such an ally, and they rightly saw in Grant an influential American, probably (they believed) the next president of the United States, who was sympathetic to their goals.

The newspaper's ultimate assessment of Grant's visit was correct, however. It described "[t]he princely hospitality of the Viceroy Li . . . and the unexpected lengths to which he and his household have gone" in making Grant welcome. Li had shown "no little moral courage to stand forth thus, before his countrymen and his detractors who are always ready to taunt him with pro-foreign tendencies, to make bold though tacit declaration that he is the open friend of foreigners, and dares to manifest his friendship to whatever extent his feelings may dictate." Because of this, Grant had left China filled with "cordial sentiments of friendship . . . which may bear their fruit in the fullness of time." This was true; but more importantly, Grant had left China with the conviction that Americans needed to think of the country neither as a source of cheap labor nor as an exotic "land of poetry and romance, antiquity and dreams." The nation's past dated "unbroken and unquestioned to the ages of our mythology," but its future would involve, for better or for worse, the United States. Young stated the question that was on Grant's mind: "What is [China's] power to-day? That is the question of the nineteenth century, and it is a question which cannot be asked too seriously."[40]

CHAPTER SEVEN

The Path to Peace Not Taken: 1879

From the moment he arrived in Nagasaki on Saturday, June 21, Ulysses Grant encouraged his Japanese hosts to ask themselves the same question about the future of Chinese power. While in the White House, Grant himself had given a lot of thought to the advent of Japanese power in Asia, much more than most Americans realized. The foreign policy of the Grant administration was associated in the public mind with the Geneva arbitration, the *Virginius* crisis, and the failed annexation of Santo Domingo (although that had been less an international issue than one between the president and Senate). But President Grant dealt with major international developments from the moment he took office. The most important of these in Europe was the Franco-Prussian War and German unification. In Asia, it was Japan's consolidation, in the Meiji Restoration, of its central government institutions and the parallel attempt to regain tariff autonomy and end the jurisdiction of western consular courts. The result of these events was the same, although more immediately apparent in Europe: the establishment of a new state with economic, political, and military power that changed, in the case of Germany, or had the potential to change, in the case of Japan, the regional, and possibly global, balance of power. By the end of Grant's years in office, Wilhelmine Germany and Meiji Japan, like the post–Civil War United States itself, were power-political factors in the international system that had not existed before 1860.

President Grant followed developments in Europe and Japan closely. He had a trinity of ministers in the three key capitals who raised the profile of the United States in the countries to which they were accredited, and who kept him and Secretary of State Fish well-informed: Elihu Washburne in Paris throughout Grant's eight years in office, George Bancroft

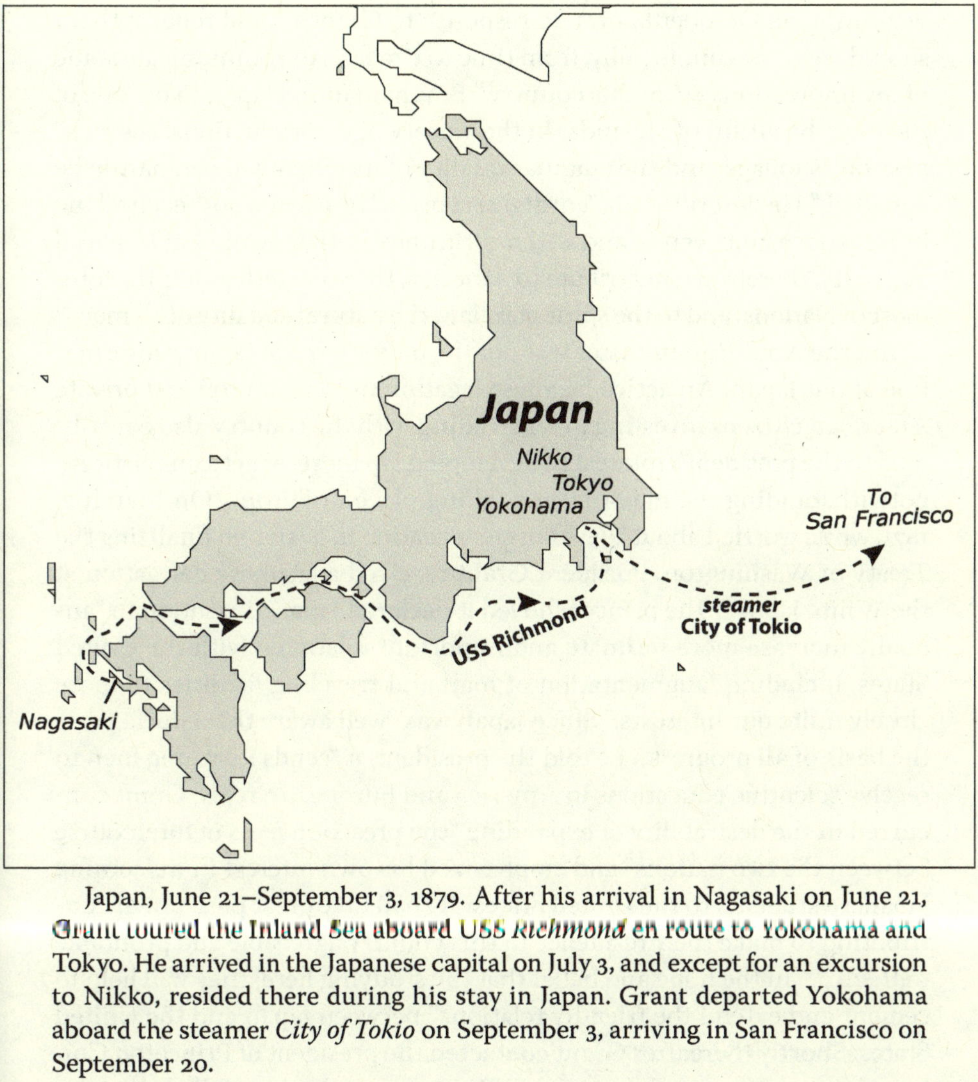

Japan, June 21–September 3, 1879. After his arrival in Nagasaki on June 21, Grant toured the Inland Sea aboard USS *Richmond* en route to Yokohama and Tokyo. He arrived in the Japanese capital on July 3, and except for an excursion to Nikko, resided there during his stay in Japan. Grant departed Yokohama aboard the steamer *City of Tokio* on September 3, arriving in San Francisco on September 20.

in Berlin until 1874, and John Bingham in Edo/Tokyo after 1873. All three shaped Grant's thinking while he was in the White House, and his expectations of what he would find when he went abroad in 1877. Once in Europe Grant's personal experiences caused him to revise, positively (as Washburne wished), his opinion of France, and negatively (contrary to Bancroft's optimism) his opinion of Germany. In Japan Grant found confirmation of what Bingham had described in long letters he wrote to the president, beginning on October 8, 1873, in response to Grant's "kind request that I should write you unofficially, from time to time, . . . to communicate some of my impressions &c of this country." Bingham found Japan to be "one of the most beautiful of all lands. In the variety of its productions, the richness of its foliage, and the singular quality of its climate, it can hardly be equalled." He described his "cordial reception" by Meiji who "received me in his palace, uncovered, and without throne or other symbol of Imperial authority, thereby paying tribute to America, the youngest, as it is the foremost of Nations, and to the spirit of its law, the natural equality of all men."[1]

But the American minister was not the only source of Grant's information about Japan. An active Japanese legation in Washington and private American citizens investing in and trading with the country also contributed to the president's interest in developing Japanese-American relations, notwithstanding the major events taking place in Europe. On March 2, 1871, while worried about Washburne's situation in Paris and finalizing the Treaty of Washington, President Grant received a Japanese delegation at the White House. The prince who led it declared Japan's intention to "annually increase more intimate and important relations" with the United States, including "augmentation of mail and traveling facilities to more closely unite our interests." Since Japan was "well aware that education is the basis of all progress," he told the president, it "sends its young men to receive scientific educations in America and Europe." In reply, Grant concurred in the desirability of expanding "the present means of intercourse between the two nations" and emphasized his own interest in welcoming Japanese students to the United States: "I shall take great pleasure in contributing to make their residence in this country agreeable and profitable to them . . . in the hope and belief that [by studying here] they will help to cement and extend the friendly relations" between Japan and the United States. Shortly thereafter Grant contacted the president of Princeton College about expanding the number of Japanese students enrolled there.[2]

In November 1871 Grant received his first extensive "background brief" on Japan in the form of a long letter from Thomas Walsh, a prominent American businessman in Japan and the son-in-law of Governor Dix of New Jersey. Walsh's letter resulted from "the wish expressed by you, at the interview with which you honored me last week, [for] some observations on American relations with Japan." It summarized relations between the two countries since 1858, when "foreigners knew but little" of Japan and the Japanese had all foreigners "equally under suspicion." But thanks to the work of the first American consul, Townsend Harris, "the Japanese learned that our nation had no other aim than to cultivate profitable commerce with them, and that intercourse with us involved no danger to their independence." As a result Japan "soon manifested a special good will towards Americans [and] American influence surpassed that of any foreign nation." Although Europeans "controlled more capital, and supplied a greater variety of useful imports," Americans initially succeeded out of proportion to "their numbers, or their capital alone." But two things happened: Townsend Harris retired in 1862, and "our civil war, and the concentration of attention upon domestic affairs, which it required, led to a neglect of American interests in Japan which afforded our European rivals an opportunity that they were not slow to seize."[3]

In addition to supporting their merchants, the European powers sent "able and earnest men, instructed both by special training and by special orders, to advance their nations' interests on every occasion, and to obtain the greatest possible power in that rich and virgin field." Britain ("through her efficient Consulates at every port, and her liberally appointed Legation"), France ("maintaining a formidable fleet in Japanese waters"), and Germany ("even during her recent great war") had advanced their mercantile and strategic interests in Japan, a country "which [is] likely, at no very distant day, to become of serious importance to whoever should seek to dominate that great [Pacific] ocean." Moreover, Walsh wrote:

> Italy, Holland, Belgium, Spain and other European nations, are also now in the field; and, though they do not pretend to vie with the three Greater Powers, and have but little commerce to protect, yet they maintain Legations, and, having naturally more sympathy with European than with American interests, frequently combine adversely to the latter, rendering the efforts of the U.S. representatives so much the more difficult and laborious.

Walsh wanted the United States to emulate the Europeans, to recoup the influence "she has well nigh lost . . . by sheer indifference."[4] He laid out for President Grant what should be done to rectify the disadvantageous situation of the United States in Japan.

Chief among Walsh's recommendations was enhancement of the capabilities of the meager US legation, which had "neither Secretary, clerk, interpreter nor attaché to aid" the American minister. Walsh told the president that his representative in Tokyo "should not have to depend for his information upon what he can gather from his [foreign diplomatic] colleagues, or from the local newspapers (all under British management), or from his mercantile friends, or from his native servants (often but spies)." The US minister should not have to depend for interpretation on "Missionary volunteers, who know little of diplomatic language" or "chance scholars in merchants' offices" or, worst of all, the "timid and obsequeous [*sic*] native employes [*sic*] of the Japanese Government, who may betray him." He "should have a staff of his own whose members he could trust, and through whom he could conduct his business in an intelligent and efficient manner." This, Walsh wrote,

> would impress upon the Japanese that this Republic is not less concerned in its foreign affairs than are the Monarchies of Europe, that it is jealous of its reputation, and careful of its interests in Japan, and that it can afford to maintain its dignity there.

Not all of these problems were rectified while Grant was in office; there was perpetual congressional hostility to funding the diplomatic and consular services. But the appointment of Bingham as minister, and of Durham Stevens as secretary of legation, in 1873 went a long way to enhance the diplomatic position of the United States in Japan.[5]

From his arrival there, Bingham made no secret of his hostility toward "European rapacity hitherto too successful in the East," incurring the displeasure of his European diplomatic colleagues, especially the British minister, Sir Harry Parkes. On December 6, 1873, Bingham wrote to Grant that "Sir Harry does not want a [treaty] revision that would open this country to American adventure, energy, & enterprize [*sic*]." And on March 9, 1874, he told the president that "the general purpose [of] the English Press here [is] to damage America and American interests." A year after his arrival, Bingham wrote Grant on October 9, 1874, that, "I offend [Europeans] only because I follow instructions from Washington rather than from London St Petersburg, Paris & Berlin."[6] The Japanese government cultivated the US minister as part of its strategy to win revision of the unequal treaties imposed on Japan in the 1860s, especially return of the American portion of the indemnity Japan paid after the 1863 Shimonoseki incident.[7] It was particularly his support for treaty revision and return of the indemnity that made Bingham unpopular with the British-dominated English-language press in Japan and with Sir Harry Parkes.

The lesson of China's failure to resist western encroachment was not lost on Japan. After the arrival of Commodore Perry in 1854, the Tokugawa shogunate lost control of the country it had ruled for over two hundred years, and Japan fought its own civil war in the 1860s. Initially favoring the shogunate because it had agreed to trade with the West, the European powers took advantage of both sides' need for the military resources and expertise that Europe could provide to expand their influence with those who opposed the shogunate and supported "restoration" of political power to the imperial house. The leaders of the Meiji Restoration eventually accepted what the West wanted—opening Japan to trade—but they were not willing to accept European tutelage over the long term. On the contrary, the new rulers of Japan in 1868, including the sixteen-year-old emperor, were determined to free the country from constraints on its freedom of action. To do so they had to demonstrate that the government was stable; that it could establish law and order throughout Japan; that a new national army and navy could maintain external security; and that the Japanese people were prepared to participate in the global political and commercial system dominated by the western powers. Above all, Japan had to present a façade to the world that there was no internal dissent about the desirability of achieving those objectives. It needed to be the "non-China" in the eyes of the West: the Asian country that unequivocally embraced both modernization and westernization. Japan's reception of Grant was an important component of this strategy, and the government mobilized all its diplomatic and political resources to achieve its goal, that he carry home a positive impression of Japan as a power worthy of respect in the West.[8]

His hosts designed a program to showcase the country's achievements in those areas about which Grant cared most deeply: primary education for both girls and boys; access to economic advancement unrestricted by class, caste, religion, or race; investment in transportation and communications infrastructure, especially railroads; and a willingness to engage in the peaceful settlement of international disputes. To be sure of success, the government called home its minister to the United States, Yoshida Kiyonari, to attend the former president throughout his visit. Yoshida was in Nagasaki on June 21. This was, of course, a courtesy to the Grants that a familiar face, "an old personal friend,"[9] as Young wrote, was there to welcome them. But bringing home its minister was an astute decision on the part of the Japanese government for other reasons. He was a source of information about Grant's impressions of Europe, the British Empire, and China, and if Grant was displeased by anything in Japan, he was more likely to tell Yoshida than anyone else because of their long acquaintance and the minister's fluent English. More likely it would be unnecessary for Grant to say anything; the minister knew the Grants well and could be counted on to anticipate anything they might need or want. Yoshida and Bingham traveled with Grant's party aboard *Richmond* through the Inland Sea from Nagasaki to Yokohama, and during the former president's more than two months in Japan, his longest continuous stay in one country, Yoshida was always close by the guest compound, Enriokan, where the Grants stayed in Tokyo. He served as interpreter for Grant's conversations with the emperor.

The Japanese government also displayed its diplomatic skills by demonstrating that it understood the significance of the Fourth of July for its American guests. Yoshida had experienced the 1876 centennial in the United States, and Bingham was, of course, another source of information on the double significance of the date for Grant. July 4, 1879, was the third Independence Day the former president spent away from home, but the first time one of his host governments made an effort to mark the occasion. In 1877 this was unavoidable. French Republicans would have gone out of their way to celebrate, but Washburne had cautioned Grant not to come to Paris. It would have been uncomfortable for all concerned had the British government attempted to commemorate the day. In 1878 Grant spent July 4 with Americans in Hamburg, Germany. It apparently never occurred to Bismarck that it might be a good idea for the German government to host a celebration in Berlin; or perhaps it did occur to him, but the prospect of stirring the republican ashes of 1848 in the Prussian-German capital was unappealing. Japan's leaders found the idea of honoring American Independence Day very appealing. They "had been impressed by the poetry of the idea of a reception to one who had been the head of the American nation on the anniversary of American independence." Grant's party "discovered, as soon as we had left Nagasaki, that our visit to Tokio was timed for the 3rd of July, and for the reception at the palace on the Fourth."[10]

Their first two weeks in Japan were spent visiting Nagasaki from June 21 to 26, and then touring the Inland Sea aboard *Richmond*. She led quite a flotilla, when seen from the small towns along the shore, including *Ashuelot* "and a Japanese man of war sent from the Capitol [*sic*] with a committee to accompany us through Japan." Grant's party initially could not disembark because of a cholera epidemic that prevented the coastal towns from welcoming the American guests as planned. After they left the area where cholera was a danger and it was safe to go ashore, Grant observed "the general neatness of the simple homes of the people, the perfection of the cultivation of their patches of ground, and the great and simple curiosity of the people, of all ages and both sexes, to see so many foreigners." He was welcomed everywhere by "miles" of schoolchildren and their teachers, who were "lined along the road to make their bow of welcome as we passed." *Richmond*'s arrival in Yokohama on July 3 "was a grand scene, the vessels of all nations being decked with flags all over, the stars & stripes being conspicuous in all, and a number of them firing salutes." Grant noted, "The English were conspicuous for their lack of courtisy [*sic*]." He knew this was "in consequence of orders from the home govt and to anno[y] exceeding[ly] the officials in these waters. No blame to them." Yokohama was a treaty port, but Japan intended to make clear that it was not Shanghai; Grant was the guest of Japan, not the country's foreign residents. He was welcomed at the landing of the Japanese Admiralty by "His Majesty's Ministers of State," as Bingham reported to Washington. In contrast to the long journey by houseboat and sedan chair from Tientsin to Peking, within three hours of arriving in Yokohama, the Grants "were installed in our quarters in Tokio," seventeen miles away. Japan's first railroad, connecting the port city and the capital, had opened in 1872, and the government was happy for its guests to experience the contrast with their travels in China.[11]

In Tokyo the emperor had placed one of his palaces at the Grants' disposal. For the next two months, when they were not traveling overnight outside the capital, they resided at "our lovely Enriokwan [*sic*], which was beginning to seem like home to us," as Julia Grant remembered it many years later. On July 4 Grant's party was received by the emperor and empress "in the presence of the Princes of the Empire, the Prime Ministers, Admiral Patterson, and several Naval officers and the officers of this Legation," Bingham reported to the secretary of state. Meiji expressed his appreciation that "while holding the high office of president of the United States you extended to our countrymen special kindness and courtesy." Japanese "of all classes feel gratified and happy to receive you," and the emperor was "especially gratified that we have been able to do so on the anniversary of American independence." Grant thanked the emperor and the Japanese people for their hospitality. Americans, he said, "without regard to party, take the deepest interest in all that concerns Japan, and have the warmest wishes for her welfare." The United States was Japan's "next neighbor, and will always give Japan sympathy and support in her efforts to advance." He wished Japan "prosperity and independence"—from what he did not say, but the implication was clear enough to the European powers.[12]

Three days later, on July 7, Meiji hosted a military review in Grant's honor. In his July 15 report from Tokyo, published in the August 31 *New York Herald*, John Russell Young described the review and pondered what role the military aspect of Japanese culture would play in the country's future. Unlike China, "Japan dearly loves a soldier," he wrote. "Her traditions are full of military adulation, and the military side of General Grant's career especially attracts the people." Writing of Meiji, Young used almost the same words with which Bismarck a year earlier had described Wilhelm I and the Prussian army: "The Emperor of Japan is fond of his army, and was more anxious to show it to General Grant than any other institution in the Empire." As it had in Berlin, this no doubt struck a false note with the former president, but, as in the German capital, he was too gracious not to accept his host's invitation. The review itself was far more pleasant than the one in the driving rain on Berlin's Tempelhof, and it was followed, not by an all-male lunch in the officers' mess, but by a breakfast hosted by the emperor at one of his palaces by the sea, at which those who had attended the review were joined by the former first lady and princesses of the imperial court. Among the guests were the Grants' hosts in Hong Kong, Governor John Pope-Hennessy and his wife, who had been visiting Japan since mid-June. Pope-Hennessy had also been at the Tokyo train station on July 3; he told the former president that "he came as a British subject to be among those who welcomed General Grant to Japan." At the breakfast, Meiji "conversed a great deal with General Grant through Mr. Yoshida [and] expressed a desire to have a private and friendly conference with the General . . . after [his] return from Nikko."[13] At that meeting, on August 10, the two men discussed the Loo Choo islands.

Until then, except for his respite in Nikko, Grant carried out the program of visits to schools, colleges, farms, military academies, and factories that the government had arranged for him, and with the effect for which it had hoped. Summing up his weeks in Japan, he wrote in his diary that "[e]very day and almost every hour of the stay was taken up in entertainments which although they became very fatiguing, were very instructive as to the rapid progress made by the Japanese Govt. & people." On July 16 Grant wrote to Daniel Ammen that "[t]he changes in Japan have been very great since you were here last, and there is much that you would not recognize." He praised the country's "very perfect school system which enables all classes, male and female, to get a fair education," and the new military and naval academies, which were "both on a better basis than ours were for many years after their establishment." Men "connected with the government in any way, and many merchants and other people, dress in European style, and not infrequently the ladies do also." The Japanese were "altogether the superior people of the East." Still, Grant saw "dawning a new era for China." He wrote to Adam Badeau on the same day that "[f]rom China to Japan the change is very great both in the people and country." However, there were "jerms [*sic*] of progress in China. The country has great resources and a wonderfully industrious, ingenious & frugal people. The end of this century will probably see China looming up." On June 22, the day after his arrival in Japan, Grant had written to Badeau from Nagasaki that "China is on the eve of a great revolution that will land her among the nations of progress. [The Chinese] have the elements of great wealth and great power too and not more than a generation will pass before [China] will make these elements felt."[14] Grant wanted to do what he could to help the Japanese government recognize that.

At the moment, though, China had no choice but to favor peaceful settlement of its issues with Japan. Grant knew that Japan could settle the Loo Choo question through the use of force. In fact, it had already done so. By bringing the islands' king to Japan against his will and annexing them as the province of Okinawa, Japan had created a *fait accompli* that China could overturn only through diplomacy. Peking had not ruled out the use of military force to restore the *status quo ante*, but Grant recognized that it had no capability to do so. For the foreseeable future, Tokyo would be able to impose its will in places like Formosa (Taiwan) and the Loo Choos, if it chose to do so. Grant wanted the Japanese government to make a different choice, to treat China's desire to negotiate as an opportunity to seize, not a weakness to be exploited. In his arrival speech in Nagasaki, he praised Japan for its "efforts to advance in all the benefits of our civilization" and expressed his "hope that all foreign nations will continue to give Japan sympathy and encouragement." But he also expressed the hope that Japan "will long enjoy peace and especially be at peace with her neighbors. This will be a blessing to her as well as to the rest of the world." The leaders of China saw Grant's statement as "evidence of the General's philanthropy and comprehensive grasp of the whole situation." On July 1 Li Hung-chang wrote to John Russell Young that he could not "sufficiently express my gratitude" that Grant had emphasized "the importance of preserving friendly relations with other countries, and especially of avoiding the interruption of long existing peaceful intercourse with neighboring Governments." Li hoped that Grant's stay in Japan meant that "means may be adopted to meet the present exigency; so that a rupture of friendly relations between China and Japan may be averted."[15]

But there were currents in both Japanese society and western statecraft in the nineteenth century that made Grant's task difficult. Young had struck an ominous note in his description of Japan as a country whose traditions were "full of military adulation." One of the results of the Meiji Restoration "was the employment of foreign officers to drill and instruct the troops, teach them European tactics and organize an army." This had been "necessary to support the central power, suppress the Daimios' clans, whose strifes kept the land in a fever, and insure some degree of respect from the outside world," but it was unclear where the marriage of modern military technology and tactics with Japan's historic fascination with the military arts would lead. Young posed the "question whether a revolution which brings a nation out of a condition of dormant peace in which Japan existed for so many centuries, so far as the outer world is concerned, into line with the great military nations, is a step in the path of progress." The West in the 1870s, at the moment at which Japan and China were forced to deal with it, was itself in the throes of "military adulation," as Young regretfully observed:

> It is the painful fact in this glorious nineteenth century . . . that no advancement is sure without gunpowder. The glorious march of our civilization has been through battle smoke, and when Japan threw off the repose and dream life of centuries and came into the wakeful, vigilant, active world, she saw that she must arm, just as China begins to see that she must arm. . . . Europe is here with a mailed hand, and Japan must mail her own or be crushed in the grasp.[16]

From Cairo to Constantinople, and throughout Asia, Grant encountered the reality that Young described; he did what he could to help Japan and China find an alternative to it.

The former president's final weeks abroad were spent at the summit, in meetings with the emperor of Japan and his senior advisers and ministers, in the attempt to put Japan and China on the path that the United States and Britain had followed eight years before with the Treaty of Washington. As president, Grant had made one of the most important and enduring decisions in the history of American foreign policy, that there must not be another Anglo-American war. In 1871 the British government had reached the same conclusion; while the two countries would continue to be competitors, and even rivals, they would never again be enemies. This decision was foundational. A hundred years after American independence, it set the stage for the next hundred years of Anglo-American relations. Grant wanted Peking and Tokyo to make the same decision—to rule out the use of force as a means to settle their current and future disputes. On July 17, the day after writing to Badeau and Ammen, the former president left for Nikko to visit the shrine of the last shogun, Tokugawa Ieyasu. He met there on July 22 with the advisers, Interior Minister Ito Hirobumi and Minister of War Saigo Tsugumichi, whom Meiji had designated to discuss the Loo Choo issue with him. Yoshida and Bingham also took part in their discussions.

As Grant saw the situation, vis-à-vis China, Japan now faced the same decision that he had faced in 1871, when senators and some of his own cabinet members had advised demanding Canada in settlement of the CSS *Alabama* claims at a moment of British distraction and (relative) weakness. In Grant's opinion, Japanese leaders should resist the temptation to take advantage of their country's momentary military superiority over China, as he had resisted the pressures put on him eight years earlier. If they did not, they would poison Sino-Japanese relations for decades. Grant told Ito and Saigo that "[a]gainst Japan China, he might say, was defenceless, and it was impossible for China to injure Japan"; but "China was a country of wonderful resources, and, although he had seen nothing there to equal the progress that delighted him in Japan, there had been great progress . . . and no one could foresee what might come from it in twenty or thirty years." He counseled that "Japan should be in a position where she could assist China, and not allow this grievance to grow up and fester and be the source of alienation and irritation now and of trouble in the future."[17] Grant had experienced in Paris French demands for *revanche* against Germany because of the "lost provinces" of Alsace and Lorraine, and in Berlin the Germans' arrogant self-satisfaction with their military prowess. He did not want Sino-Japanese relations to go down a similar path. Nothing would be worse for both countries, but at the moment it was Tokyo that risked following in the footsteps of Berlin. Grant did his best to dissuade Japanese leaders from emulating Prussia-Germany in their relations with China, but he ultimately failed.

When Grant and Meiji met on August 10, the young emperor invited the former president to "talk generally upon affairs in Japan." For over two years Grant had been observing and comparing the state of the nations he had visited around the world; Meiji had never left Japan. Grant made no attempt to be circumspect in expressing his belief that "the policy of some of the European Powers was to reduce Japan and China into the dependence which had been forced upon other nations." He was particularly incensed by the opium trade "forced upon the people" of China. In Nikko he had called this trade "as great a crime against civilization as slavery." Grant told Meiji that European control over the picture of Asians painted in the press was part of the problem: "This side of Singapore I have found but few newspapers or periodicals that are capable or willing to reason things upon common footing between the Asiatics, and European[s] and American[s]." He was also outraged by the Europeans' willful disregard of Japanese law, even when they foolishly exposed themselves and others to the cholera that had kept him aboard *Richmond* on the Inland Sea. He told Ito and Saigo in Nikko that

> only the other day, he saw the Germans deliberately violate a Japanese quarantine by sending down a German gunboat and taking a German merchantman out of quarantine. No European power would dare to do such a thing in the United States. But it illustrates European policy in the East.

Grant told Meiji, as he had the two ministers in Nikko, that it made his "blood boil" to see the Europeans' "unfairness and selfishness" in dealing with Asians.

Grant warned the emperor to "avoid . . . owing money abroad," exhorting him to "[l]ook at Egypt, Spain, or Turkey; how helpless they are!" Spain had an "extravagant rate of internal taxes of all sorts" because of "superfluous foreign loans"; those taxes had led to "corruption among revenue officials of all grades [that was] fast ruining the nation, a nation of great capacity and resources." And "[i]n Egypt the Kedief [*sic*] is forced to abdicate!" Grant saw clearly that there was policy behind the creation of such indebtedness. He told Meiji that "some nations are very desirous to loan money to weaker nations whereby they might establish their supremacy and exercise undue influence over them. They lend money to gain political power. . . . They would be glad, therefore, to see Japan and China . . . at war with each other so that they might loan them on their own terms and dictate to them the internal policy which they should pursue." Grant was blunt: "European powers have no interests in Asia, so far I can judge from their diplomacy, that do not involve the humiliation and subjugation of the Asiatic people."

This brought the discussion to the Loo Choo islands. Despite all he had read since June—Grant had spent a good deal of time studying background papers prepared for him by both governments—he understood that he was not "in a position to know definitely the merits of the case." But he realized the near impossibility of Japan's backing down: "A nation having gone as far as Japan . . . must consider what is due to her people." China's national pride was equally involved, and that aspect of the issue was, Grant told Meiji, "the only point that I would care to mention." China saw "Japan's action as wanting in respect and friendship, and as indicating a disposition upon the part of Japan to again occupy Formosa and in doing so bar the channel between China and the Pacific Ocean. The result of this is that the Chinese statesmen feel a sense of wrong and irritation towards Japan." Grant suggested that "this feeling in the minds of Chinese statesmen should be well-considered by Japan, and that Japan in a spirit of magnanimity and justice should make concessions to China." The two countries should deal bilaterally with the issue, "approaching this question in a spirit of friendship and concession, as ancient allies and of the same race." If they did so, they could "adjust it in a manner honorable to both, and lay the foundations of a lasting peace."

The extension of Japanese influence in Asia could, in theory, have been accomplished by diplomatic means, in keeping with Grant's advice. But his counsel collided with the reality of the profound, and ultimately fateful, disagreement among Japan's leaders about the desirability of using the country's armed forces not only to defend the home islands, but to expand beyond them. Those who favored such expansion had three reasons to do so: the employment "of the dispossessed warrior class by making new territory available to them for exploitation"[18]; the straightforward desire to improve Japan's economic and strategic situation through the acquisition of new territory and resources; and the belief that the successful use of force abroad, more than anything else that Japan could do, would win it the respect of the European powers. For the Meiji elite who observed the great power status that came with the success of Prussian-German arms in 1870–71, and of Grant's own armies in 1865, it seemed obvious that Japan had an interest in enhancing the capabilities and reach of its armed forces, not negotiation and compromise. That interest was reinforced, as Young had observed, by the status Japanese society accorded to the warrior. For centuries the loyalty of those warriors had belonged to the daimyo, the feudal lords of the great clans. The government had abolished the daimyo, their domains, and the samurai in 1871,[19] but the clan leaders who fought the wars of the Meiji Restoration, some on the side of the emperor, some opposing him, and some at various times on both sides, still had the ability to destabilize Japan. As Young wrote, "The daimios appear to accept the revolution and give allegiance to the present government of the Mikado, but their acceptance is not hearty."[20]

It was only two years before Grant's visit that forces loyal to the emperor had defeated the rebellion of the Satsuma clan, and in 1879 Meiji and his advisers could not be certain that another such danger would not arise. While trying to cope with the demands placed on Japan by the foreign powers, the government also needed to placate the daimyo and secure their commitment to peace and stability at home by pursuing aims that were important to them. Beginning with the 1874 Formosa expedition, the country's first foray overseas, "Japan [found] it necessary to make war to avert a revolution."[21] That venture created not only a crisis with China, but a potential new *Virginius* issue for the United States because, as Bingham wrote to the president on July 18, 1874, of "the employment of . . . an American vessel . . . in violation of our Treaty obligations & of our laws & also of the sovereignty of China." The US minister called the expedition a "wild & foolish adventure" that "Japan was forced into by the clamor of the clans lately engaged in insurrection."[22] Five years later, Japan's claim to the Loo Choos rested in part on China's (apparently inadvertent) recognition of Japan's right to mount the 1874 expedition and in part on the tribute that the king of those islands had paid to the Satsuma clan for centuries, while simultaneously paying tribute to China.[23]

Whatever the validity of Grant's argument about China's future economic and military strength, Meiji and his advisers faced the reality that, in the here and now, the "men of Satsuma" and the other domains had political power at home. Grant had told Ito and Saigo that Japan needed "a complete and amicable understanding with China," because "[t]he only Powers who would derive any benefit from a [Sino-Japanese] war would be foreign Powers." But any sign of internal disunity, perhaps even a renewal of civil war and the possible toppling of Meiji, would present an even greater opportunity for foreign interference. Since concessions to China would alienate powerful elements at home, even those Japanese leaders most receptive to Grant's arguments could persuade themselves that Japan could not afford to pursue such a policy in the short term. And many members of the Japanese elite were not receptive to his advice. They did not believe that their country would win respect from the European powers by conciliating China. Two decades later, the respect that Japan did win from those powers (and the United States) by its victories in the Sino-Japanese and Russo-Japanese wars confirmed the expansionists' belief that the successful use of military force was all that mattered.[24]

In discussing Japan's domestic political system, Grant warned Meiji to avoid a too-rapid expansion of the franchise. By all accounts, this made a strong impression on the emperor, "who had already demonstrated his preference for a gradual approach to the creation of a parliament"[25]; but what prompted the former president to give such advice requires some speculation. It seems, at first glance, out of character. He told Meiji that "[y]ou do not want to see anarchy as the result of any premature creation of an assembly" and recommended "that the first step should be an advisory assembly, a counsel [*sic*] of the leading men in Japan, with power to debate but not to legislate." Grant coupled the specter of "anarchy" with the observation that while, "[i]n all civilized countries . . . political parties" were "very useful for checking each other from misrule," there were also "leading men who might be called in our country demagogues [who] must find some pretext against government to secure followers." He warned Meiji that "parties trying to destroy the existing government" were "very mischievous. I dare say there are also [such] parties here."

What was this about? Grant thought comparatively; whatever he mentioned to his hosts abroad almost always reflected an issue with which he had dealt at home, whether or not he made the analogy explicit. In this case it seems unlikely that he was thinking of the Fifteenth Amendment. Grant certainly recognized the educational challenge posed by the enfranchisement of former slaves; but that required schools for adults and children, preferably, in Grant's opinion, public schools, but if necessary, privately supported Freedmen's Schools. It was not an issue of anarchy or demagogy. There was such an enfranchisement issue in the United States, however, and Grant had corresponded with his close friends about it while traveling abroad: the emerging "Solid South" in the states of the former Confederacy. The end of federal election supervision; the reestablishment of white-controlled state governments; the manipulation of the votes of semiliterate white southerners; the intimidation of black voters in blatant disregard of the Fifteenth Amendment; and the prospect that an alliance of southern and northern Democrats would win control of the federal government all troubled Grant greatly. The unreconstructed South shared with

Tammany Hall and California's anti-Chinese rabble-rouser, Denis Kearney, a common cause in demagogic manipulation of voter blocs susceptible to their appeals to ethnic solidarity and racial stereotypes.

Thanks to Bingham and Yoshida and his own experiences since June, Grant was well-informed about recent Japanese history. Most likely, he saw a parallel to post-Reconstruction developments in the United States in the continued strength of the great clans like Satsuma and Choshu, "whose real power rested on the authority they enjoyed as hereditary lords of the counties and chiefs of the local Samurais."[26] There was no racial component to the Japanese situation, but as with working-class whites in the former Confederacy and recently arrived immigrants in the large cities of the North, a sudden expansion of the franchise could bring to the polls voters who would cast their ballots as the former daimyo and samurai ordered them to, for candidates selected by the clans. There was no point in making this analogy explicit; it was unlikely that what Meiji knew of the history of the United States would have enabled him to understand it. Moreover, with an eye on domestic American politics, Grant's general exhortation to proceed cautiously in establishing an assembly was as far as it was prudent to go, at least in conversations that Young put in the public record. He could only create problems for the Republican Party by making pointed comments about American issues. With regard to his hosts, Grant was too prudent a diplomat to suggest outright the possibility of another Satsuma Rebellion through manipulation of the ballot box; Meiji had invited his frank opinions, but such a reference would have been unacceptable interference in the domestic politics of Japan.

Unfortunately, "Grant's recommendation that Japan proceed slowly before creating a legislative body accorded perfectly with what most Japanese statesmen favored anyway"[27]; for some members of the Meiji elite, it confirmed their reluctance to establish one at all. The Prussian-German model had far greater appeal to them than the ever-widening franchise that Grant saw as characteristic not only of republics like France and the United States, but of constitutional monarchies in the Netherlands, Scandinavia, and Britain.[28] The young royals and aristocrats who founded the modern Japanese state in 1868 became the genro—the elder statesmen who, throughout the Meiji and Taisho years and even into early Showa (Hirohito) in the 1920s, constituted the "counsel [*sic*] of the leading men of Japan" that Grant had recommended. But as ministers and advisers to a theoretically absolute monarch, the council of the genro became not the first step on the road to constitutional monarchy that Grant envisaged, but a roadblock to it.[29] The former president could not have foreseen this in 1879, when the threat that a manipulated franchise might pose to the central government was highly plausible; but it was consequential for Japan's future that Meiji and his ministers were as receptive to Grant's advice in this case as they were reluctant to embrace his recommendation that Japan use diplomacy to pursue its foreign policy aims.

It must have been strange for Grant to realize, as he finished his August 10 conversation with the emperor, that he had less than a month remaining in his travels overseas. In his last weeks in Japan, amid a final round of festivities, he was threatened with assassination. On August 4 the US legation received a letter announcing the intent to murder the two most prominent foreigners then in Japan, Grant and Pope-Hennessy. The letter claimed that Meiji had been betrayed by his advisers, whose hosting of "many foreign visitors" produced "boundless extravagance, and needless expenses . . . the like of which have never been seen in our country in ancient or modern times." Because "the safety and reputation of the country are at stake," it was necessary "to kill . . . Okuma Shigenobu and Ito Hirobumi, the guilty ringleaders, and . . . to assassinate Grant and Hennessy." Bingham immediately reported the threat, enclosing the English translation of the letter done by the legation, to Foreign Minister Terashima Munenori, and asked him to determine "whether the statement . . . has any real foundation or . . . is the fiction of some inventive or diseased mind." On August 8 Terashima replied that the government did not know "what frantic person has ventured to act in such injurious tendencies," but had undertaken "serious inquiries by the proper authorities." Bingham informed the State Department of the threat on August 16, telling Evarts that he had asked the Japanese government to ensure that "the conspirators might be detected and arrested before the execution of their declared purpose." After nearly two weeks, however, the police had "not been able to ascertain the author of the letter nor the truth of its statement that there is such a conspiracy."[30]

Like the disagreements within the country's political elite, the threat to Grant's life belied the façade of Meiji Japan. The government did its best to project the image of a nation unanimous in its embrace of political and commercial intercourse with the rest of the world, but there remained a good deal of dissatisfaction with what had happened to the country in the previous twenty-five years. Grant wrote to Daniel Ammen on August 7, "The changes that have taken place here are more like a dream than a reality."[31] He was on to something. The changes were not a dream, but they were to some extent a mirage. Even had western diplomats, merchants, and missionaries been less arrogant than most of them were, the upheaval and turmoil of civil war, establishment of the new educational system that Grant so much admired, pressure to wear western dress,[32] abolition of the daimyo and samurai, and the disruptive speed of railroads and steamships were all disconcerting. Although Meiji Japan presented a united front to the outside world, the silent, hostile faces that Young had observed in the streets of China also existed in Japan, some of them at the highest levels of government. Even Iwakura Tomomi, the emperor's principal adviser and old friend who had done "more than anyone else" to westernize Japan, had "ceased to look kindly upon the changes," and "his eyes are turned with affection and sorrow toward the lamented and irrecoverable past."[33]

Grant's final letters from Japan reflected his awareness of the bitter legacy that the interaction between the West and Japan would leave to the future. Three days after meeting the emperor, he wrote on August 13 to Prince Kung, with a copy to Iwakura, reporting on his conversations with Meiji and his advisers about the Loo Choo issue. Grant repeated what he had, by then, said and written often since China had requested his involvement in the matter, that the two countries should resolve their dispute through bilateral diplomacy, without interference from foreign powers. But he added one thought that he had not emphasized before—that the long term interests of foreigners themselves were not well-served by their present policies:

> I can readily concieve [*sic*] that there are many foreigners, particularly among those interested in trade, who do not look beyond the present, and who would like to have the present condition remain, only grasping more from the East, and leaving the natives of the soil merely "hewers of wood and drawers of water," for their benefit. I have so much sympathy for the good of their children if not for them, that I hope the two countries will disappoint them.

This letter, which was sent with Meiji's approval, was not made public at the time. Three years later, on October 9, 1882, while serving as US minister in Peking, John Russell Young sent a copy of it to Secretary of State Frederick Frelinghuysen, telling him that it had "never to my knowledge before been printed or even made a matter of record in the Department. At the time . . . it was held as a confidential communication at the request of Mr. Iwakura. . . . It had the effect . . . of preventing what threatened to be a serious disagreement, and perhaps war. It is much to be regretted that the advice given by the Ex President was not followed to a complete settlement."[34]

On August 10, the same day he met with Meiji, the former president gave free rein to his dislike for European behavior in Asia in a letter to his daughter, Nellie: "The course of the average Minister, Consul & merchant in this country & China towards the native is much like the course of the former slave owner towards the freedman wh[en] the latter attempts to think for himself in matters of choice of candidates. The present policy towards these two countries cannot continue much longer without a terrible calamity and one that will fall heavy upon life and property." Grant told his daughter, "How the Government & the people retain their temper and kind treatment to the foreigner under the insults heaped upon them and overbearing and bullying policy of the foreigner and their diplomatic representatives I cannot understand." There should be "a speedy change" of western officials in Asia, including "the most of our representatives" in China and Japan; but reflecting his admiration for Bingham, Grant concluded: "Not our Minister here however." Grant wrote to Adam Badeau on August 25 that he had "never been so struck with the heartlessness of Nations as well as individuals as since coming to the east. But a day of retribution is sure to come. These people are becoming strong and China is sure to do so also. When they do a different policy will have to prevale [*sic*] from that enforced now."[35]

That evening, Tokyo celebrated its twelfth anniversary as Japan's capital with a grand festival in Ueno Park, attended by the emperor and all the members of the diplomatic corps. Postponed for over a month because of the cholera epidemic, the festival also became the people of Tokyo's farewell to the former president. Five days later, on August 30, Grant paid a final, formal call on the emperor. The assassination threat was not mentioned that day. Grant told Meiji that, in more than two months in Japan, he had "not witnessed one discourtesy towards myself nor a single unpleasant sight." He commented that "while no signs of great individual wealth exist, no absolute poverty is visible," which he found "in striking and pleasing contrast with almost every other country I have visited." He assured Meiji of his "sincere desire . . . to see Japan realize all the strength and greatness she is capable of, to see her as independent of foreign rule or dictation as any western nation now is, and to see affairs so directed by her as to command the respect of the civilized world." The emperor expressed his conviction that Grant's "visit to our Empire, which enabled us to form very pleasant personal acquaintance with each other, will facilitate and strengthen the friendly relations that have heretofore happily existed between the two countries."[36]

On Wednesday, September 3, Ulysses, Julia, and Fred Grant and John Russell Young sailed for home aboard the Pacific Mail Steamer *City of Tokio.* Young described the "clear and beautiful" morning on which the Grants left the Tokyo palace that had been their home since July 3:

> Shortly after eight the state carriages came. We drove slowly away, the cavalry forming around us, the infantry presenting arms. . . . Troops formed in double line . . . along the whole line of our route, even to the railway station. . . . The crowd was enormous and increased as we came to the railway. . . . At twenty-five minutes past eight the train pushed out from Tokio, the troops presenting arms, the band playing our national air, the people waving their farewell, while the General stood on the platform and bowed his acknowledgments. Our engine was draped with the American and Japanese flags.

Grant's "train was a special one" that "stopped at none of the intermediate stations. But as we whirled past each station we observed the crowds assembled to have a last glimpse of the General." The train "came in sight of Yokohama bay [and] we saw the ships dressed from stem to stern with streamers, flags, and emblems"; at "Yokohama station the crowd was apparently as large as what we had left in the capital." Grant's party made its way to the pier along a "road [that] was decorated with Japanese and American flags, and when we came to the Admiralty there was a display of day fireworks . . . and amid the noise of the exploding fireworks and strains of the naval band we pushed off." As *City of Tokio* headed for open water, "[a]round us were men-of-war shimmering in the sunshine, so it seemed, with their multitudinous flags," including USS *Ranger*, USS *Monongahela*, and the two vessels that had flown Grant's flag in Asia:

> We pass the "Richmond" near enough to recognize our friends on the quarter-deck—the Admiral and his officers. You hear a shrill word of command, and seamen go scampering up the rigging to man the yards. The guns roll out a salute. We pass the "Ashuelot," and her guns take up the iron chorus. . . . For an hour or so the Japanese man-of-war, the same

> which met us at Nagasaki and came with us through the Inland Sea, keeps us company. The Japanese cabinet are on board . . . and we hurry to the side of our vessel to wave farewell to so many friends. . . . The man-of-war fires twenty-one guns. The Japanese sailors swarm on the rigging and give hearty cheers. Our steamer answers by blowing her steam whistle. The man-of-war turns slowly around and steams back to Yokohama. Very soon she also becomes a phantom, vanishing over the horizon.[37]

The day before Grant's departure, Bingham wrote his report to the secretary of state summing up the former president's visit to Japan. It was the last of many such dispatches that Evarts had received since his circular note of May 23, 1877. Like the first reports from London and, since then, from capitals throughout Europe and Asia, this final message from Tokyo confirmed the impact of Grant's summitry and public diplomacy on American relations with the countries he visited. "I do not hesitate to say," Bingham told the secretary, "that no such imperial and popular reception as that given to General Grant by His Majesty and His Majesty's Ministers and people was before given in this Empire to any foreign visitor. . . . It is not to be doubted that the extraordinary attentions shown to our illustrious citizen were shown alike in honor of the Ex President and of the government and people of the United States of America." Bingham concluded by telling the secretary that "[t]he Emperor and people of Japan look with a confiding trust to our government and people."[38]

The leaders of Japan had been flattered by Grant's visit and impressed by his modest dignity, but they did not take to heart the content of his diplomacy. In the years after 1879 Japan instead chose to travel the path of territorial conquest in Asia that Grant had urged it to avoid. As a result, sixty-six years to the day after Bingham's dispatch to Evarts, on September 2, 1945, another delegation of Japanese cabinet members traveled from Tokyo to Yokohama on "a surprisingly cool day for early September. The sky was dull gray with clouds hanging low." A Foreign Office diplomat, Kase Toshikazu, described their journey "on the battered and bumpy road to Yokohama":

> Along the highway, we could see nothing but miles and miles of debris and destruction where there had once flourished towns containing a great number of munitions factories. The ghastly sight of death and desolation was enough to freeze my heart. These hollow ruins, however, were perhaps a fit prelude to the poignant drama in which we were about to take part for

> were we not sorrowing men come to seek a tomb for a fallen Empire? . . . There were few men on the road and none probably recognized us. Our journey was kept in utmost secrecy in order to avoid publicity lest extremists might attempt to impede us by violence.[39]

As the delegation approached Yokohama, there were no festively dressed ships, but there were foreign troops, because "the spearhead of the Eighth Army" had arrived and was "heavily guarding the streets through which we rode slowly to the port area." Kase's delegation had been commanded by Meiji's grandson, the Showa emperor, Hirohito, to make this journey of surrender. They had come to meet General Douglas MacArthur, grandson of a friend of Ulysses Grant:

> All the cars had removed the flags on the bonnet and officers had left their swords behind. . . . Diplomats without flag and soldiers without sword—sullen and silent we continued the journey till we reached the quay. . . . We boarded . . . the *Lansdown* [and a]s the destroyer pushed out of the harbor, we saw in the offing lines on lines of gray warships, both heavy and light . . . of the Allied navies. . . . After about an hour's cruise the destroyer stopped in full view of the battleship *Missouri*, which lay anchored some eighteen miles off the shore.[40]

"The Emperor and people of Japan look with a confiding trust to our government and people," Bingham had written on September 2, 1879. Despite, or perhaps because of the choices Japan made in the intervening decades, that statement was as true on September 2, 1945, as it had been on the day sixty-six years before when *City of Tokio*, with Ulysses Grant onboard, "breast[ed] the sea with an earnest will—for California and for home."[41]

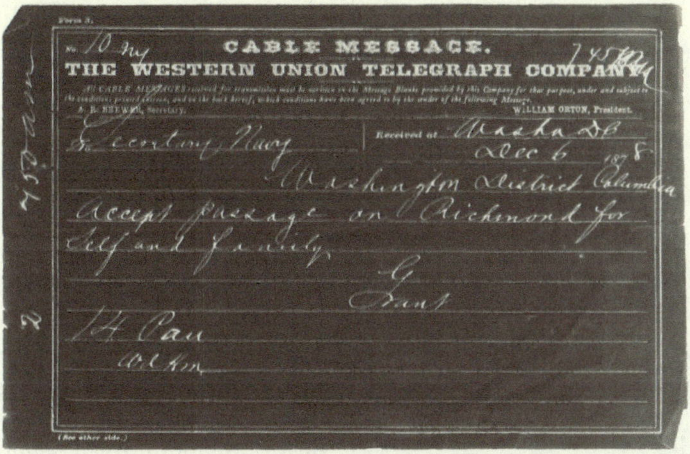
CABLE MESSAGE.

THE WESTERN UNION TELEGRAPH COMPANY

WILLIAM ORTON, President.

To Secretary Navy

Received at Washn DC Dec 6 1878

Washington District Columbia

Accept passage on Richmond for self and family

G Grant

14 Pau

Grant decided while in Pau, France, on his return to Paris from a two-month visit to Spain, Portugal, and Gibraltar, to accept the invitation of Secretary of the Navy Richard Thompson (1809–1900) to travel from Europe to the Far East aboard USS *Richmond*, designated as the new flagship of the Pacific Squadron at Yokohama, Japan. Ulysses S. Grant Association's Ulysses S. Grant Presidential Library, Mississippi State University.

Grant's party arrived in Calcutta, India, on March 10, 1879, about the time that USS *Richmond* reached Port Said, before its transit of the Suez Canal. Delayed for a month in departing Norfolk, *Richmond* suffered further delays en route and only met Grant off the coast of China in June 1879, five months after he had expected to board her in France. The delay angered the former president, but it also gave him the opportunity to meet many Europeans with years of experience in Asia while traveling aboard commercial vessels from Europe to Hong Kong.

Michael Hicks-Beach (1837–1916), Britain's colonial secretary in 1879, declared that Grant, as a former president, was only a "distinguished foreigner" and not entitled to the twenty-one-gun "royal" salute accorded to heads of state. The Royal Navy had rendered the salute to Grant in Europe, and other European countries, Siam, China, and Japan all rendered the salute to him in Asia. Author's collection; scan courtesy of John Wilkes, The *Vanity Fair* Print Company, www.vanity-fair-prints.com.

Lord Lytton (1831–91), the viceroy of India, hosted the Grants in Calcutta in March 1879 at the end of their month-long tour of India. A Confederate sympathizer who had served at the British legation in the 1850s in Washington, DC, Lytton told John Russell Young that he had wanted the South to win, but "never believed that [it] would succeed." Author's collection; scan courtesy of John Wilkes, The *Vanity Fair* Print Company, www.vanity-fair-prints.com.

Robert Hart (1835–1911) was the world-renowned "I.G.," inspector general of China's Imperial Maritime Customs Service, for almost fifty years. Hart built a multinational civil service that developed China's ports, collected customs duties, and tried to lay a sound financial foundation for the country's future development. He was a trusted adviser to Prince Kung and Viceroy Li Hung-chang. Grant spent a week with Hart aboard ship from Singapore to Hong Kong in April 1879, an unplanned encounter that prepared the former president for the diplomacy he would conduct in Tientsin, Peking, and Tokyo. Author's collection; scan courtesy of John Wilkes, The *Vanity Fair* Print Company, www.vanity-fair-prints.com.

Grant and Li Hung-chang (1823–1901), China's northern viceroy, formed an immediate bond during the former president's visit to Tientsin in May–June 1879. For more than a quarter century, Li was China's principal negotiator with foreign powers, and he welcomed the opportunity to receive "wisdom and information and sympathy" from the former president. Grant was impressed by the "wonderful shrewdness and industry" of the Chinese people, and he urged Li to open his country to the West and pursue "a policy that would give new greatness to China." Author's collection; *Harper's Weekly*, October 4, 1879.

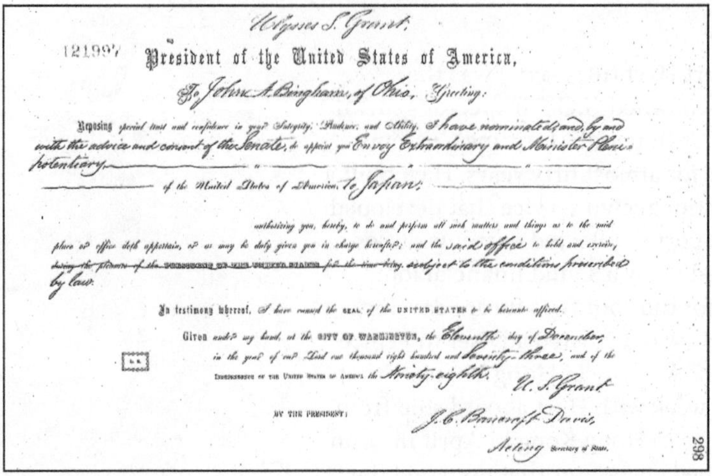

Ulysses S. Grant,

121997

President of the United States of America,

To John A. Bingham, of Ohio, Greeting:

Reposing special trust and confidence in your Integrity, Prudence, and Ability, I have nominated, and, by and with the advice and consent of the Senate, do appoint you Envoy Extraordinary and Minister Plenipotentiary of the United States of America to Japan; authorizing you, hereby, to do and perform all such matters and things as to the said place or office doth appertain, or as may be duly given you in charge hereafter; and the said office to hold and exercise, ~~during the pleasure of the President of the United States for the time being~~, subject to the conditions prescribed by law.

In testimony whereof, I have caused the seal of the United States to be hereunto affixed.

Given under my hand, at the City of Washington, the Eleventh day of December, in the year of our Lord one thousand eight hundred and Seventy-three, and of the Independence of the United States of America the Ninety-eighth.

U. S. Grant

By the President:

J. C. Bancroft Davis,

Acting Secretary of State.

298

On December 11, 1873, President Grant named John A. Bingham (1815–1900) as US minister to Japan, where he remained until 1885 under Presidents Hayes, Garfield, and Arthur. Bingham traveled with Grant throughout the former president's time in Japan, June–September 1879, his longest continuous stay in any country. In his final report to the secretary of state on Grant's visit, Bingham told Evarts on September 2, 1879, that "no such imperial and popular reception . . . was before given in this Empire to any foreign visitor." Ulysses S. Grant Association's Ulysses S. Grant Presidential Library, Mississippi State University.

Seventeen days out of Yokohama, Ulysses, Julia, and Fred Grant and John Russell Young arrived at the Golden Gate on Saturday, September 20, 1879. This engraving shows their ship *City of Tokio* inside the Gate, with Fort Point on the left and the Marin headlands on the right, escorted by the flotilla of ships and boats that met it to welcome the Grants home. Author's collection; *Harper's Weekly*, October 25, 1879.

This Thomas Nast engraving hailed Grant's return home. With his trident, Neptune is steering a boat named *Tokio,* as Minerva crowns the former president with fresh laurels for his achievements abroad. The caption quotes Homer's *Odyssey,* "Much-enduring, modest Ulysses was then glad, rejoicing in his own land." Author's collection; *Harper's Weekly,* October 11, 1879.

Although San Francisco was ecstatic to welcome Grant home, many of its residents were not pleased by his generally positive stance on Chinese immigration. The former president refused to receive the city's anti-Chinese rabblerouser, Denis Kearney, saying, "I won't see a ruffian." But despite pressure to decline, he met with Chinese consular officials and merchants at the Presidio home of General Irvin McDowell. Facsimile courtesy of Melissa Trombley-Prosch, Grant Cottage Association, Mount McGregor, New York.

Many festivities were held in Grant's honor during his stay in San Francisco. As Generals Sherman and Sheridan had predicted, Californians were flattered that the Grants returned home to the West Coast, rather than to one of the usual ports on the Atlantic seaboard. The "sand lots" were famous as the site of Denis Kearney's anti-Chinese demagogy, but as *Harper's Weekly* reported, they hosted "a magnificent display of fireworks" in salute to the former president. Author's collection; *Harper's Weekly*, October 25, 1879.

When Assistant Secretary of State John Hay (1838–1905) and Secretary of State Evarts met with Grant in December 1879 in Washington, DC, Grant sought to impress on them the importance of US engagement in the Far East. During the 1900 Boxer Rebellion, then secretary of state Hay worked with Chinese ambassador Wu Ting-fang, who had met Grant in Hong Kong in 1879, to rescue the besieged legations in Peking and prevent the foreign powers from dismembering China. Hay's "Open Door" notes of 1899 and 1900 made explicit the US commitment to the sovereignty and territorial integrity of China. Author's collection; scan courtesy of John Wilkes, The *Vanity Fair* Print Company, www.vanity-fair-prints.com.

Grant's political enemies sought to torpedo his chances of returning to the White House in this 1880 cartoon by proclaiming him the "Hero of a Thousand Feeds," whose travels abroad were an attempt to "eat [his] way" back to the presidency. Original in author's collection; Ulysses S. Grant Association's Ulysses S. Grant Presidential Library, Mississippi State University.

CHAPTER EIGHT

Home: 1879

Lieutenant Ulysses Grant first saw San Francisco in early September 1852, when he arrived from Panama aboard one of the Pacific Mail Steamship Company's wooden side-wheelers, *Golden Gate*. Twenty-seven years later Grant returned to a very different city on September 20, 1879, aboard the same company's *City of Tokio*, after more than two years and four months overseas.[1] He received a tumultuous welcome, akin to that accorded ninety years later to Apollo astronauts returning from the moon. The *San Francisco Chronicle* reported on Tuesday, September 23, that, "in anticipation of a large demand," it had printed "50,000 copies of the [September 21] SUNDAY CHRONICLE containing the description of the reception of General Grant and the sketch of his life"; but "at a comparatively early hour on Sunday the entire issue was exhausted." The *Chronicle* printed an additional ten thousand copies on September 22, "but this proved utterly inadequate to supply the wants of the public," and an additional 15,000 copies, which would "probably supply all demands," were issued the next day. But the paper was wrong, and two days later it issued a fourth edition of 10,000 copies. Even before the fourth press run, this was "the first time in the history of California journalism" that demand had been so high for "any issue of a paper published on this coast."[2]

Thanks to Jules Verne's novel *Around the World in Eighty Days*, published in 1873, the high Victorian age was fascinated by circumnavigation of the globe, starting from one point and returning to the same location, as Phileas Fogg did in Verne's book. Americans who had closely followed Grant's travels, as well as, it seems, the former president himself, did not regard his "world tour" as complete until he was welcomed home in Philadelphia. Supporters of a third presidential term had their own reasons to prolong the enthusiasm generated by his journey abroad for a few more months. By this measure, Grant's travels did not end until December 16, 1879, when he returned to Philadelphia, the city from which he had embarked on May 17, 1877, almost exactly two years and seven months from the date of his departure. But his postpresidential diplomacy, by definition, had ended on September 3, the day he left Japan. Home in the United States, Grant defined for himself a role that he hoped would allow the country to benefit from his years abroad, especially his months in China and Japan. He used what was not yet called the bully pulpit to focus Americans' attention on the future of Asia and on their own identity as part of a trans-Pacific, as well as transatlantic, community of nations. His speeches, interviews, and conversations emphasized four themes. Grant tailored his approach and matched the theme to the decisive point where his influence was likely to have the most impact. With the State Department and President Hayes, and eventually with Presidents Garfield and Arthur, he focused on reform of the diplomatic and consular services. With the people and press of California he emphasized the importance of mutual respect and political-commercial reciprocity in Sino-American relations. To members of the Universal Peace Union (UPU) he gave his thoughts on prospects for the peaceful settlement of international disputes. And in many contexts across the country the former president sought to awaken American interest in Japan.

Since he returned home in San Francisco, the first item on Grant's agenda had to be China; a reporter asked his opinion of the "Chinese Question" on the day he arrived. Grant replied that he had "left [the United States] before it attained any prominence or political importance whatever" and "had no opportunity of examining it in its California bearings." He repeated what he had said in Penang, "that the importation of a race of slaves to this coast, if such were their condition, was a great evil; but if they came as citizens of other countries did, I saw no objection." Grant told the reporter that "the highest dignitaries of the [Chinese] empire" were "opposed to Chinese emigration to this country, except for commercial purposes, and that they are ready to co-operate with the United States in ameliorating the evil." The man whipping up Californians' frenzy for Chinese exclusion, Denis Kearney, attempted to meet Grant, but the former president refused. John Russell Young told the *Philadelphia Times* that Grant "did not wish to go out of his way to snub Kearney," so he initially claimed to be too busy to see him. But Kearney, refusing to take the polite hint, "persisted in calling not twice, but three times, and at the fourth visit the General was so vexed at the persistence of the man that he sent word that he 'couldn't and wouldn't' see him. Then Kearney attacked him on the sand lots, to which General Grant remarked: 'I would see any working man or any man in California, but I won't see a ruffian.'"[3]

Focusing Californians on the opportunities of closer relations with China, and away from their obsessive demand for exclusion, was no easy task. The fixation of Golden State politics on Chinese labor had an effect that Grant described in a September 28 letter to John Bingham relating his attempts to awaken interest in Japan. "The fact is," Grant wrote, that "the people here are so absorbed with their anti-Chinese discussions that they hardly know anything about Japan except that there is such a country that one has to pass to reach the territory of their aversion."[4] But he persevered, taking on California's exclusionary hysteria when he insisted on receiving the consular officers of China and a group of local Chinese merchants at the Presidio home of Major General Irvin McDowell, commander of the Military Division of the Pacific, on September 24. Grant's socializing with the Chinese, Young wrote, was a "delicate question," and "there were strong objections from some quarters, for fear that it would give offense to the people of California." The former president resisted pressure to cancel the meeting, saying "that the kindness he had received from the statesmen and rulers of China was so marked that he would be only too happy to return it by any courtesy he could show to Chinamen in America."[5]

The location was chosen, as Young noted, because "the home of General McDowell is a [federal] government property, [and] it was thought better that the Chinese delegation should there present their address." The *Chronicle*'s report of the event emphasized its "exotic" nature by describing in detail "the court dress of their native land" worn by Chinese officials and "the prismatic hues" of the merchants' garments; "[t]he united effect of so many unique and brilliant costumes were [*sic*] pleasing and picturesque." The newspaper described the arrival of the merchants as "a new Mongolian invasion" and did not include their names in the published guest list. Instead, it noted that "the Chinese Consul . . . and suite . . . were also present, having participated in the presentation ceremonies," and the "merchants and officials *mingled with the guests*, conversing on various topics in fluent English."[6] The ceremony itself was one with which Grant was, by now, very familiar. The Chinese presented an address and a scroll to him and gifts to the former first lady, on this occasion given to her directly since Julia Grant was present, as she often was not in Asia.

The consuls and merchants were "deeply gratified," they told Grant, that he had "consulted with [China's] rulers and become familiar with the important features of both Government and people." Unlike "other foreign nations [that] had used force to establish commercial relations" with China, the United States "had always approached the imperial power of China with the olive branch of peace." They hoped that Grant's visit would "bring the people of the oldest and youngest nations in still closer friendly and commercial relations." This gave the former president a welcome opportunity to respond with comments that he knew would make their way across the Pacific to Li Hung-chang. He had had, he said, "a most interesting visit, one that I shall always remember, especially because of the kindness and hospitality shown me by the people and the authorities of China." He was "grateful" to China, and "glad of the opportunity of expressing that gratitude so soon after my arrival at home." As he had so often overseas, Grant expanded the sentiment expressed in the Chinese address into the broader point he wished to make:

> I hope that the remark you make about China breaking down the seclusion in which she has been shrouded for ages will prove true, in all senses, and that China will continue to draw near to her the sympathy and the trade of the civilized world. The future of China will largely depend upon her policy in this respect. A liberal policy will enlarge your commerce and confer great advantages upon the outside world. I hope, as an American, that America will have a large share in this.[7]

In speeches and interviews throughout California the former president attempted to awaken American commercial and political interest in both China and Japan. Sometimes, skirting the political minefield, he simply encouraged trans-Pacific trade, as he did in an October 9 speech to the San Francisco Board of Trade and Chamber of Commerce. Grant's message was clear, though. The *Chronicle* reported the next day that the speech was thought by "many of the gentlemen present . . . to be an expression upon the Chinese question," as, indeed, it was. Fear that China would retaliate against exclusionary legislation by restricting American access to its markets was widespread among Bay Area businessmen, who welcomed the former president's statement that "the prosperity of the State [of California], as well as of the nation," depended on trade.[8]

Grant's thoughts on American relations with China and Japan were most fully expressed to the American public during his October 22–23 visit to

Sacramento. On November 1, in an article entitled "Grant as a Talker," the *Sacramento Record-Union* published the former president's "interesting observations concerning foreign countries."[9] Grant's "reputation for reticence was not only not sustained," the paper wrote, but "upon topics of conversation in which he feels a real interest he becomes almost voluble, and never fails to be entertaining." He "discusses all questions of home and foreign policy without apparent caution, especially Japan's 'progress in civilization.'" Unlike China, Japan was a new topic for Americans in 1879. A handful of people, including the owners of the Pacific Mail Steamship Company, the Walsh Brothers of Kobe and Yokohama, US naval officers, John Bingham, and Grant himself, had personal and professional interest in cultivating Japanese-American relations, but the few Japanese in the United States had come as students or diplomats, and most Americans had had no contact with them at all. To the extent that there was an impression of the Japanese, it was of an earnest young man in a western business suit, entirely different from the negative stereotype of the Chinese cultivated in California.

In Sacramento Grant spoke at length about his experiences in Japan. Asked if he had "witness[ed] any military display," he said that he had, and had "never seen in any country a more thoroughly martial exhibition." The Japanese army was "thoroughly drilled and disciplined" and equipped with "arms of modern invention and precision." It was "in all respects . . . equal to those of European nations." The country's new navy yards "would compare favorably in point of machinery and other equipments with those of the European nations and with those of our country." Japan had accepted changes that "within a single generation will make that Government a first-class power." Grant declared, "Nothing can arrest the present tendency to adopt our civilization on the part of the Japanese Government. The national character and the national characteristics of mind are such as to readily assimilate civilized ideas and adopt civilized customs." He was particularly enthusiastic about the "most rapid progress . . . made in the science of government" and the new role of the emperor, formerly "a sacred being, a veritable child of the sun, never to be looked upon by common mortals." But Meiji, "a young man about 30 years of age . . . goes about the country freely, mingling everywhere with the people and seeming to have an ardent desire to understand their wants and to meet and to mingle with them."

Grant showed his awareness of the resistance of the daimyo and samurai to the changes effected by the Meiji Restoration. Asked if there was "no conservative party in Japan" opposed to the "rapid revolution of social customs and ideas of civil government," he replied, "Most certainly." Resistance, he said, came from the "very old" and "the most ignorant" and "the class privileged under the old order of things, and who will lose their dominance from the present tendencies to adopt broader and more liberal principles of government." They were "[t]he two-sword fellows of the old time, whose . . . privileges and immunities . . . are very rapidly passing away." It was "but natural to suppose that they would not give up these good things without some resistance, but as a party or an element in the government they are growing smaller and weaker." This statement must have pleased the Japanese government, desiring as it did to play down the extent of any internal dissent from the policies of the Meiji leaders. Unfortunately the influence of the "two-sword fellows" on the future of Japan was not as limited as Grant believed.

While he sought to awaken American interest in Japan, Grant also had a great deal to say about China, a country "where human labor [was] the cheapest thing known" and the government worried about the impact of western technologies on the livelihood of its people. China's army was "very inferior," with "cast-off and rejected weapons . . . of the American and European nations." He "did not believe the Chinese in any sense to be a military people." Grant praised Chinese agricultural techniques, which had produced crops on the same land "for five thousand years without deterioration of the fertility of the soil," but the country needed transportation infrastructure that "would enable the more favored districts to supply the destitution in localities of want." He was an astute observer of the reasons for the lack of a mercantile middle class in China itself, except in the treaty ports, where "the Chinese deposit their money in foreign banks [since] wealth deposited there escapes [China's] confiscating process of unequal taxation." Although the poorer Chinese residents of Hong Kong were treated there "very much as they are treated by the hoodlums of San Francisco . . . [t]heir compensation is that the authority extended over the city by the British Government gives them protection for whatever property they may possess—a protection they would not have under their own Government." Grant called attention to China's complaints about the opium trade, declaring, in what the paper called the "severest reprobation" of British policy, that "no greater injustice was ever practiced by one people upon another, and particularly by a strong Government against a weaker one." Opium brought "large revenues" to Britain, but for China it meant "misery, poverty and death, and yet the Government was powerless to arrest the evil."

Within the article containing Grant's observations, the *Record-Union* published excerpts from an August 23 letter to the former president from Owen Denny, the US consul in Tientsin. Denny reported China's "unlimited confidence" in Grant, as "shown in their asking you to come forward in behalf of the United States and settle the question of Chinese emigration to our country, and by the good results already beginning to flow from your visit here, as well as those which are sure to follow." Denny's example of those "good results" was probably what Grant most wanted the American public to read, as evidence that China, if more slowly than Japan, would open itself to western ideas. Li Hung-chang's wife, who had hosted Julia Grant on her last night in Tientsin, "a few weeks ago was taken dangerously ill, and came so near dying that all the native physicians gave her up and said she must die." Li, "as a last and vain hope," called in western doctors, "and in their hands she soon recovered," Denny wrote. Since then Li had employed one of the doctors "as his family physician" and asked another to "conduct a regular dispensary that has been opened in the Temple where the Viceroy entertained you at dinner." Li paid all the bills "for the benefit of the poor people, and every day hundreds come to be treated." But in addition to the poor, "[o]fficials, as well as rich and influential Chinese also come, who would have rather died than been treated by the foreigners three months ago." Denny commented that "[t]he news of the success of the foreign doctors . . . will be the means, coming as it does from the Viceroy, of breaking down an infinite amount of prejudice among the official classes against progress and foreign skill." He expressed the opinion that not even Li "could have been induced before your visit to have thought of such a thing." An unprecedented development, it was "only the first of many more which are sure to follow from your visit here."

Grant was an astute observer of other governments and societies, but his most interesting and prescient comments in Sacramento concerned foreign attitudes toward the United States and the distinction he saw between Americans and the people of other nations. There was nothing racial in his remarks—he did not at all regard his country as a partner of European governments in bearing what would later be called the "white man's burden" of colonialism. On the contrary, Grant contrasted America with all countries where uniforms and gilded helmets held sway, declaring that "[o]ur institutions are in a measure a rebuke to the aristocratic classes of the old civilizations." Because of that, "America is respected throughout the world, but it must not be presumed from that fact that she is necessarily loved." The former president understood that it was American economic and military potential that interested the governments that had hosted him. Although he had exhorted Japan to negotiate with China, he knew that the United States was now regarded with interest overseas because of the navy it had built and the armies it had fielded from 1861 to 1865. He saw without blinders that what impressed the European powers was the ability to make war.

Asked in Sacramento if other nations feared the United States, Grant replied that America was not seen as "a menace to the peace of other countries," but it was now taken seriously, as it had not been before 1865. The reasons he gave for this showed a shrewd understanding of what would be the underpinnings of American power in the two world wars of the approaching twentieth century:

> Our navy is not equal to the navy of a third class power, but there is no power possessed of a navy greater than we can build on very short notice. We have all the resources of power, the wealth, the materials of war, with the necessary mechanical capacity to make them effective. . . . We have . . . no standing army, but every man . . . under 40 years of age can become a good soldier in five minutes. . . . There are more Americans who are employers of labor, or in positions where they direct other men, than any other people on the earth. . . . This produces and develops among our people the faculty of accomplishing a desired result through others, and this capacity is of the highest value in an army. The command of an army in the aggregate sense resides in the entire rank; . . . and the higher this capacity in the people from which the army is drawn the higher its manifestations in the operations of war. . . . Whoever knows best how to command knows best how to obey.

Grant had had ample opportunity to compare the armed forces of his hosts abroad with those he had commanded, and he declared, in praise of the American soldier and sailor: "Discipline is not the result of mere docility; it is the intelligent perception of the necessity of obedience."

After more than a month on the West Coast, Grant left San Francisco on Saturday, October 25, and arrived at his home in Galena, Illinois, on Wednesday, November 5. A week later, he was in Chicago, where he told the Society of the Army of the Tennessee that his "receptions [abroad] have been your receptions. They have been everywhere a kind of an acknowledgment that the United States is a Nation, a strong, independent, and free Nation, composed of strong, brave, and intelligent people, capable of judging of their rights, and ready to maintain them at all hazards." Grant was, he said, proud of the United States, "proud that I am an American citizen." At an earlier ceremony welcoming him to Chicago, he told the crowd gathered at the Palmer House that

> our country stands differently abroad in the estimation of the Europeans and Eastern nations from what it did a quarter of a century ago. . . . At that time it was believed that we had not a nation, that it was merely a confederation of States tied together by a rope of sand, that would give way upon the slightest friction. They have found out their grand mistake.

Consciously or unconsciously, in his Chicago speeches Grant paraphrased the cadence and content of Gladstone's (in)famous October 2, 1862, Newcastle speech pronouncing the Confederacy "a nation"; but Grant was speaking, more triumphantly than was usual for him, of the victorious United States. His tone in Britain had been conciliatory, but at home, after circling the globe, he struck a defiant, deterrent note, emphasizing the latent power of his country.[10]

The former president linked growing American influence overseas with the energies released by the Civil War when he spoke at Chicago's Union Veterans Club on November 13 and to the Grand Army of the Republic in Philadelphia on December 18. He had "not been in hardly a country, in hardly a town, or hardly a place in the two and a half years that I have been away from my own country that I have not met some of your number," he told the veterans in Chicago. "People who grow up in a time of profound peace are very much accustomed to vegetate and live along in or near the place of their birth." But the upheaval of war changed that; men, "having been torn away from their homes, as all of you were," sought after 1865 "the best place for the development of their energy and their talents" and were now "scattered over all of this broad land," as well as overseas. "They . . . are making our country felt and known and appreciated wherever a flag can float." Grant developed this theme in Philadelphia. The man who was "carried away in the great struggle" of the Civil War saw "a wider field than he contemplated at his home," and after the war he "struck out for new fields" in the United States and abroad:

> The ex-soldier has become the pioneer, not only of our own land, but has extended our commerce and trade and knowledge of us and our institutions to all other lands, and when brighter days dawn upon other nations, particularly those nations of the East, America will step in for her share of the trade, which will be opened, and through the exertions of the ex-soldier, the comrade, veterans, and I might say members of the Grand Army of the Republic.[11]

By the time he left Chicago in late November for a brief stay in Galena before heading to the East Coast, Grant had spent two months giving interviews and speeches designed to awaken Americans' interest in China and Japan and in their own country's role in Asia—the role it already played, and the role Grant believed it must play in the future. He thought that his labors had been worthwhile. From Chicago on November 16 he wrote to John Bingham that Japan "has been a constant source of conversation with me since my return," and he could "safely say that an interest in Japan and the Japanese has been awakened in this country that was never known before. It is safe to predict that the number of visitors from the U.S. to Japan will multiply very rapidly hence forward." Grant's most important partner in his efforts to influence American opinion was John Russell Young, through his *New York Herald* articles and book describing Grant's travels. Young wrote from New York on November 19 to Julia Grant, to whom the book was dedicated, that *Around the World with General Grant* "should be out by Christmas." Parts of it had already been published by subscription and attracted a good deal of interest. Young must have been particularly pleased on his return home to find waiting for him an August 27, letter from Commander Robeson, *Vandalia*'s captain in 1877–78, who wrote from Newport, Rhode Island, that the "first installment of my subscription to your book" had arrived, and "brings very vividly to mind my recent cruise and its pleasant associations."[12]

In December, Grant finally returned to Philadelphia, where he shifted his focus from influencing public opinion about China and Japan to the other two topics on his agenda, the peaceful settlement of international disputes and reform of the diplomatic and consular services. While in Galena he had accepted "with much pleasure" a November 18 invitation from Alfred Love, founding president of the Universal Peace Union, to meet with its members in Philadelphia so that they might "testify their appreciation of your eminent services in behalf of peace." Love, who had refused military service during the Civil War, and the organization he established in 1866 to "remove the Causes and abolish the Customs of War," had a long-standing relationship with the former president. Love promised Grant a "reception [that] would be comparatively a plain one and yet a very sincere one," honoring "those noblest acts of your life, which have advanced the cause of Christian civilization." It took place Friday morning, December 26. As a prelude to Grant's appearance, the UPU's monthly newsletter, *The Voice of Peace*, reported on "Ex-President Grant as a Peace-maker" between China and Japan. The article contained extensive extracts from the *New York Herald* report of Grant's conversations in Peking, and quoted approvingly his remark to Prince Kung that "[a]n arbitration between nations may not satisfy either party at the time; but it satisfies the conscience of the world, and must commend itself more and more as a means of adjusting disputes."[13]

In Philadelphia the UPU wanted to hear from the former president about "the prospects and means for disarmament and arbitration." In his welcoming speech, Love praised the accomplishments of the Grant administration, including "the immortal Geneva Arbitration, which has been followed by at least fifty important and successful arbitraments throughout the world," as well as Grant's personal conviction that "standing armies [are] a constant menace of war, a heavy burden to the people, and a ruinous expense to Governments."[14] The UPU wanted Grant's support for its effort to establish an International Court of Arbitration. During his presidency, in 1874, Congress had authorized the president to appoint a commission to promote such a court in the United States, but had appropriated no money for its work. The UPU in 1879 was lobbying both President Hayes and Congress finally to establish and fund the commission. "We deem it opportune," Love said to Grant, "that President Hayes is now on his way to Philadelphia and will call upon you today. . . . It would be gratifying if this matter could claim your attention." He asked Grant if he had "found more of a peace than a war feeling abroad" and if "there is not good reason to hope that some general system of disarmament could be adopted, and that a tribunal of arbitration could be established between some, if not all nations, wherein all difficulties could be settled."

No doubt disappointingly for his audience, while the UPU could "hope" for such a change, Grant did not think there was "good reason" to expect it any time soon, and he told its members why. It was true, he said, that he "look[ed] forward for a day when there will be a Court established, that shall be recognized by all nations, which will take into consideration all questions of difference between nations, and settle by arbitration or decision of such court, those questions, instead of keeping up large standing armies as in Europe." But what Grant wanted and what he had observed were two different things, and he did not confuse the two:

> In the course of my travels, from what I have seen, I am constrained to believe, however, that the day is yet distant when such a result may be hoped for. The differences between some European powers are such at the present time that if one was to reduce its armament it would be in danger from those who are stronger. This is the gravest objection.

Grant recognized the beginnings of what would be a full-blown arms race among the European powers by the turn of the twentieth century, and the increasingly frenetic "scramble" for overseas colonies and concessions:

> The European powers have to look abroad, beyond their own continent, for trade and support. They each and all of them are looking, more or less, to the East. Each nation is jealous of the advance made by all the others in that direction in the acquisition of territory or establishment of commercial relations.

On these questions Grant said, "[I]t will be a long time before the nations interested will consent to arbitrate." He encouraged the UPU to continue its work, but concluded by reiterating the difference between their common aspiration to "a great reform" and the reality of global politics: "I only wish it was susceptible of speedy solution, but, as I remarked, I do not think it is."

In the February 1880 issue of *The Voice of Peace*, Love wrote an editorial on Grant's meeting with the UPU, describing it as an opportunity to hear from "the greatest warrior on this side of the Atlantic," with "the epaulets off the shoulder." Grant's speech had been telegraphed across the Atlantic, and on December 30, "only four days after the meeting, the telegraph brought back from Europe . . . a favorable endorsement" that made the UPU believe "that the great reformation we have conceived is both popular and possible." Love optimistically quoted an Associated Press report that "[t]he leading German, French, Russian and English papers" contained "considerable comment" on Grant's speech. "A majority of them," reported the AP, "treat his views . . . as worthy of the attention of their own statesmen and generals." In his optimism, Love appeared to forget that Grant's "views" were that there was no prospect of success, at least not in the short term, for the UPU's cause; but he was right to be "deeply impressed with the scientific achievement" of transatlantic telegraphy that made possible a true dialogue among Europeans and Americans on the future of the international system, almost in real time. Grant had already been part of this dialogue two years before, when reports of his welcome in Britain had rapidly crossed the Atlantic and favorably impressed Americans with the interest of the British government and people in Anglo-American reconciliation. At the end of 1879, since they thought Grant likely to reenter the White House in 1881, the chanceries of Europe paid close attention to what he had to say about arbitration, disarmament, and the use of force.

In December 1879, however, Grant needed to speak with the current president if he wished to encourage reform of the diplomatic and consular services. From Galena on November 30, he had replied to a November 25 letter from President Hayes inviting the Grants to stay at the White House when they visited Washington in December. Grant told the president he was not yet sure that he would be in the capital before leaving for Cuba in January, but he was "very desirous of seeing you and the Sec. of state before leaving the country again, and hope I may have the opportunity of doing so." Meanwhile, John Russell Young was writing to the new assistant secretary of state, John Hay, about the subjects that Grant wanted to discuss with the president. Hay and Young had known each other for almost twenty years; they met at the beginning of their careers during the Civil War, Hay serving in the Lincoln White House and Young as a war correspondent. Young found when he returned home from Asia that Hay had accepted the position in the State Department, and he wrote to him from New York on November 16 that "I know of nothing that has rejoiced me more than your appointment as Ass't Sec'y State." After wishing Hay "all success in your office, and I have no doubt of that, because I know you will have a brilliant and enviable career," Young came to the point:

> There is one department of our service abroad that will merit your attention,—the service in China and Japan and Siam. We have great interests in those countries and they are paralyzed by a degraded public service. General Grant said to me that one of the reasons why he was anxious to go to W[ashingto]n was to talk with Mr Hayes and Mr Evarts on the subject.[15]

A month later, on December 16, Young wrote again to Hay, this time from "dingy, dreary" London where he had taken over the *Herald*'s European operations. He congratulated the State Department on the promotion of Owen Denny from consul in Tientsin to consul general in Shanghai. "We have no better man in our service" than Denny, Young wrote. He reiterated the scarcity of such men in the consular service: "We have thrown away many chances by our bad appointments, and I never heard Gen. Grant grieve over anything so much, as over what he learned in China. As he said in his Shanghae [*sic*] speech he wished he had known ten years ago what he knew now." Young had "seen more of China and Japan, than any American now living except Gen. Grant," and like the former president he "came away profoundly convinced that we had no diplomacy worth half as much, for our own interests, as what opened to us in these two nations." Before leaving for London, Young had met with President Hayes and Secretary Evarts and told them that "[t]he three points where we want strong men are Bangkok, Yokohama, & Peking,—beyond all things Peking." He reiterated to Hay that "Peking is the most important place in the gift of the President, for the good that can be done." He admitted to his old friend that "I could bore your life out on this theme if I had no pity for you," and warned Hay that he would "find Gen. Grant very earnest on the subject."[16]

On the day Young wrote to Hay from London, Grant was being welcomed in Philadelphia. Ten days later, on December 26, as Love had announced at the UPU reception that morning, President Hayes arrived in the city. He was the guest of John Welsh, the US minister in London with whom Grant had dined en route back to Paris from Ireland at the beginning of the year. That evening Welsh gave a small dinner party for the incumbent and former presidents, and Hayes and Grant also had, as the president wrote to his wife, "[a] most agreeable talk . . . for two hours alone." The next day Grant left Philadelphia for Washington. John Hay wrote to Young on December 30, telling him that "General Grant was in the Department yesterday and made several suggestions exactly in the line of your letter, and approved, as you did, in the heartiest way, the change the Department has made at Shanghai." Hay told Young that he was "very glad to have your suggestions in regard to those Eastern matters." He regretted "that I was not able to see you here and talk with you more fully in regard to them" but was "glad that you saw the Secretary and the President."[17]

It cannot have been a surprise to the president, the secretary of state, or John Hay to hear what Grant had to say about American diplomatic and consular representation in Asia. Even had Hay not been alerted by Young's letters, Grant had made headlines with a December 19 speech on the subject to the members of the Philadelphia Commercial Exchange, and a December 21 interview with the *St. Louis Globe-Democrat.* The president of the Commercial Exchange, John Bailey, welcomed him with words reminiscent of those used by the secretary of the navy when he offered Grant passage on USS *Richmond.* Grant had, Bailey said, "shown to the world the simplicity and dignity of character of an American citizen" and "made this citizenship honorable in every country you have visited." Grant's "simple presence [had] drawn from them the most decisive expressions of respect for your country and for yourself. We are proud of these testimonials, and grateful for your agency in procuring them," as well as "for the great practical work accomplished by your mission in the interest of commerce." As Secretary Thompson had hoped, Grant's travels had "already led to a better knowledge of the products and manufactures of the United States, and an increased demand for them in the markets of the world."[18]

In reply Grant told the leading businessmen of Philadelphia that he did not worry about the future of American trade with Europe: "The merchants of our country have their correspondents all over Europe, and understand exactly what they are to do to increase their trade in that quarter." But the situation in Asia was different. American "trade might be very much increased with the East," but the United States must adopt "a more positive" approach to its consular service. Grant proposed that "Congress . . . say to the Chambers of Commerce of the United States, as I said to the religious societies of the country in appointing Indian agents, if you will suggest men whom you are willing to trust with your business, let them be appointed and let them act as American agents for the merchants and manufacturers and commercial interests." This would be preferable to the present situation in which competent men were scarce because the salaries paid would "not support respectably even a single man, let alone a man with a family." In some ports, where there was no American willing to serve, Grant said, "our Consul Generals [*sic*] are compelled to appoint some one to act as American Consuls," often European merchants who were "not interested in extending the commerce of the United States, but on the contrary interested in suppressing it and keeping it out of that country."[19]

Grant's comments received extensive press coverage throughout the country. The *St. Louis Globe-Democrat* reported on Sunday, December 21, that "[t]he allusion in General Grant's speech in Philadelphia to the Consular service of the United States attracts much attention, both in Administration and Congressional circles."[20] According to these "official circles," Grant's observations overseas would "stimulate the disposition to radically reorganize the consular system, and greatly enlarge its dignity, credit and usefulness." The *Globe-Democrat* provided further details to its readers, based on a "conversation with your correspondent a few days ago [in which Grant] mentioned very fully his views on the Consular and Diplomatic service, and said that a revision of the Consular system could be made at once." As he had in the speech, Grant emphasized that his concern was not American consuls in Europe. They were "near home"—an interesting comment that showed how the transatlantic telegraph and steamship had affected the perception of time and space—and "subject to local laws and the surveillance of diplomatic representatives." But the scope of consular jurisdiction was different at "the Oriental Consulates," and many of the consuls "failed to appreciate the importance and duties of their positions."

Grant made it clear that he favored reform of the service not only to increase American commercial competitiveness in Asia, but to enhance the reputation and standing of the United States in the region and among the European powers. In the foreign concessions where extraterritoriality was provided by treaty, "extraordinary authority [was] vested in the consular office" and "a degree of responsibility which amazed him." Unfortunately, he had seen "in the exercise of judicial functions by the Consuls . . . such an utter disregard for judicial forms and the dispensation of justice that the whole system was a subject of severe comment among officers and subjects of foreign nationalities, not to speak of the oppressions they heaped upon American citizens." The newspaper reported that the former president "attributed this, in a great measure, to the manner in which selection for these offices are [*sic*] made, in which influence outweighs a lack of fitness," and not only to the "inadequate" salaries "that doubtless prevented the Government from securing a higher class of fitness." This comment was fairly scathing self-criticism, since many of the men concerned had been appointed by President Grant, and all of them by Republican administrations. Grant contrasted American consuls with the "consular officers of foreign governments," who "were liberally compensated and were surrounded by a proper staff of assistants where trade was important. They were also educated for the duties, and advanced in rank for meritorious service that they contributed under the auspices of their governments to the extension of commerce and advancement of trade and influence." Grant's comments reflected what he had learned about the British civil service while traveling from India to Hong Kong, and from Robert Hart about China's Maritime Customs Service, both of them staffed by men chosen by competitive examination and promoted on merit.

In addition to espousing consular reform, Grant again took the opportunity to stress "the wonderful progress of affairs in Japan, and compared, at much length, the condition of affairs in the Empire of to-day with ten years ago." Although he almost never referred to American officeholders by name in an interview, whether to praise or criticize, Grant made two exceptions in this case. George Seward, the US minister in Peking and former consul general in Shanghai, had been absent from China until the very end of Grant's visit there. In Washington because of impeachment investigations by Congress, Seward was not convicted, but his long tenure in the country (nephew of the secretary of state, he was appointed to Shanghai in 1861 by Abraham Lincoln; Grant, against his better judgment, named him minister in 1876) was coming to an end.[21] In the *Globe-Democrat* interview, Grant called it "unfortunate" that Seward

> had placed himself in a position which destroyed his usefulness, and that the report of the condition of affairs at the Consulate General at Shanghai in 1870, and the subsequent investigation by Congress, had exposed a state of things which had lost him the consideration which a Minister of the United States should enjoy from the Government to which he is accredited.

On the other hand, the former president "could hardly find terms," the newspaper reported, "in which to express his admiration of the American Minister" to Japan. Before Bingham's arrival there, "foreign diplomatic representatives treated the Government more as a dependency than as an equal as a nation." Bingham's behavior toward the Japanese government had "revolutionized" the situation, "and Japan occupies her proper position in the list of nations." This was an overstatement, as Grant realized, but the interview was one of his last opportunities to draw attention to Japan and to create support for revision of the United States' unequal treaties with that country when the issue came before Congress, as Grant knew it would.[22]

The former president also knew that interest in his experiences overseas was coming to an end. The public would buy John Russell Young's book, but since Philadelphia had welcomed him home, Grant's now-completed circumnavigation of the globe was no longer news to the daily press. Moreover, he was leaving the country again. Grant departed Washington, D.C., on December 30, 1879, by train to Florida, the only state he had never visited, en route to Cuba and Mexico. On January 22, 1880, only four months after *City of Tokio* had brought him home through the Golden Gate, he was again on foreign soil, in Havana. The 1880 Republican convention lay ahead, and a possible third term in the White House. But for the moment, the former president left behind the issues that had preoccupied him from 1877 to 1879. He had said what he had to say to the American public and to the president and secretary of state. He was off to see something new, Florida and Cuba, and to show Julia Grant something old, the Mexico he had known as a young soldier. Before he departed, on Christmas Eve 1879, Grant visited his mother at her home in Jersey City. The week before, on December 17, Hannah Grant had told a reporter from the *Philadelphia Press* that "[t]he General was always a good traveler . . . and I do not think he would ever tire of it."[23] Apparently, she was right.

Conclusion

When her son Ulysses visited her on Christmas Eve 1879, Hannah Grant was eighty-one years old. She died in May 1883, in her eighty-fourth year. Her husband had died a decade before at age seventy-nine. In his memoirs Grant wrote that his mother's oldest sister "still lives in Clermont County at this writing, October 5th, 1884, and is over ninety years of age"; and "[h]er brother, next of age and now past eighty-eight, is also still living in Clermont County within a few miles of the old homestead, and is as active in mind as ever." Given this family history, the former president, fifty-seven years old on December 24, 1879, had every reason to expect that he would see the twentieth century; in fact, he had exactly four healthy and physically active years remaining to him. His fall on an icy sidewalk on Christmas Eve 1883 dislocated his hip, and as Julia Grant remembered this "distressing and cruel accident," her husband "never passed a well day afterwards."[1] In those four years Grant's attention was also divided. As much as he cared about the issues he had discussed across the United States in the fall of 1879, he was equally, if not more, concerned with two questions of foreign and commercial policy closer to home: a transisthmian canal and railroad development in Mexico. Much of his time from 1880 to 1883 was spent promoting those two projects. President Arthur named Grant to a commission negotiating a commercial treaty with Mexico, and in early 1883 the former president "spent weeks in Washington, D.C., renewing old contacts, enjoying capital society, and successfully concluding a treaty with the help of his Mexican counterpart and friend, Matias Romero."[2] But Grant's efforts failed to produce the results for which he had hoped; the treaty failed in the Senate, and the Nicaraguan canal project languished.

The first two years after Grant's return home were also dominated by electoral politics and their aftermath. First, there was the divisive fight at the 1880 Republican convention in Chicago, which failed to nominate him for a third term. The machinations at Chicago produced a rupture between Grant and Elihu Washburne that never healed, and that deprived both of them not only of a close friend, but of an important ally on questions of foreign policy. Fearful of the consequences for the country of a Democratic victory, Grant spent the fall of 1880 campaigning, for the first and only time in his life, for his party's presidential nominee. James Garfield probably owed his election to Grant's efforts, and his victory might have meant a cabinet or diplomatic appointment for the former president. Grant, however, disavowed all interest in any formal position in a November 11, 1880, letter to the president-elect, telling him that "[t]here is no position within the gift of the President which I would accept. There is no public position which I want." He offered instead to "serve the country . . . freely and without reward . . . by advice in relation to our affairs with Mexico and the East, especially China & Japan."[3] If Grant hoped to shape the conduct of American foreign policy, this preemptive refusal of a presidential appointment, while gracious, was a mistake.

Until the early twentieth century, with the establishment of such organizations as the American Society of International Law (1906) and the Carnegie Endowment for International Peace (1910), there were no nonpartisan institutional frameworks within which former elected and appointed officials could influence the policy planning of current officeholders.[4] If Grant wanted his voice to be not just heard but heeded, he needed a title that was in Garfield's power to give him. But, in fact, despite their common interest in a Republican victory in November 1880, the prospects of the two men finding a political *modus vivendi* were slim, as events proved in the short four months between Garfield's inauguration and the July 2, 1881, shooting that resulted in his death two months later. Grant was in Mexico again in early 1881, and by the time he returned to the United States, he had had a public falling out with the president over the distribution of patronage jobs to New York Republicans.[5] The shock of Garfield's incapacitation and death in September 1881 briefly dampened the vitriol of the Republicans' internecine disputes and ended what would likely have been a prolonged intraparty battle involving Grant.

Six months before, on February 18, in the afterglow of Garfield's electoral victory, Grant had written the incoming president a long letter with specific advice on diplomatic and consular appointments to Mexico, China, and Japan. The president had no time to act on them, even had he been so inclined, and on December 5, 1881, Grant wrote an even longer letter to the new president, Chester Arthur, making many of the same recommendations. The most important was to promote Owen Denny from consul general in Shanghai to minister in Peking, and to name John Russell Young as Bingham's successor in Tokyo. Grant had already told Arthur on October 8, 1881, that "Judge Denny . . . is the person who I spoke to you about personally as being the fittest person I know of for the Chinese Mission." In his December 5 letter, Grant elaborated on his support for both Denny and Young. He repeated much of what he had said in his speeches and interviews two years before about the inadequacy of American diplomacy compared to that of European countries, "represented by men whose career is in the diplomatic or consular service and who give the whole of their time and their energies to the cultivation of trade between their respective countries and the East." The United States' need for "proper representatives" led Grant to "take the liberty" of reiterating his support for Denny's appointment to Peking and suggesting Young for Tokyo. Young "was with me in all my travels in those countries," Grant told Arthur, "and by his being with me, had access to all the places that I had, and had the advantage of observation that he could not have had if he had been traveling alone." His "appointment would be well received by the highest officials in Japan," and he "would be of great assistance to whoever might be his colleague in China." In recommending Denny for that position, Grant was even more emphatic: "He is a man of intelligence, understands the Chinese people and their institutions well [and] would have more the confidence of the Chinese people and government than any person who could be appointed. I believe it is a matter of national importance that he should receive that appointment."[6]

In fact, Denny was not appointed to Peking. Grant's proposals were contingent on Bingham willingly leaving his post in Tokyo, either by promotion (Grant suggested he be named to Vienna), or, as seemed likely at the time, to become "Judge of a [mixed] court which is to be established by the Japanese government in that Empire." But that did not happen. Bingham continued as minister to Japan, Arthur appointed Young to Peking, and Denny remained as consul general in Shanghai until October 1883, when he resigned and returned to the United States.[7] Arriving in Peking in 1882 at a delicate moment in Sino-Japanese-Korean-American relations (made more so by the diplomatic missteps of Commodore Shufeldt in his third attempt to open Korea to trade with the United States),[8] Young proved to be "a really finished diplomat." Because of "the very cordial personal relations established" with Prince Kung and Li Hung-chang during Grant's visit in 1879, he arrived in China "already more familiar with the pressing problems than was usual in those days or even later."[9] During his three years in Peking, Young corresponded regularly and intensively with the former president, until Grant's health and the pressure to finish his memoirs no longer permitted him to do so. He told Grant on March 8, 1883, "I have faithfully tried to do out here, what I know would meet with your approval."[10]

Grant's original suggestion to Arthur, although it did not come to fruition, to send Denny to Peking and Young to Tokyo, said even more about his grasp of diplomacy and the quality of his strategic thinking than did Young's performance as minister to China. Grant saw Asia *whole.* In an age when diplomatic and consular appointments were rewards for partisan political service (a moment that has not yet passed in the naming of American ambassadors to the more "glamorous" capitals of the world), there was little thought given to the need for the country's diplomats to work with each other across a region. Some of them did so, on their own, when they saw a reason to do so, but more often the minister and consuls in one country existed in a "stovepipe," dealing only with the court and government to which they were accredited, not with their colleagues next door. This had not been true when the survival of the United States was at stake—the approach of Seward's State Department to the European powers from 1861 to 1865 required coordination among all the American legations in Europe; but absent such a crisis, neither the US government nor its representatives abroad thought in terms of a regional grand strategy. Grant did. He recognized that, because of greater mobility and connectivity, the consequences of an event in one country spilled over to its neighbors with greater effect than ever before, and because of his travels throughout Asia, he knew how the countries of the region stood in relationship to each other, as few other Americans did. The conduct of diplomacy was organized bilaterally, but the issues confronting the United States were regional and global. Grant understood this a good three decades before the idea began to be accepted, and a century before its acceptance was universal.

In 1882, Grant made another recommendation to the president that showed the breadth of his thinking on the future of American diplomacy. He wrote to his friend, Judge Arthur MacArthur, on June 10, 1882, that "I have a letter from your son, Capt. McArthur [*sic*], requesting my interest in his behalf to get him attached to [the US] Legation [in China]." The former president believed "that the appointment of such an Attaché to our Chinese Legation might be attended with good results," and he assured the judge that he would "willingly give my views in favor of such an Appointment, and of the selection of Capt. McArthur [*sic*] for the place." With this endorsement, Judge MacArthur wrote the president that his son "desires to suggest to the President the expediency of a military Attachée [*sic*] to our Embassy in China," and informed him that "General Grant is quite willing to furnish his views in favor of the measure, and I have reason to believe that our minister the Hon John Russell Young will address a communication upon the subject to the Department of State."[11]

While it is interesting to speculate about the different future Captain MacArthur's son, Douglas, two years old at the time, might have had if he had grown up in Peking, the position did not materialize. Secretary of War Robert Lincoln replied on April 9, 1883, to Secretary of State Frelinghuysen's transmittal of the message he had received from Young in Peking, supporting MacArthur's appointment. Lincoln had "read Mr. Young's despatch with care," but did "not perceive that the War Department has any interest in sending a military attaché to our Legation to China; and . . . I would not recommend its being done." He feared that "such a step . . . would form a precedent for the detaching of military officers from their proper duties and sending them where they would be of little use, to other countries, and that in administering the War Department, much embarrassment and difficulty would be occasioned by it." If Frelinghuysen nevertheless believed that such an appointment would serve "the general interests of the country," Lincoln felt that "[i]t might be possible to spare an officer of the grade of major . . . if the President should wish to have one sent"; but "Captains of Companies [were] especially needed" for duties on the frontier.[12] Making allowances for the fact that Lincoln and General Sheridan, in whose Division of the Missouri MacArthur served, were both annoyed by his efforts to escape life as a company commander in the West,[13] the secretary's blunt statement that the War Department had no interest in sending military officers abroad "where they would be of little use" is still startling in its shortsightedness.

Far from causing the department "much embarrassment and difficulty," military attachés at US embassies became indispensable in the twentieth century, but in the early 1880s Grant was, once again, the exception in recognizing what the future had in store. He had traveled the route from the Taku forts to Peking that the Boxer relief force would take in the summer of 1900; seen the Baltic approaches and the "ground" from Moscow to Warsaw and Vienna; observed the work of British armed forces in building the "partnership capacity," to use a later term, of Indian armed forces; and responded to Said Pasha's request for the textbooks used at West Point and Annapolis. Grant recognized around the world the tasks that would be the "proper duties" of US military officers in the years to come, and he understood why, despite budgetary and manpower constraints, it was very much in the country's interest to begin to prepare its officers to undertake those tasks. His support for MacArthur as military attaché, although unsuccessful, like his recommendation of a diplomatic post for Young, also reflected the former president's conviction that the United States needed to be represented abroad by a higher caliber of men. More qualified presidential appointees were not the thoroughgoing reform of the diplomatic and consular services for which Grant had called since his return home, and would continue to support for the rest of his life,[14] but they were a start.

Grant's early death cut short his counsel to his successors in the White House, but his diplomacy from 1877 to 1879 had a lasting impact on the United States' expanding global role. The Constitution enumerated the executive's foreign-policy powers, but it was no help in defining the desired and necessary behavior of the president as diplomat in chief. Grant's world tour provided the definition. Wherever he traveled, he left behind an indelible impression of what an *American* head of state looked, acted, and sounded like, and it was like nothing that the countries he visited had ever seen. Except when formal occasions required formal attire, Grant wore the clothes of a prosperous European businessman. Because of that, and because he had no entourage, people waiting long hours to see him often failed to recognize him. He walked and, where it existed, took public transportation. He talked with coachmen and doormen. Where he could avoid it, no plumes, epaulettes, or prancing horses announced his arrival.

One of the former president's, and the United States', principal diplomatic assets was Julia Grant. Not only was she an intrepid traveler who inspired admiration and affection among her male traveling companions and the officers of the US Navy, she was a natural buster of negative stereotypes about the "frontier women" of America. The first first lady born west of the Mississippi more than held her own among the crowned heads and aristocrats who entertained the Grants. Nothing fazed her, neither the donkeys of Egypt nor the palaces of Berlin, and like her husband, she found something of interest everywhere, from the Escurial to the working elephants of Moulmein. Because of gender segregation in many of the countries they visited, Julia Grant frequently had a separate program of activities with the wives and daughters of the diplomatic corps, the court, and host government officials. Even in Western Europe, the former first lady was often on her own, when the ladies "retired" from the gentlemen after dinner, to represent the United States. She was not shy about doing so, telling one smug diplomatic wife who had, with apparent horror, "heard that a man was sent to Congress whose wife had once been a factory girl," that "[i]n America we are all equal. . . . Our men . . . select their own wives. They like beauty and intelligence, and generally think *their* wives have both."[15]

When he returned home in September 1879 Grant had seen more of the world than any American except a few naval officers, and he had seen it from a unique perspective that no other American could have, meeting with national decision makers like Li Hung-chang, Bismarck, and Disraeli; traveling on both US naval and commercial vessels; and bringing to his observations his own experience as commanding general, secretary of war, and president. The failure of USS *Richmond* to appear before he was in Tientsin was both a blessing and a curse. Commercial travel gave Grant the unexpected opportunity to discuss the past, present, and future of Asia with Europeans who had long experience there, most notably Robert Hart, and the former president took full advantage of that opportunity. As a result, he was fully prepared to conduct the diplomacy that awaited him in China and Japan. But because Grant spent only a few weeks aboard *Richmond*, the origin of his diplomacy east of Suez, in a request from the United States government, has been lost. When Secretary Thompson issued orders to *Richmond* and *Ticonderoga* in the fall of 1878, he and Secretary Evarts saw Grant's mission aboard *Richmond* as complementary to that of Commodore Shufeldt aboard *Ticonderoga*; but while Shufeldt's diplomatic and commercial accomplishments are still heralded by the State Department,[16] Grant's are largely unknown. Had *Richmond* carried the former president from France to Japan, as originally expected, his diplomacy would not have been as easily forgotten.

From the moment Grant set foot in California, he spoke to all who would listen to him about American foreign-policy interests, particularly how he thought they should be defended and advanced in the western Pacific.

More than any other American leader of his time, the former president recognized the evolving nature of the international system and understood the role that the United States could play, indeed, would have to play, in the coming century. Unfortunately, whether meeting with President Hayes, the secretary of state, members of Congress, journalists, businessmen, or students, Grant was unlikely to encounter anyone who had had similar experiences, especially not outside of Europe. Indeed, this became one of his problems. It was hard to convince people who had not been where he had been and seen what he had seen of the importance and urgency of the courses of action he proposed. There was a perhaps inevitable failure of imagination on the part of both political leaders and the public. It was especially difficult for them to grasp the significance of China and Japan politically, as Grant did, rather than see the two countries only as fields for American commercial and missionary activities. Grant's experiences were *sui generis* in 1879.

Looking back from 1924, one of the leading interwar historians of US-Asian relations wondered whether Grant, "had he again been elected President, . . . would not have taken up the Far Eastern question in earnest and made the American government an active participant nearly twenty years before John Hay was compelled to step in and do what he could to regain the ground lost by his provincially minded predecessors."[17] As William McKinley's and Theodore Roosevelt's secretary of state from late 1898 until his death in July 1905, Hay dealt with the political and military consequences of the American acquisition of the Philippines in 1898, the 1900 Boxer Rebellion, and the 1904–5 Russo-Japanese War. His 1899 and 1900 Open Door notes committed the United States to the sovereignty and territorial integrity of China. Unfortunately for Hay, he had neither Grant nor John Russell Young to call on for counsel. Young and Hay finally served together in a Republican administration when McKinley in 1897 appointed Hay ambassador to Britain and Young Librarian of Congress, but Young died in January 1899, soon after Hay returned home from London to become secretary of state.[18]

As Hay must have realized, however, much of his diplomacy in Asia depended for its success on leaders whose positive opinion of the United States began with Grant's diplomacy in 1879. Most notably, during the Boxer Rebellion, the viceroy who had hosted Grant in Canton, Liu Kun-i, kept the violence from spreading to southern China, where the potential for death and destruction involving foreigners was far greater than in the north. China's ambassador to Washington, Wu Ting-fang, was Hay's link to the besieged legations in Peking, and his partner in seeking to prevent the western powers and Japan from waging war on and dismembering China. Known as Ng Choy during his early years in Hong Kong, Wu was the first Chinese member of Hong Kong's governing council, appointed by John Pope-Hennessy, and he spent time with Grant at Government House in 1879. In the aftermath of the rebellion, Li Hung-chang, almost eighty, was still negotiating for China.[19]

Because Grant neither returned to the White House in 1881 nor lived long enough to participate in shaping American foreign policy two decades later, the importance of his postpresidential diplomacy has gone unrecognized. Grant's summitry and public diplomacy confirmed the United States' commitment to Anglo-American cooperation; demonstrated the country's interest in the territorial integrity of China; affirmed American faith in universal (male) suffrage as the basis for governmental legitimacy; and asserted the importance of an international order based on equality and justice for all states and their citizens, not just the European powers. Circling the globe from 1877 to 1879, Grant prepared the ground for America's international role in the twentieth century. He saw the modern age of international relations dawning, but the infrastructure and human capacity needed to support the American role in the new era were not yet accepted, or even understood, by most of Grant's countrymen. It took another twenty years for men like John Hay and Elihu Root, Hay's cabinet colleague as secretary of war and successor as secretary of state, to begin to put Grant's ideas into practice. If Grant had lived to the ripe old age of some of his ancestors, he might have witnessed the Fourteen Points, the Armistice of 1918, and Woodrow Wilson's arrival the next year in Paris.

One man who did live to such an age was Secretary Root. Born in 1845, Root died in 1937, having experienced as an adult every major international event from the American Civil War to the eve of World War II. He was in Berlin in July 1870 when the Franco-Prussian War began, in St. Petersburg on a mission for President Wilson in 1917, and at the 1921–22 Washington Conference that seemed, briefly, to have reached agreement with Japan on the territorial integrity of China. As secretary of state in 1906, Root began the professionalization of the consular service that Grant had so vigorously supported.[20] Two years later he introduced the texts of the 1899 and 1907 Hague Peace Conferences by recalling the impact on international law of the *Alabama* arbitration established by the 1871 Anglo-American Treaty of

Washington. Like Grant, who recognized that governments' acceptance of disarmament and arbitration would be a slow process, Root urged Americans to understand that "the question about each international conference is not merely what it has accomplished, but also what it has begun and what it has moved forward."[21] Cofounder of both the American Society of International Law and the Carnegie Endowment for International Peace, Root served as president of the former from 1906 to 1924, and of the latter from 1910 to 1925. He won the 1912 Nobel Peace Prize for his work to advance international arbitration.

In the centennial year of Grant's birth, Root published an article, "A Requisite for the Success of Popular Diplomacy," in the inaugural issue of the journal *Foreign Affairs*. In this, as in so many of his writings, Root's sentiments echoed those expressed by the former president, his fellow member of the Union League Club of New York, where Grant entertained many foreign guests in the early 1880s. "In a world of universal trade and travel and inter-communication," Root wrote, "no nation . . . need consider whether or not it will be a member of the community of nations. It cannot help itself. It may be a good member or a bad member, but it is a member by reason of the simple fact of neighborhood life and intercourse." Grant had seen firsthand what Root called "the differences of thought and feeling and selfish desire which separate nations"[22] from each other, and the former president did not underestimate those differences. But Grant also estimated that individuals like Root would eventually recognize and act on their countries' common interests in an increasingly mobile and interconnected global society. As a representative of the United States around the world from 1877 to 1879, Grant practiced diplomacy as he had once waged war, without hubris or fear, but with unwavering confidence in himself and in his fellow citizens' ability to meet whatever challenges came their way. Those qualities served him and his country well.

Appendix

Notes

Bibliography

Index

Appendix: Chronology of Grant's Diplomacy

May–December 1877

17 May	Departed Philadelphia, Pennsylvania, aboard steamer *Indiana*
28 May	Arrived Liverpool, United Kingdom
5 July	Departed Folkestone, England, for Ostende, Belgium; toured western Germany, Switzerland, and northern Italy
late August	Returned to Britain; toured Scotland and England for two months
24 October	Arrived Paris, France
1 December	Departed Paris for Nice, France

December 1877–April 1878

13 December	Embarked on USS *Vandalia*; visited southern Italy and Malta
5 January	Arrived Alexandria, Egypt; visited Cairo and the Upper Nile
9 February	Rejoined *Vandalia* at Port Said after transiting the Suez Canal south to north; visited Ottoman Syria (the Holy Land)
1 March	Arrived Constantinople (Istanbul), Turkey
8 March	Arrived Athens, Greece
18 March	Arrived Naples, Italy; disembarked from *Vandalia*; visited Rome, Florence, Venice, Milan, and Turin

May–September 1878

7 May	Arrived Paris
14 June	Departed Paris for the Netherlands
24 June	Arrived Germany; visited Hannover, Berlin, and Hamburg
7 July	Arrived Copenhagen, Denmark; toured Norway, visited Stockholm, Sweden, and Helsingfors (Helsinki), Finland
30 July	Arrived St. Petersburg, Russia; visited Moscow

18 August	Arrived Vienna, Austria, via Warsaw, Poland; visited Ischl, Salzburg, and Gastein
25 September	Arrived Paris via Munich, Germany, and Zurich, Switzerland

October 1878–January 1879

12 October	Departed Paris for Spain, Portugal, and the British Crown Colony of Gibraltar
12 December	Returned to Paris via Pau, France
2 January	Departed Paris for Ireland; visited Dublin, Belfast, and Londonderry
10 January	Returned to Paris via London
21 January	Departed Paris for Marseilles, France

January–April 1879

23 January	Departed Marseilles aboard steamer *Labourdonnais* for Alexandria, Egypt
31 January	Departed Suez aboard steamer *Venetia* for Bombay, India, via Aden
13 February	Arrived Bombay; toured India for one month
16 March	Departed Calcutta aboard steamer *Simla* for Singapore via Rangoon and Penang
1 April	Arrived Singapore
9 April	Departed Singapore aboard steamer *Kongsee* for Bangkok, Siam (Thailand)
22–23 April	Returned to Singapore and departed aboard steamer *Irrawaddy* for Hong Kong

April–June 1879

30 April	Arrived Hong Kong via the French colony of Saigon (Vietnam)
5 May	Embarked on USS *Ashuelot* for Canton, China
10 May	Returned to Hong Kong via the Portuguese colony of Macao
12 May	Departed Hong Kong aboard *Ashuelot* for Shanghai, China, via Swatow (Shantou) and Amoy (Xiamen)
17 May	Arrived Shanghai
23 May	Departed Shanghai aboard *Ashuelot* for Tientsin, China
27 May	Arrived Tientsin; visited Peking (3–10 June)
15 June	Departed Tientsin aboard *Ashuelot*; transferred to USS *Richmond* for Nagasaki, Japan, via Chefoo, China

June–September 1879

21 June	Arrived Nagasaki; toured Inland Sea aboard *Richmond*
3 July	Arrived Yokohama/Tokyo, Japan
3 September	Departed Yokohama aboard steamer *City of Tokio* for San Francisco, California

September–December 1879

20 September	Arrived San Francisco, California
5 November	Arrived Galena, Illinois
16 December	Arrived Philadelphia, Pennsylvania

Notes

Abbreviations

AB	Adam Badeau (US consul general in London, 1871–81)
AT	Alfred Torbert (US consul general in Paris, 1873–78)
DA	Daniel Ammen (boyhood friend, US Navy admiral)
EBW	Elihu B. Washburne (US minister to France, 1869–77)
EFB	Edward F. Beale (US minister to Austria-Hungary, 1876–77)
EMB	Elizabeth M. Borie (Adolph E. Borie's wife, in US during his travels with USG)
HF	Hamilton Fish (secretary of state, 1869–77)
JAB	John A. Bingham (US minister to Japan, 1873–85)
JDG	Julia Dent Grant
JK	John Keating, MD (Adolph Borie's physician; traveled with Grants, 1879)
JRG	Jesse R. Grant (son, traveled with parents, 1877–78)
JRY	John Russell Young (journalist, was with Grants on USS *Vandalia*, 1877–78; in Berlin and Iberia, 1878; and east of Suez, 1879)
LHC	Li Hung-chang (Northern Viceroy of China)
PUSG	*Papers of Ulysses S. Grant*
TD	Travel Diary
USG	Ulysses S. Grant
USGPL	Ulysses S. Grant Presidential Library
WTS	William Tecumseh Sherman (commanding general, US Army, 1869–83)

Preface

1. Joan Waugh, *U.S. Grant: American Hero, American Myth*, 156–62.

2. For her most recent perspective, see Charlotte Ku, *International Law, International Relations, and Global Governance* (London: Routledge, 2012), esp. 160–66, "Governance in a Westphalian Order."

3. John F. Marszalek, introduction, *Papers of Ulysses S. Grant* (hereinafter *PUSG*), 32:xv.

4. John Russell Young (hereinafter JRY), "Grant: An Estimate," in *Men and Memories*, 2:467.

Introduction

1. *Philadelphia Inquirer*, Wednesday, December 17, 1879, in file USG Speech, December 19, 1879, USGPL. See bibliography, note on the *Papers of Ulysses S. Grant* and unpublished primary sources.

2. Osterhammel, *The Transformation of the World*, 502.

3. Jesse R. Grant (hereinafter JRG), *In the Days of My Father*, 212, 231, 261.

4. As Rosenberg, ed., *A World Connecting*, points out in her introduction, 6–7, after 1870 there was a "dramatic shrinking of time and space as a result of the revolution in communications and transportation," and an "accompanying acceleration in mobility of people, goods, and ideas." See also Henrikson, "Beyond Global-Regional Thinking," 199–205, on "the overspreading of the world in terms of time and space" that contributed to a new American approach to foreign policy decision-making in the late nineteenth century. Grant's diplomacy was an early, and at the time unprecedented, manifestation of these developments.

5. Foster, *A Century of American Diplomacy*, 403.

6. JRG, 310–11.

7. Ammen (hereinafter DA), *The Old Navy and the New*, 521.

8. Richard W. Thompson (hereinafter RWT) to Ulysses S. Grant (hereinafter USG), October 23, 1878, *PUSG*, 29:15.

9. McPherson, *This Mighty Scourge*, 111–12.

10. Bradford Perkins, *The Creation of a Republican Empire*, 230, quoting an 1866 comment from the *Spectator* (London).

11. JRY, *Around the World*, 2:445.

12. Badeau (hereinafter AB), *Grant in Peace*, 268, 270, 297–98.

13. JRG, 311, 321–22.

14. For the foreign concessions in China, see Westad, *Restless Empire*, 60–63, and for the efforts of China, Japan, and the Ottoman Empire to abolish extraterritoriality, Kayaoglu, *Legal Imperialism*.

15. JRY, *Around the World*, 2:448–49, 281.

16. Ibid., 403. Young was referring to demands for an audience with the seven-year-old emperor, but the comment described broader western behavior in China as well.

17. Ibid., 260.

1. Europe Welcomes America's "Tyneside Skipper": 1877

1. William M. Evarts to USG in file USG to Ulysses S. Grant, Jr., May 26, 1877; see also JRY, *Around the World*, 1:3–4.

2. *PUSG*, 28:204–5, 224.

3. Ibid., 210–11.

4. Ibid., 207–8.

5. JRG, *In the Days of My Father*, 208, 250.

6. Simon, ed., *Personal Memoirs*, 204.

7. For Van Buren's postpresidency, including his visit to Europe, see Skidmore, *After the White House*, 52–54.

8. "Grant's Birthday, 1888," 32–33, in file Grant—Miscellaneous Speeches and Memorials, USGPL.

9. Ibid., 34–35.

10. Grant told John Russell Young, *Around the World*, 2:279, that the chair of the Senate Foreign Relations Committee, Charles Sumner, had demanded "that our first condition of peace with England should be the withdrawal of her flag from the American continent. That suggestion was a declaration of war, and I wanted peace, not war."

11. *PUSG*, 28:213, 232. The Windsor incident involved the question of whether Jesse and Badeau would dine at the queen's table. (Jesse eventually did; Badeau did not.) Simon, 206–7, contains a brief description of it, but the memory was still fresh in Jesse's mind fifty years later, and his book, 221–23, provides a detailed account of what he regarded as a personal insult.

12. The Royal United Services Institute (RUSI), www.rusi.org, remains one of the most influential defense and security think tanks in the world.

13. *PUSG*, 28:237–38.

14. Ibid., 237.

15. Ibid., 232.

16. Ibid., 226.

17. Ibid., 232.

18. Ibid., 239.

19. Although Washburne's (hereinafter EBW) *Recollections of a Minister to France* covers his eight years in Paris, the vast majority of it is devoted to his experiences during the war, siege, and commune in 1870–71; see also Hill, *Elihu Washburne*.

20. EBW, 2:338–48.

21. *PUSG*, 28:214–15, 219.

22. Ibid., 229–30.

23. Simon, 209; see Owsley, "Henry Shelton Sanford and Federal Surveillance Abroad," and Meyer, "Henry S. Sanford and the Congo."

24. *PUSG*, 28:242.

25. On Grant laying the cornerstone of Emmanuel Church, Geneva, see JRY, *Around the World*, 1:48–50, and http://www.emmanuelchurch.ch/history.htm; Simon, 210–16, provides details on the Grants' sightseeing and visits to friends in the summer of 1877.

26. James M. McPherson, "'The Whole Family of Man': Lincoln and the Last Best Hope Abroad," in May, ed., *The Union, the Confederacy, and the Atlantic Rim*, 137, 140; for the international relations of the Civil War, see Jones, *Blue and Gray Diplomacy*.

27. *PUSG*, 28:223, 289.

28. Ibid., 290; for a summary of the enfranchisement issue at the time of Grant's visit, see Kennedy, *The Realities behind Diplomacy*, 36–43.

29. JRG, 248–50.

30. *PUSG*, 28:290–91.

31. JRY, *Around the World*, 1:129; see also Hardy, "South of the Border," 63–86.

32. *PUSG*, 28:297; Simon, 217.

33. *PUSG*, 28:298, 316.

34. Ibid., 323, 316.

35. Ibid., 303.

36. Hill, quoting EBW diary entry, December 18, 1870, 112; JRY, *Around the World*, 1:134–35.

37. *PUSG*, 28:303; for the Comte de Paris's support for the Union, see his July 29, 1862, letter, Sideman and Friedman, 155–57. See also Mahin, *The Blessed Place of Freedom*, 40–41: "The Comte de Paris's four-volume history of the American war was published in Paris in 1874 . . . He was regarded by British historians as prejudiced in favor of the North, and aroused great anger in the South."

38. *PUSG*, 28:319; on President Grant and the Statue of Liberty, see Harris, *A Statue for America*, 12–13, and Khan, *Enlightening the World*, 62, 102–3, 123–24, 128–32, and 135–36.

39. *PUSG*, 28:332.

40. Harris, 114, and Khan, 173.

2. *On the Mediterranean with the US Navy: 1877–78*

1. Simon, 218.

2. *PUSG*, 28:327.

3. Ibid., 327, 332. Ammen was promoted to Rear Admiral on December 11, 1877.

4. Simon, 219.

5. *PUSG*, 28:327.

6. JRG, 260–61.

7. JRY, *Around the World,* 1:215; Caldwell letter, December 31, 1877, in file USG to AB, November 27, 1877, USGPL.

8. For the Ottoman Empire at the time of Grant's visit, see Hourani, *A History of the Arab Peoples,* chap. 17, "European Empires and Dominant Elites, 1860–1914," 279–98, and Lewis, *The Middle East,* chap. 7, "New Ideas," 315–31; see also Kennedy, *The Realities Behind Diplomacy,* 82–90.

9. *PUSG,* 28:334, 336–37.

10. Ibid., 343, 345–46.

11. Ibid., 344, 358.

12. Lewis, 284.

13. JRY, *Around the World,* 1:231; JRG, 279; *PUSG,* 28:349, 353; Simon, 232–33. Although most biographers assume that he did, Grant did not transit the Suez Canal en route to India a year later.

14. JRG, 282; Simon, 234. Julia Grant (hereinafter JDG), on the other hand, was rather pleased "by this gorgeous, gleaming pageant, entering Jerusalem." See also Sarna, *When General Grant Expelled the Jews,* 127–31.

15. JRG, 286–88.

16. *PUSG,* 28:353–54, 356.

17. Ibid., 358–59.

18. Ibid., 354, 356. The sultan, in fact, gave two horses to Grant. They were shipped directly from Constantinople to New Haven, Connecticut, aboard the steamer *Norman Monarch.* US Legation Constantinople to Department of State, April 15, 1878, in file USG to Edward F. Beale (hereinafter EFB), March 6, 1878, USGPL. On Grant's friendship with Beale, see Thompson, *Edward F. Beale and the American West,* 211–27.

19. *PUSG,* 28:360; Sherman (hereinafter WTS) to Schofield, April 8, 1878, and Said Pasha to WTS, May 29, 1878, in file USG to WTS, March 21, 1878, USGPL.

20. US Legation Constantinople to Department of State, No. 230, March 7, 1878, in file USG to EFB, March 6, 1878, USGPL; *PUSG,* 28:354; Simon, 239.

21. JRG, 296; Field, *From Gibraltar to the Middle East,* 121, describes the philhellenism that was rampant throughout the 1820s in the United States.

22. Simon, 240.

23. US Legation Athens to Department of State, No. 366 and No. 367, March 9, 1878, in file USG to Alfred T. A. Torbert (hereinafter AT), March 9, 1878, USGPL; JRY, *Around the World,* 1:354.

24. US Legation Athens to Department of State, No. 366, March 9, 1878, and (no number), March 15, 1878, in file USG to AT, March 9, 1878, USGPL; Simon, 239.

25. US Legation Athens to Department of State, (no number), March 15, 1878, and John Meredith Read to Hamilton Fish (hereinafter HF), US Legation, Athens, March 22, 1878, in file USG to AT, March 9, 1878, USGPL.

26. *PUSG*, 28:364, 366.

27. Caldwell letter, March 19, 1878, in file USG to DA, March 25, 1878, USGPL; *PUSG*, 28:358, 365. JRG, 297, wrote that the Grants left *Vandalia* at Piraeus, but this is incorrect.

28. Interview with JRY, *Philadelphia Times*, October 20, 1879, in file Speech, Tokyo, August 30, 1879, USGPL; JRG, 312.

29. All quotes from Marsh's dispatch to Evarts are from US Legation Rome to Department of State, No. 753, April 17, 1878, in file USG to WTS, March 21, 1878, USGPL.

30. The Vienna and Aix-la-Chapelle rank and precedence order known as the *Reglement* was, in fact, meant to end "acute wrangles about precedence" by doing away with "the conception of [diplomats'] royal if vicarious dignity [that] precluded them from entering into contact with any persons other than those of royal or semiroyal blood." Nicolson, *Diplomacy*, 14. See also Nicolson, *The Congress of Vienna*, 216–18.

31. Six years before, Marsh had given General Sherman a more hospitable welcome, but Sherman's position as commanding general was clear, and his visit posed no unusual protocol questions. Sherman wrote to President Grant from Rome on February 21, 1872, that Marsh was "a scholar & gentleman—universally esteemed by our people and the Italians." *PUSG*, 22:358.

32. Caldwell letter, March 19, 1878.

33. *PUSG*, 28:380, and J. Schuyler Crosby letter to George P. Marsh, April 19, 1878, in file USG to J. Schuyler Crosby, April [n.d.], 1878, USGPL. Emphasis in original. All correspondence between Crosby, McMillan, Marsh, and the Department of State, with their various versions of what happened at the Florence train station, is in this file.

34. *PUSG*, 28:379, and 29:51–52. Sherman did contact Evarts about the McMillan-Crosby contretemps on January 22, 1879.

3. A Summer of Summitry from the North Sea to the Neva: 1878

1. For the cultural significance of world's fairs in the late nineteenth and early twentieth centuries, see Rosenberg, 887–904, and Osterhammel, 14–15.

2. Osterhammel, 29–39, discusses the worldwide rise of the independent (of governments and political parties) press in the last quarter of the nineteenth century, especially in the United States and the British Empire. It was characterized, 36, by "owners and chief editors [who] were able to give free rein to their own convictions and obsessions." The sale of newspapers more than quintupled in the United States from 1870 to 1900, from 2.6 million copies to "at least fifteen million" per day.

3. In command for the first time and pursuing an enemy unit with his heart "in his throat," Grant learned that "[the enemy] had as much reason to fear my forces as I had to fear his. The lesson was valuable." USG, *Personal Memoirs*, 132.

4. *New York Herald*, July 20, 1878, in file Conversation with Otto von Bismarck, June 30, 1878; *New York Times*, July 21, 1878, in file USG to J. Schuyler Crosby, April [n.d.], 1878, USGPL; Simon, 244–45.

5. *New York Times*, July 21, 1878.

6. *Philadelphia Times*, October 20, 1879; Mahin, 11, 20; *PUSG*, 21:164.

7. *PUSG*, 21:163–67.

8. The United States did participate in the 1884 Berlin Congress on the Congo, a "break with long-standing precedent" caused by "the lure of free trade." John Kasson, who became US minister to Germany in 1884, represented the United States, but there was bipartisan opposition to the Berlin agreement, and it was never submitted to the Senate. Herring, *From Colony to Superpower*, 287–88. See also Pletcher, *The Awkward Years*, chap. 17, "The Berlin Congo Conference," 308–24; Kasson, "The Congo Conference"; De Leon, "The Conference at Berlin"; and Shepperson, "The Centennial of the West African Conference."

9. Taylor, *On Two Continents*, 283, quoting a letter from her husband.

10. JRY, *Around the World*, 1:51–78.

11. WTS, "General Sherman's Tour of Europe," 738–40.

12. Thanks to Munich historian Dr. K. Michael Prince, author of *War and German Memory* (Lanham, MD: Lexington Books, 2009), for his search of contemporary press coverage of Grant's visit to Germany.

13. JRY, *Around the World*, 1:404.

14. See Pletcher, chap. 7, "The Mongrel Tariff," 139–57, and chap. 8, "The Pork Controversy," 158–69; also Snyder, "The American-German Pork Dispute."

15. The description of Grant's activities in Berlin and all quotes are from JRY's report in the *New York Herald*, July 20, 1878, in file Conversation with Otto von Bismarck, June 30, 1878, USGPL. See also *PUSG*, 28:407–10.

16. JRG, 252.

17. US Legation Berlin to Department of State, no. 26, July 1, 1878, in file Conversation with Otto von Bismarck, June 30, 1878, USGPL.

18. Ibid.

19. *PUSG*, 28:440.

20. Ibid., 399–401.

21. Ibid., 441.

22. Ibid., 412.

23. Ibid., 443. The prince imperial was fourteen when his father abdicated in 1870. He attended the Royal Military Academy after he and his mother found refuge in Britain, and was killed in the Zulu War on June 1, 1879. See Wade, "The Prince Imperial."

24. *PUSG*, 28:440, 443, 445–46, 449–50, 454, 478–79.

25. US Legation Stockholm to Department of State, No. 21, July 29, 1878, in file USG to AB, August 4, 1878, USGPL.

26. Gade, "General Grant in Norway," 290; *Chicago Tribune*, August 11, 1878, in file USG to AB, August 4, 1878, USGPL.

27. *Chicago Tribune*, August 11, 1878.

28. US Legation Stockholm to Department of State, No. 21, July 29, 1878.

29. *PUSG*, 28:453. For the Grant administration's problems with Catacazy, see *PUSG*, 22:130–33 and 147–57. On Grand Duke Alexis's reception in the United States in 1871–72, see Scott, Bleed, and Damm, *Custer, Cody, and Grand Duke Alexis*, 28.

30. *PUSG*, 28:453, 460.

31. Ibid., 443–45, 450.

32. *PUSG*, 30:176–78.

33. JDG wrote in her memoirs, Simon, 254, that the Grants went directly from Moscow to Warsaw, but she was mistaken. See *PUSG*, 28:450, 459, USG to DA, August 22, 1878, and USG to Frederick Dent Grant, August 22, 1878.

34. US Legation Vienna to the Department of State, No. 109, August 27, 1878, in file USG to HF, August 22, 1878, USGPL. On Kasson, see Younger, *John A. Kasson*; *The Biographical Dictionary of Iowa*, University of Iowa Press Digital Editions, http://uipress.lib.uiowa.edu/bdi/DetailsPage.aspx?id=201; and *The Iowa Legislature*, www.legis.iowa.gov/legislators/legislator?ga=14&personID=4963.

35. *PUSG*, 28:459; US Legation Vienna to the Department of State, No. 109, August 27, 1878.

36. *PUSG*, 28:474–75; Younger, 280.

37. Horstmann, *Consular Reminiscences*, 196–98.

38. *PUSG*, 28:467–68.

4. A Decisive Letter from Washington: 1878–79

1. *PUSG*, 28:459, 461, 467, 479.

2. The neutrality proclamation, *PUSG*, 20:307–9, did not mention any group by name, but was directed against "divers evil disposed persons" who "within the territory and jurisdiction of the United States" contributed to "military expeditions to be carried on thence against the Territories or Dominions of Powers with whom the United States are at peace." It was understood that this principally meant Fenian excursions into Canada and support for the Cuban insurrection, since Grant had already signed separate neutrality proclamations related to the Franco-Prussian War on August 22 and October 8, 1870. Ibid., 235–40, 302–5. On operations against the Sioux and the Canadian-US border, see Wooster, *The Military and United States Indian Policy*, 97–99, and Hedren, *After Custer*, 153–63.

3. Sexton, "The United States, the Cuban Rebellion," 338–39; Dulles, *Prelude to World Power*, 162–63.

4. Sexton, "The United States," 348. In Grant's first State of the Union message, on December 6, 1869, he told Congress "that in due time Spain and other European powers will find their interest in . . . establishing their present dependencies as independent powers—members of the family of nations." USG, *Complete State of the Union Addresses*, 6.

5. USG, *Personal Memoirs*, 102–5, and "The Nicaragua Canal," 109.

6. *New York Herald*, December 30, 1878, in file USG to AB, October 27, 1878, USGPL.

7. US Legation Madrid to Department of State, October 29, 1878, in file USG to AB, October 27, 1878, USGPL.

8. *PUSG*, 29:11.

9. Ibid., and *New York Herald*, January 19, 1879, in file USG to AB, October 27, 1878, USGPL.

10. *New York Herald*, January 25, 1879, in file USG to AB, October 27, 1878, USGPL.

11. *PUSG*, 29:13, 16.

12. Ibid., 13, 16–17.

13. *PUSG*, 21:11.

14. Ibid., 213.

15. *PUSG*, 29:18.

16. Ibid., 36; see also 30:340, 342.

17. Simon, 258–59. Caldwell wrote to his mother on March 19, 1878, that Grant "has taken rather a fancy to me because I play a good game of whist—says he never saw anyone play better—we play Boston every night—learn it—its [*sic*] the best game I ever saw." *PUSG*, 28:368.

18. *PUSG*, 29:14–15.

19. "Commodore Robert W. Shufeldt's Voyage to Africa, the Middle East, and Asia, 1878–1880," Office of the Historian, Department of State, http://history.state.gov/milestones/1866–1898/CommodoreShufeldt. See also Paullin, *Diplomatic Negotiations*, 292–302, and Dennett, *Americans in Eastern Asia*, 455–56.

20. *PUSG*, 29:14–16.

21. Ibid., 17, and 28:480.

22. *PUSG*, 29:18–20, 26–28; *Philadelphia Press*, December 7, 1878, in file USG to Anthony J. Drexel, December 13, 1878, USGPL.

23. *New York Times*, December 22, 1878, and *Washington Post*, December 24, 1878, in file USG to Anthony J. Drexel, December 13, 1878, USGPL; *PUSG*, 29:30–31. Sherman conveyed McCrary's decision to Sheridan on December 20. Fred was kept "on [Sheridan's] staff, with the Same pay and allowances he would receive if remaining with you on duty at your HeadQuarters." He did not receive "the usual travelling allowance" because his travel was not "strictly official" and he could "be Summoned back to his Post, at any time the public Service requires his presence,

at his own Cost." He was required to report his whereabouts to the War Department regularly while he was abroad, and he did so from Aden (February 5, 1879), Lucknow, India (March 6, 1879), Singapore (April 3, 1879), Peking (June 5, 1879), and Tokyo (July and August 1879); copies of reports in file USG to Frederick Dent Grant, December 12, 1878, USGPL.

24. Simon, 261. JRG, 314, wrote that his mother was in London during his father's visit to Ireland, but this is incorrect.

25. *PUSG*, 29:36, 41–42, 45–46.

26. *PUSG*, 29:45–46; see also Fiore, "When General Grant to Ireland Came," 18–20. On September 29, 1875, President Grant laid out the importance of free, secular public schools to the future of a democratic republic in a speech to the reunion of the Army of the Tennessee in Des Moines, Iowa. Irish nationalists claimed the speech was anti-Catholic because of Grant's opposition to the use of public funds for parochial schools. See *PUSG*, 26:342–51.

27. *PUSG*, 29:47.

28. Ibid., 31, 40–41, 50.

29. Ibid., 27, 40, 50–51.

30. Ibid., 51.

5. The "Distinguished Foreigner" East of Suez: 1879

1. See Robert May, ed., *The Union, the Confederacy, and the Atlantic Rim*; Howard Jones, *Blue and Gray Diplomacy*; and Crook, *Diplomacy During the American Civil War*.

2. *PUSG*, 20:255, 257–58.

3. Earle, "A Half-Century of American Foreign Policy," 168.

4. Quoted in Stuermer, *Bismarck*, 73–74.

5. *PUSG*, 20:256. In "The Funded Loan and the *Alabama* Claims," Jay Sexton paints a different picture of Boutwell, as focused on the effect of the unsettled *Alabama* claims on the "funding bill" designed to refinance the United States' public debt, and, therefore, a moderate voice in the cabinet pressing Secretary of State Fish to reach accord with the British government. As usual in assessing Grant's foreign policy, the ghost of Allan Nevins lurks in the background: the president rarely appears as a decision maker, and when he does, he allegedly needs reining in by men like Fish and Boutwell. See, for example, the claim that the two secretaries "checked Grant's appetite for Canada in the cabinet," 461, in contrast to the Boutwell letter cited herein and the contrary evidence in *PUSG* and JRY. Sexton's article is an important contribution to understanding the political-economic context of the Treaty of Washington, but it contains not one reference to the relevant material in *PUSG*.

6. *PUSG*, 21:352–53.

7. *PUSG*, 29:48.

8. USG Travel Diary (hereinafter TD), *PUSG*, 29:61, 63; Simon, 267, 272.

9. TD, *PUSG*, 29:63–64; *PUSG*, 29:97, 110, 100.

10. *PUSG*, 29:179; Vice Admiral Alexis Pothuau to Edward Noyes, January 18, 1879, in file USG to Elizabeth M. Borie (hereinafter EMB), January 20, 1879, USGPL.

11. *Bombay Gazette*, February 15, 1879, in file USG to Anthony J. Drexel, February 16, 1879, USGPL.

12. Ibid.; *Statesman and Friend of India* (Calcutta), March 4, 1879, in file USG Travel Diary, USGPL.

13. *PUSG*, 29:113–14; TD, *PUSG*, 29:69.

14. Ibid., 69, 99, 107

15. Both the viceroy and his father, the novelist, M.P., and Colonial Secretary (1858–59) Edward Bulwer-Lytton, had been supporters of the Confederacy. JRY told the *Philadelphia Times*, October 20, 1879, that Lytton "said that while his sympathies during the war had been with the South, he never believed that the South would succeed . . . and now that the war was over, if he were an American, he would be in favor of the party which would make every sacrifice to preserve the Union." His father was "uncompromisingly pro-South in his speeches and writings." In an April 1865 letter lamenting Lee's surrender, he wrote, "I had indulged the hope that your country might break up into two or perhaps more fragments. I regard the United States as a menace to the whole civilized world, if you are allowed to go on developing as you have been, undisturbed." Sideman and Friedman, 92, 282.

16. *PUSG*, 29:105–6; Simon, 275. Lytton alleged that Grant was "drunk and licentious" at a March 15 dinner (*PUSG*, 29:107) at which the viceroy was not even present, having left Calcutta the day before. There is no credibility to the story.

17. TD, *PUSG*, 29:70–73.

18. Julia Grant recalled indignantly that in Rangoon "[o]ur American consul had been compelled to return home, as the consulate fees would not support him, and the consulship had been turned over to an English merchant." Simon, 277–78.

19. *Philadelphia Times*, October 20, 1879.

20. *Straits Times and Overland Journal* (Singapore), April 5, 1879, in file USG to EMB, April 3, 1879, USGPL; *PUSG*, 29:111–12.

21. Ibid.; see also Anderson, *Imperialism and Idealism*, 43–44, and Cole, "Chinese Exclusion," 24–27.

22. *Straits Times*, April 5, 1879; *PUSG*, 29:112–13.

23. Speeches such as these, quoted here from newspaper coverage, were not written down in advance. The journalists covering the events often mixed first- and third-person references.

24. *Straits Times*, April 5, 1879; *PUSG*, 29:112–13.

25. Ibid.

26. *Straits Times*, March 31, 1879, and April 5, 1879, and *China Mail* (Hong Kong), April 16, 1879, in file USG to EMB, April 3, 1879, USGPL.

27. *Straits Times*, April 5, 1879; US Consulate Singapore to Department of State, No. 265, May 14, 1879, in file USG to George W. Childs, April 5, 1879, USGPL; see also *PUSG*, 29:116.

28. US Consulate Singapore to Department of State, No. 265, May 14, 1879.

29. Anson, *About Others and Myself*, 362, found Grant "a very agreeable and interesting guest. He had visited every crowned head in Europe, and been to India, Burmah, etc., and when chatting in the verandah of an evening, after dinner, I found him very entertaining." When Anson asked "what he thought of his chance" of returning to the White House, Grant replied, "'Were the elections going to take place this year, I think I should have a fair chance, but as they do not, I cannot be sure of the stability of public sentiment.'"

30. *Straits Times*, April 5, 1879; on Whampoa and his famous residence, Bendemeer House, see the National Library of Singapore online: http://eresources.nlb.gov.sg/infopedia/articles/SIP_798_2004-12-14.html and http://eresources.nlb.gov.sg/infopedia/articles/SIP_759_2005-01-11.html.

31. US Consulate Singapore to Department of State, No. 265, May 14, 1879.

32. Ibid. Studer's opinion apparently did not influence Grant, who described the maharajah in his diary as "a very progressive man [who] is doing much for his country & people." TD, *PUSG*, 29:75.

33. US Consulate Singapore to Department of State, No. 265, May 14, 1879.

34. Simon, 281; *PUSG*, 29:109; *New York Herald*, September 22, 1878, in file USG Speech, Bangkok, April 16, 1879, USGPL.

35. US Consulate Singapore to Department of State, No. 265, May 14, 1879; *PUSG*, 29:118–19; *New York Herald*, June 9, 1879, in file USG Speech, Bangkok, April 16, 1879, USGPL.

36. *New York Herald*, June 9, 1879, and *China Mail*, May 2, 1879, in file USG Speech, Bangkok, April 16, 1879, USGPL; TD, *PUSG*, 29:75–76. The primary sources contain more discrepancies about the dates of the Bangkok trip than any other phase of Grant's travels. Studer reported that Grant departed Singapore on Tuesday, but gave the date as April 9, which in 1879 was a Wednesday. JRY's *Herald* report and JDG's memoirs both give the arrival date in Siam, incorrectly, as April 14. The correct dates are in Grant's diary: on April 8, "to-morrow leave for Bangkok," and arrival "off the bar of Bangkok" the morning of Saturday, April 12, "one hour less than three days from Singapore." The date JDG gave for the Grants' return to Singapore, April 27, is also incorrect; they returned on April 22. Simon, 281, 283.

37. *North China Daily News* (Shanghai), May 8, 1879, and *China Mail*, May 2, 1879, in file USG Speech, Bangkok, April 16, 1879, USGPL; Simon, 281–82.

38. *PUSG*, 29:118; TD, *PUSG*, 29:78. The text of the March 20, 1833, treaty is at: http://bangkok.usembassy.gov/relation/175usth/timeline-of-u/spotlight-on-treaty-of-amity.html.

39. These conversations were "on the record." Like Grant's past meetings with Bismarck and his future ones with Meiji and Li Hung-chang (hereinafter LHC), Young reported them in the *New York Herald*. Foreign leaders who talked with Grant in Young's presence expected, and wanted, their words to be reported in the United States.

40. *New York Herald*, June 22, 1879, and June 9, 1879, in file USG Speech, Bangkok, April 16, 1879, USGPL.

41. *New York Herald*, June 22, 1879; see also *PUSG*, 29:119.

42. *New York Herald*, June 22, 1879; *North China Daily News*, May 8, 1879.

43. David B. Sickels to JRY, October 8, 1879, and November 22, 1879, in file USG to King Chulalongkorn, May 16, 1879, USGPL.

44. *PUSG*, 29:129.

45. *New York Herald*, June 9, 1879.

46. Adolph Borie died on February 5, 1880, only a few months after his return to the United States. The Grants cabled their condolences to Elizabeth Borie from Havana, Cuba, on February 7. See *PUSG*, 29:360.

47. *PUSG*, 29:121. Weather delayed the departure from Bangkok until 2:00 A.M., Saturday, April 19.

48. TD, *PUSG*, 29:79–80; *PUSG*, 29:122–23.

6. The "King of America" and the Viceroys of China: 1879

1. Keating (hereinafter JK), *With General Grant in the East*, 160; JRY, *Around the World*, 2:286–87. Hart wrote from Shanghai on May 6, 1879, to J. D. Campbell that he had traveled with Grant from Singapore to Hong Kong. See Fairbank, Bruner, and Matheson, eds., *The I.G. in Peking*, Letter No. 246, 1:294, and, for a biographical sketch of Hart, the introduction by L. K. Little, 3–30.

2. JK, 160–61, 164; TD, *PUSG*, 29:79–80.

3. *PUSG*, 29:123–25; Keating, 165–66; TD, *PUSG*, 29:80–81. Grant likely meant the Colonial Office, not the colonial government. Perkins had not known Grant before, but he soon formed the same opinion of him as had the officers and men of *Vandalia*. He wrote on May 4 to his family in New Hampshire that "[t]he General gets up early mornings and walks about the city and seems to take in everything. I am a good deal impressed by him. I never saw less airs or pretension, which I believe is like all really great men." Susan G. Perkins, ed., *Letters of Capt. Geo. Hamilton Perkins*, 210–12.

4. *Hong Kong Government Gazette*, May 14, 1879, 245–47, and *Celestial Empire* (Shanghai), May 6, 1879, in file USG to EBW, May 4, 1879, USGPL; see also *PUSG*, 29:125.

5. *North China Daily News* (Shanghai), May 8, 1879, and *China Mail* (Hong Kong), May 2, 1879, in file USG Speech, Hong Kong, May 12, 1879, USGPL; see also *PUSG*, 29:128, and Charles Wells Russell, ed., *Memoirs of Colonel John S. Mosby*, 398.

6. US Consulate Canton to Department of State, "Annual Trade Report for Year Ending 31st August, 1879," September 18, 1879, and US Consulate Canton to Department of State, No. 67, May 16, 1879, in file USG to EBW, May 4, 1879, USGPL; TD, *PUSG*, 29:81–82; see also *PUSG*, 29:126.

7. TD, *PUSG*, 29:82.

8. Ibid., 81–82; JK, 172. All quotes describing Grant's visit to Viceroy Liu are from JRY's report in the *New York Herald*, June 27, 1879, in file USG to EBW, May 4, 1879, USGPL.

9. Susan G. Perkins, ed., 197.

10. Gideon Nye to Secretary of State James Blaine, May 27, 1881; "Address of the American residents of Canton to His Excellency General Ulysses Grant"; and *Celestial Empire* (Shanghai), May 27, 1879, in file USG to EBW, May 4, 1879, USGPL; see also *PUSG*, 29:125.

11. *Daily Press* (Hong Kong), May [10?] and May 13, 1879, enclosure to US Consulate Canton to Department of State, May 16, 1879; see also *New York Herald*, June 27, 1879.

12. *Daily Press* (Hong Kong), May [10?], 1879; TD, *PUSG*, 29:82; JRY, *Around the World*, 2:351. In 1888, Wade became the first professor of Chinese at Cambridge University; see http://www.lib.cam.ac.uk/exhibitions/shelf_lives/wade.html.

13. *New York Herald*, June 27, 1879; JK, 202; *North China Daily News*, May 23, 1879, in file USG to EFB, May 23, 1879, USGPL. See also JRY, *Around the World*, 2:351.

14. *Celestial Empire* (Shanghai), May 6, 1879; *New York Herald*, June 27, 1879.

15. *New York Herald*, June 27, 1879.

16. *PUSG*, 29:128–30, 132.

17. *Japan Daily Herald*, June 5, 1879; *North China Daily News*, May 23 and May 24, 1879; and *Celestial Empire* (Shanghai), May 27, 1879, in file USG to EFB, May 23, 1879, USGPL; *PUSG*, 29:136; TD, *PUSG*, 29:83.

18. JK, 214–15; see also JRY, *Around the World*, 2:370, and Simon, 286. Borie and Keating departed Shanghai on *Nagoya Maru* to Nagasaki, arriving on May 23. They spent a week sailing the Inland Sea and visiting Hiogo (Kobe), Kyoto, and Osaka, arriving in Yokohama on May 30. Admiral Patterson sent a launch to transfer their luggage to *City of Tokio*, which departed Yokohama the morning of Saturday, May 31. She sailed through the Golden Gate at daybreak, Monday, June 16, 1879. See JK, 215–27.

19. *Japan Daily Herald*, May 31, 1879, and *North China Daily News*, May 21, 1879, in file USG to EFB, May 23, 1879, USGPL.

20. *PUSG*, 29:136; *North China Herald and S.C & C. Gazette*, May 27, 1879, in file USG to EFB, May 23, 1879, USGPL; TD, *PUSG*, 29:83.

21. TD, *PUSG*, 29:83–84.

22. US Consulate Tientsin to Department of State, No. 28, August 12, 1879, in file USG to Prince Kung and Iwakura Tomomi, August 13, 1879, USGPL.

23. *New York Herald*, August 11, 1879, in file USG Speech Tientsin, May 30, 1879, USGPL.

24. *Celestial Empire*, June 24, 1879, in file USG Conversations with LHC, Tientsin, June 12–14, 1879, USGPL; TD, *PUSG*, 29:85–86; *New York Herald*, August 11, 1879; Simon, 290.

25. *New York Herald*, August 12, 1879, in file USG Speech Peking, June 5, 1879, USGPL; TD, *PUSG*, 29:85–86.

26. *PUSG*, 29:143–45; for the railroad's impact on Missouri River commerce, see Hedren, *After Custer*, 77, 89–90.

27. *PUSG*, 29:141–42.

28. *New York Herald*, August 12, 1879.

29. *PUSG*, 29:145–46, 148–49.

30. Owen Denny to JRY, June 3, 1879, in file USG Conversations with LHC, June 12–14, 1879, USGPL; TD, *PUSG*, 29:86; *PUSG*, 29:149–51.

31. *PUSG*, 29:151–57.

32. *New York Herald*, August 16, 1879, and August 17, 1879, in file USG Conversations with LHC, June 12–14, 1879, USGPL; see also *PUSG*, 29:158–68.

33. *New York Herald*, August 17, 1879.

34. Ibid.

35. Ibid.; *New York Herald*, August 18, 1879, in file USG Travel Diary 1879, USGPL.

36. *New York Herald*, August 18, 1879; TD, *PUSG*, 29:87.

37. *New York Herald*, August 18, 1879.

38. US Consulate General Shanghai to Department of State, No. 87, July 15, 1879, enclosure, "Reception of General U.S. Grant at Peking and Tientsin (Extracted from the '*North-China Daily News*')," in file USG Speech Tientsin, June 13, 1879, USGPL.

39. On Li's hope to find an ally in the United States, see Hunt, *The Making of a Special Relationship*, chap. 4, 115–42. Hunt's analysis at least takes Grant's diplomacy seriously, but he is too willing to ascribe to the former president attitudes that may have been characteristic of many Americans, but were not Grant's; for example: "Grant was certain that Asians were as ready to accept the United States as protector and tutor as Americans were suited and obliged to claim the role" (122). Hunt asserts that Grant returned home with "his head filled with dreams of an American century in Asia" (123). The opposite was true; Grant wanted Asian countries to be free of any western tutelage, including that of the United States.

40. *New York Herald*, August 18, 1879.

7. The Path to Peace Not Taken: 1879

1. Calendar, *PUSG*, 24:458–59.

2. *PUSG*, 21:206–8. James McCosh, president of Princeton, wrote to Grant on May 16, 1871, that "we could teach a dozen as easily and more effectively than two [Japanese students already at Princeton]. . . . My only aim . . . is to help the East to profit by what we have in the West. You have been helping this cause and I would be glad to aid you."

3. Ibid., 311–12, 316–17. For the Walsh Brothers, the Kobe Paper Mill, and the founding of Mitsubishi, see www.mitsubishi.com/e/history/series/walsh.

4. *PUSG*, 21:312–13.

5. Ibid., 313–14, 317–18. Twenty-two years old in 1873, Stevens was a graduate of Oberlin College and Howard University. He served as secretary of the US legation in Tokyo from 1873 to 1883, after which he entered Japan's diplomatic service. He was assassinated by Korean-American nationalists in San Francisco in 1908 because of his association with Japan's policy in Korea. See Houchins and Houchins, "The Korean Experience in America," 556–58.

6. Calendar, *PUSG*, 24:460, 462, 464. The Europeans complained to Secretary of State Fish about Bingham's lack of cooperation with their ministers in Japan. Although Bingham feared otherwise, Fish was more supportive of him than the US minister knew. Approached in May 1874 by Sir Edward Thornton, "on further instruction from Lord Derby," and by the German charge d'affaires, Baron Bunson, whose "government wishes to know" whether there had been a change of US policy toward cooperation with the other powers, Fish wondered to Thornton if British diplomats in Tokyo might not exert "influences . . . to the disadvantage of Americans in favour of British subjects. He thinks that could scarcely be. I tell him I have reason to apprehend that there is cause for complaint." With Bunson, Fish was more direct. While the United States was "in favour of joint or co-operative action on the part of the Treaty powers," Bingham was "not bound to a servile adoption of the policy of his colleagues but is to act with them whenever in his judgment the interests of the country would justify it. . . . [W]e desire cooperation whenever it can be done without the sacrifice of a principle or some large interest." Bingham (hereinafter JAB) kept up a lively correspondence with both President Grant and the secretary of state. See HF Diary, 256–57, 304–5, 310–11, and 315–16, in file October 8, 1873, Calendar, *PUSG*, 24:458; JAB to USG, October 12, 1874, Calendar, *PUSG*, 32:245. See also Calendar, *PUSG*, 24:458–64, for extracts from letters from JAB to USG on October 8, December 6, and December 23, 1873, and January 21, February 23 (twice), March 9, March 23, April 24, May 20, and October 9, 1874.

7. See Treat, "Return of the Shimonoseki Indemnity."

8. See Richard T. Chang, "General Grant's 1879 Visit to Japan," 375–76, for Japan's extensive preparations to welcome Grant.

9. *New York Herald*, August 22, 1879, in file USG to AB, June 22, 1879, USGPL. Yoshida presented his credentials to President Grant on December 18, 1874. Over the next two years, he and his family became friends with the Grants, and Yoshida maintained a direct friendship with Bingham, who had been minister to Japan for about a year before Yoshida left for America. On September 21, 1876, he wrote to Bingham that "the other day I went to the White House," and the president "intimated to me that he is intending to make a tour of [the] World soon after the next March—& that he desire[s] to go to Japan where he would likely stay a few weeks to travel in the country. I trust this will be realized for I know that our people—to say nothing of His Majesty & his Cabinet—will be exceeding glad & happy to welcome him." In file USG to JAB, September 28, 1879, USGPL. See also *PUSG*, 29:247, and Simon, 292–93.

10. *New York Herald*, August 31, 1879, in file USG Speech, Tokyo, July 4, 1879 (second of two July 4 speeches), USGPL.

11. TD, *PUSG*, 29:88–90; *New York Herald*, August 31, 1879. JDG (Simon, 296) incorrectly recalled that British vessels saluted Grant. Bingham reported to Secretary of State Evarts on July 15, 1879, that "[t]he English men-of-war in port made no recognition of the General, owing to the order issued by Her Britannic Majesty's Colonial Secretary Sir Michael Hicks-Beach to the effect that Her Majesty's war vessels should not salute General Grant as he was but a private gentleman." *PUSG*, 29:179.

12. Simon, 303; *PUSG*, 29:178–79.

13. *New York Herald*, August 31, 1879. In the 1870s the young emperor was an asset to Japan in presenting a public face to the western world. He appeared vigorous and dynamic, and left the impression of willingly adopting western ideas and manners. In other words, he embodied the way Japan's government wanted foreigners to see Japan. See the portrait of "Meiji, the 'restored' emperor," in Large, *Emperors of the Rising Sun*, 17–73, and Keene, *Emperor of Japan*, especially 188–97, and, for Meiji's meetings with Grant, 308–19. Whether Meiji was actually "fond" of his army is disputed by historians. Japan had learned from its emissaries abroad that heads of state, particularly royal and imperial ones, were expected to take a keen interest in their armed forces, and so, Meiji seemed to do so. However, see Large, 34–35: "In 1881, [Meiji] told the minister of education he was distressed to see that school textbooks made too much of the emperors as military figures in Japanese history. He allowed that children like to read about war but he would much prefer them to know that historically, and in his own reign, the imperial house was more important for its cultural achievements and sponsorship of the peaceful arts." Still, Keene, 310, maintains that Meiji by 1880 "was manifesting increasing interest in military drills and maneuvers."

14. TD, *PUSG*, 29:91; *PUSG*, 29:183–85, 171, 173.

15. *New York Herald*, August 31, 1879; *PUSG*, 29:175.

16. *New York Herald*, August 31, 1879.

17. All quotes from Grant's conversations with Meiji, Ito, and Saigo are from *PUSG*, 29:200–207.

18. Borton, *Japan's Modern Century*, 88.

19. Nagao Ariga, "Diplomacy," in Stead, ed., *Japan by the Japanese*, 154.

20. JRY, *Around the World*, 2:597.

21. Dennett, "American 'Good Offices' in Asia," 10.

22. *PUSG*, 29:208–9.

23. See Leung "The Quasi-War in East Asia."

24. On the impact of Japan's military victories on its international status, see Osterhammel, 480–82, 492–93, 915.

25. Keene, n. 39 (chap. 31), 787.

26. Ariga, in Stead, ed., 149.

27. Keene, 317.

28. See Osterhammel, 612–13, on Japan's development of "a rational bureaucracy" within "a modern authoritarian state" that had "many parallels with the post-1871 German Reich." For a fuller discussion of "the German influence" on Meiji Japan, see chapter 5 in Pittau, *Political Thought in Early Meiji Japan*, 131–57.

29. Borton, 144: "[T]he old leaders were neither willing nor able to relinquish control," and "the informal conferences of two or more of the older statesmen came to be formalized into" an "extraconstitutional body" that "for several years was the strongest body in the governmental structure." In American terms, it was as if US government decision-making had remained in the hands of John Adams and Thomas Jefferson into the 1820s.

30. US Legation Tokyo to Department of State, No. 937, August 16, 1879, with Enclosures Nos. 1–3, in file USG to AB, August 1, 1879, USGPL; see also *PUSG*, 29:194.

31. *PUSG*, 29:195.

32. At one banquet in Grant's honor, "the reception committee insisted that the wives and daughters of committee members should be present" in western dress, and the women were encouraged to dance. Only one had the courage to do so, the others "watching her with our eyes wide open in astonishment." One attendee recalled that she "felt as tense as a soldier going into the battlefield for the first time," and "[o]n the way home in our horse carriage my mother and I felt quite relieved and we once again breathed freely." They were apprehensive about meeting Grant, "[n]ever having been close to a Westerner before," but as in Siam, his modesty and silent dignity were "more like an Oriental man than an American gentleman," and he made an excellent impression. Quoted in Chang, 387–88.

33. JRY, *Around the World*, 2:607–8.

34. *PUSG*, 29:214–15.

35. Ibid., 211–12, 228.

36. Keene, 317; *PUSG*, 29:229–30; see also JRY, *Around the World*, 2:570–75.

37. JRY, *Around the World*, 2:609–13.

38. US Legation Tokyo to Department of State, No. 956, September 2, 1879, in file USG Speech, August 30, 1879, USGPL.

39. Quoted in MacArthur, *Reminiscences*, 311–13.

40. Ibid.

41. JRY, *Around the World*, 2:613.

8. Home: 1879

1. *PUSG*, 29:264. On the Pacific Mail Steamship Company, see Weinstein, "North from Panama."

2. *San Francisco Chronicle*, September 23, 1879, in file USG Memorandum, October 23, 1879, and September 25, 1879, in file USG Speech, September 24, 1879, USGPL.

3. *PUSG*, 29:238; *Philadelphia Times*, October 18, 1879, in file USG to JRY, November 3, 1879, USGPL; see also *PUSG*, 29:280.

4. *PUSG*, 29:247.

5. JRY, *Around the World*, 2:629–30.

6. Ibid.; *San Francisco Chronicle*, September 25, 1879, emphasis added.

7. *San Francisco Chronicle*, September 25, 1879; *PUSG*, 29:241–42.

8. *PUSG*, 29:255–56; see also Cole, "Chinese Exclusion."

9. All quotations from Grant's visit to Sacramento and from Owen Denny's letter to USG are from the *Sacramento Record-Union*, November 1, 1879, in file USG Memorandum, October 23, 1879, USGPL. Extensive excerpts from the newspaper article are in *PUSG*, 29:265–70.

10. *PUSG*, 29:282, 292–94. Gladstone had declared: "We may have our own opinions about slavery; we may be for or against the South; but there is no doubt that Jefferson Davis and other leaders of the South have made an army; they are making, it appears, a navy; and they have made what is more than either, they have made a nation." Sideman and Friedman, eds., 186.

11. *PUSG*, 29:297, 332.

12. *PUSG*, 29:302–3; Robeson to JRY, August 27, 1879, in file Conversations with LHC, June 12–14, 1879, USGPL. Young left the Grants on the West Coast earlier than planned because his father died in Philadelphia. He "could not go to Chicago [for the Army of the Tennessee reunion because] business matters arising out of my father's death, and the closing of my book have absorbed all my time." Robeson told Young that several of his "old messmates," including Lieutenant Commander Caldwell, had been in Newport, and commented that "the talk about the Presidency [a third Grant term] seems to be more than a nine days wonder, and the papers are still full of it."

13. *PUSG*, 29:310; *The Voice of Peace* 6, no. 10 (January 1880): 153–54, in file USG to Prince Kung and Iwakura Tomomi, August 13, 1879, USGPL.

14. All quotations from Love's and Grant's remarks to the UPU, and comments thereon, are from *The Voice of Peace* 6, no. 11 (February 1880): 161–63, 167, in file USG Speech, December 26, 1879, USGPL; see also *PUSG*, 29:340.

15. *PUSG*, 29:313; see also Taliaferro, *All the Great Prizes*, 202, 184–85.

16. JRY to John Hay, December 16, 1879, in file USG to Rutherford B. Hayes, November 30, 1879, USGPL; *PUSG*, 29:313–14.

17. *PUSG*, 29:314; John Hay to JRY, December 30, 1879, in file USG to Prince Kung and Iwakura Tomomi, August 13, 1879, USGPL. Grant also saw Secretary Evarts at a dinner on December 29 given by New York congressman Levi Morton and attended by Daniel Ammen. *PUSG*, 29:334–35.

18. *Philadelphia Public-Ledger*, December 20, 1879, in file USG Speech, December 19, 1879, USGPL.

19. *PUSG*, 29:328–29. The issues that Grant raised of trade promotion and foreign relations at the intersection of the private sector and public policy have not yet been, and perhaps can never be, fully resolved. See, on the US Foreign Commercial Service of the Department of Commerce, Daniel Harris, "Facing the Unthinkable," and www.trade.gov/cs.

20. All quotes from Grant's interview are in the *St. Louis Globe-Democrat*, December 21, 1879, in file USG Speech, December 19, 1879, USGPL.

21. On Seward, see David L. Anderson, *Imperialism and Idealism*, 91, 94–95, 99–105.

22. Grant's aversion to the unequal treaty regime dated to his presidency. On January 7, 1876, Japan's commissioner to Europe, George B. Williams, wrote to Bingham that he had met with President Grant, who "said he was not aware that the customs duties of Japan were determined by Treaty and that he did not see the justice or necessity of so determining them, that possibly some reason existed when the Treaty was made but that the times had changed and he thought Japan should be left untrammeled in this matter." Grant told Williams that "if Japan wanted a change for me to tell Yoshida to present some proposition from the Japanese government, or to advise his government to take some action that could be acted upon by the United States. . . . The president told me to talk to Mr. Fish, which I did. Mr. F. was non-committal beyond saying he could do nothing until Japan presented a proposition, when he was prepared to act promptly." *PUSG*, 29:212.

23. Ibid., 337.

Conclusion

1. USG, *Personal Memoirs*, 8; Simon, 326.

2. USG, "The Nicaragua Canal"; John Y. Simon, introduction, *PUSG*, 31:xv.

3. John Y. Simon, introduction, *PUSG*, 30:xi, 74–75.

4. See http://www.asil.org/about/asil-history and www.carnegieendowment.org/about/?lang=en. There is a growing literature on the activities of former presidents and the institutionalization of the American postpresidency since the mid-twentieth century. One of the best articles is Lisa Anderson, "The Ex-Presidents," which considers, 66, "the opportunities and incentives for democratic leaders' postpolitical lives" in many countries, not only the United States. As Anderson notes, ibid., although "most countries do not wholly squander the resource that they have in their former leaders, neither do they provide clear guidelines for how their skills ought to be deployed." See also Schaller and Williams, "The *Contemporary Presidency*"; Belenky, "The Making of the Ex-Presidents"; Skidmore, *After the White House*; and Benardo and Weiss, *Citizen-in-Chief.*

5. Simon, *PUSG*, 30:xiii. The vitriol of the intra-Republican party battle for control of New York is well captured in Taliaferro, 201–8. On Garfield's death, see Millard, *Destiny of the Republic.*

6. *PUSG*, 30:149–52, 303–8.

7. Ibid., 307. On Denny's later role in Korea, see Swartout, *Mandarins, Gunboats, and Power Politics.* Denny's American supporters in China were angry that he did not become minister, and they blamed Grant for, they believed, securing the position for John Russell Young. See *PUSG*, 30:447. Grant's correspondence, however, shows clearly that he was a strong supporter of Denny, but neither he nor (more importantly) President Arthur was willing to force Bingham out of Tokyo.

8. "Commodore Shufeldt's treaty with Corea promises more complications than any other recent act of Eastern diplomacy," wrote the *New York Times* on July 12, 1882, in file USG to JRY, November 28, 1882, USGPL. On Shufeldt's three missions to Korea, 1866–67, 1880, and 1881–82, see Dennett, *Americans in Eastern Asia*, 454–65. Li, Young wrote to Grant from Peking on September 23, 1882, "was angry with Shufeldt, but said he was too good a friend of yours and of America to cherish resentment towards America because of Shufeldt." *PUSG*, 30:445. For the story of Shufeldt and growing US involvement in Korea, see Pletcher, *The Awkward Years*, 208; Paullin, *Diplomatic Negotiations of American Naval Officers*, 282–328; Deuchler, *Confucian Gentlemen and Barbarian Envoys*; Gordon H. Chang, "Whose 'Barbarism'? Whose 'Treachery'?"; Treat, "China and Korea, 1885–1894"; and Dennett, "Early American Policy in Korea." An early (1883) introduction of Korea to an American audience was Everett Frazar, *Korea and Her Relations to China, Japan and the United States*, in file USG to JRY, November 1884, USGPL.

9. Dennett, "American Choices in the Far East in 1882," 84–85; see also his *Americans in Eastern Asia*, 508–9, and "American 'Good Offices' in Asia," 14–17. More recent scholarship on Young's years as US minister includes chapter 6, "Attempts at an Independent Policy: James B. Angell and John Russell Young in Peking," in David L. Anderson, *Imperialism and Idealism*, 115–43; Hunt, *The*

Making of a Special Relationship, 133–36 and 173–74; and a brief consideration of Young's diplomacy in Pletcher, *The Awkward Years,* chap. 11, "The Far East," 195–18. There is still no biography of Young.

10. Grant's letters to Young, and extensive extracts of Young's letters to Grant from China, are in *PUSG,* 30:443–47 (USG to JRY, November 28, 1882; JRY to USG, September 23, 1882, and January 27, 1883) and 454–56 (JRY to USG, December 12, 1882); and *PUSG,* 31:35–38 (USG to JRY, May 18, 1883; JRY to USG, March 8, 1883, January 31, 1883, and February 3, 1883); 59–60 (USG to JRY, August 25, 1883); 95 (JRY to USG, January 26, 1884); 101 (USG to JRY, January 21, 1884); 192 (USG to JRY, August 20, 1884); and 241–42 (USG to JRY, November [n.d.], 1884). Working on his memoirs in the midst of his financial and worsening health problems, Grant told Young in November 1884, "I am always willing to help when I can to establish trade and commerce with the East."

11. *PUSG,* 30:388–89.

12. Robert Lincoln to Frederick Frelinghuysen, April 9, 1883, in file USG to Judge Arthur MacArthur, June 10, 1882, USGPL.

13. Kenneth Ray Young, *The General's General,* 142: "Nearly every officer stationed on the frontier was attempting to pull strings to be reassigned to other duties." In 1872, President Grant withdrew his support for MacArthur's assignment as a military instructor at the University of Wisconsin after learning that "Captain MacArthur[']s services [were] imperatively needed with his company." *PUSG,* 30:389.

14. Despite his financial and physical issues and while writing his memoirs, Grant gave extensive testimony on the need for diplomatic and consular reform at an October 9, 1884, hearing in New York City, held by a commission established by President Arthur to look into ways to expand American trade and commerce with Latin America. See *PUSG,* 31:219–26.

15. Simon, 224, 237–38, 246, 255, 279–80.

16. See http://history.state.gov/milestones/1866–1898/CommodoreShufeldt.

17. Dennett, "American Choices in the Far East in 1882," 85.

18. In a cruel repetition of what happened to Grant, Young "suffered a severe fall on Christmas Eve, 1898, and . . . died on January 17, 1899, after only nineteen months" as Librarian of Congress. He nevertheless had a major impact on the library; see http://www.loc.gov/about/librarianoffice/young.html.

19. For Hay, the Open Door, and the Boxer Rebellion, especially the secretary's cooperation with Wu, see Taliaferro, 364–66 and 376–89, and Dennett, *John Hay,* 297–323. See also Westad, *Restless Empire,* 126–32; Hunt, *The Making of a Special Relationship,* 190–202; Moskin, 219–23; and Graebner, 28–33. Li Hung-chang died in November 1901, two months after concluding the treaty with the western powers that was his final negotiation for China, the Boxer Protocol.

20. Root's reforms "classified officers by salary, increased the overall pay scale, and provided for the creation of a corps of consular inspectors who were to report on the operation of each consular post at least once every two years." Lamont and Cohen, "In the Beginning: The Rogers Act of 1924," 27. See also Moskin, 233–37; Graebner 56–58; and https://history.state.gov/departmenthistory/short-history/professionalism.

21. James Brown Scott, ed., *Texts of the Peace Conferences at the Hague, 1899 and 1907,* prefatory note by Elihu Root, iii–iv.

22. Root, "A Requisite for the Success of Popular Diplomacy," 7–8. As US Attorney for the Southern District of New York, Root deposed Grant in the Grant and Ward case on March 26, 1885. See *PUSG,* 31:323–36. The Root and Grant families were related by marriage after 1907, when Root's daughter, Edith, married Grant's grandson, Ulysses S. Grant III.

Bibliography

The Papers of Ulysses S. Grant *and Unpublished Primary Sources*

Under the editorial direction of Professor John Y. Simon for more than four decades, and of Professor John F. Marszalek since 2008, the *Papers of Ulysses S. Grant* (*PUSG*), comprising thirty-two volumes, were published by Southern Illinois University Press from 1967 to 2012.

The Ulysses S. Grant Presidential Library (USGPL), Mitchell Memorial Library, Mississippi State University, has digitized all thirty-two volumes. They are available at http://digital.library.msstate.edu/cdm/landingpage/collection/USG_volume. The period of Grant's overseas travels, May 17, 1877–September 20, 1879, is covered in volumes 28 and 29, respectively, *November 1, 1876–September 30, 1878*, and *October 1, 1878–September 30, 1880*. Grant's travel diary (TD) is in volume 29.

The *PUSG* volumes are an extraordinary resource, meticulously edited and annotated. Each volume contains extensive notes that support Grant's letters, speeches, and other writings published in that volume. But even more extraordinary is the wealth of primary material in the USGPL files from which those notes were compiled. This material, sometimes, but not always, extracted in the published notes, offers new insights on the life and work of Ulysses S. Grant and provides context to Grant's published writings. Searching instructions are at http://www.usgrantlibrary.org/access/database.asp. All unpublished primary sources used in the writing of this book are from USGPL. The endnotes provide the information needed to locate unpublished material in the library's files, where each unpublished item is linked to a published document in *PUSG*. The first time that an unpublished source is cited, the endnote will indicate that it is "in file" of the related *PUSG* document.

John Russell Young's Around the World with General Grant *and* New York Herald *Articles*

This book makes extensive use of the *New York Herald* articles that John Russell Young wrote while traveling with Ulysses Grant, copies of which are in the USGPL files. The first volume of *Around the World with General Grant* was compiled from Young's articles and appeared while he was still overseas because his publisher faced competition from unscrupulous "authors" publishing books about Grant's world tour by plagiarizing Young's articles. Young supervised publication of the second volume after his return home in 1879. Some chapters in Young's book reproduce his articles word for word, but in many cases there are details and comments in the articles that do not appear in the book, and for that reason they are more often cited here.

Published Material

Adams, Henry. *The Education of Henry Adams*. Boston: Houghton Mifflin, 1918.

Ammen, Daniel. *The Old Navy and the New*. Philadelphia: J. B. Lippincott, 1891.

Anderson, David L. "The Diplomacy of Discrimination: Chinese Exclusion, 1876–1882." *California History* 57, no. 1 (Spring 1978): 32–45.

———. *Imperialism and Idealism: American Diplomats in China, 1861–1898*. Bloomington: Indiana University Press, 1985.

Anderson, Lisa. "The Ex-Presidents." *Journal of Democracy* 21, no. 2 (April 2010): 64–78.

Anson, Archibald E. H. *About Others and Myself*. London: John Murray, 1920.

Badeau, Adam. *Grant in Peace from Appomattox to Mount McGregor*. Hartford, CT: S. S. Scranton, 1887.

———. "Two Great Wars: An Historical Parallel." *Fraser's Magazine* 2, no. 12 (December 1870): 793–805.

Ballard, Michael B. *U. S. Grant: The Making of a General, 1861–1863*. American Crisis, edited by Steven E. Woodworth. Lanham, MD: Rowman and Littlefield, 2005.

Barnhart, Michael A. *Japan and the World since 1868*. International Relations and the Great Powers, edited by John Gooch. London: Arnold, 1995.

Bartlett, Christopher J. "British Reaction to the Cuban Insurrection of 1868–1878." *Hispanic American Historical Review* 37, no. 3 (August 1957): 296–312.

Beale, Howard K. *Theodore Roosevelt and the Rise of America to World Power*. New York: Collier Books, 1962.

Becker, William H., and Samuel F. Wells, eds. *Economics and World Power: An Assessment of American Diplomacy since 1789*. New York: Columbia University Press. 1984.

Bibliography

Belenky, Irina. "The Making of the Ex-Presidents, 1797–1993: Six Recurrent Models," *Presidential Studies Quarterly* 29, no. 1 (March 1999): 150–65.

Benardo, Leonard, and Jennifer Weiss. *Citizen-in-Chief: The Second Lives of the American Presidents.* New York: William Morrow, 2009.

Bensel, Richard [Franklin]. "Comments" [on Edwards and John articles, as part of the "Forum: Should We Abolish the 'Gilded Age'?"]. *Journal of the Gilded Age and the Progressive Era* 8, no. 4 (October 2009): 481–85.

Bensel, Richard Franklin. *The Political Economy of American Industrialization, 1877–1900.* Cambridge, UK: Cambridge University Press, 2000.

Borton, Hugh. *Japan's Modern Century.* New York: The Ronald Press, 1955.

Buell, Raymond Leslie. "The Development of the Anti-Japanese Agitation in the United States." *Political Science Quarterly* 37, no. 4 (December 1922): 605–38.

Bunting, Josiah, III. *Ulysses S. Grant.* American Presidents, edited by Arthur M. Schlesinger Jr. New York: Times Books Henry Holt, 2004.

Burlingame, Michael, ed. *Lincoln's Journalist: John Hay's Anonymous Writings for the Press, 1860–1864.* Carbondale: Southern Illinois University Press, 1998.

Carlson, Peter. "Ulysses S. Grant Talks War with Otto von Bismarck." *American History* 47, no. 2 (June 2012): 26–27.

Chang, Gordon H. "Whose 'Barbarism'? Whose 'Treachery'? Race and Civilization in the Unknown United States–Korea War of 1871." *Journal of American History* 89, no. 4 (March 2003): 1331–65.

Chang, Jung. *Empress Dowager Cixi: The Concubine Who Launched Modern China.* London: Jonathan Cape, 2013.

Chang, Richard T. "General Grant's 1879 Visit to Japan." *Monumenta Nipponica* 24, no. 4 (1969): 373–92.

Chatfield Taylor, H. C. "American Diplomats in Europe." *The North American Review* 163, no. 476 (July 1896): 125–28.

Clyde, Paul H. "The Shadow of the Open Door." *Far Eastern Survey* 18, no. 2 (January 24, 1949): 13–16.

Clyde, Paul H. and Burton F. Beers. *The Far East: A History of the Western Impact and the Eastern Response, 1830–1965.* 4th ed. Englewood Cliffs, NJ: Prentice Hall, 1966.

Cole, Cheryl L. "Chinese Exclusion: The Capitalist Perspective of the *Sacramento Union*, 1850–1882." *California History* 57, no. 1 (Spring 1978): 8–31.

Coolidge, Louis A. *Ulysses S. Grant.* 2 vols. Boston: Houghton Mifflin, 1924.

Cortazzi, Hugh. "The Pestilently Active Minister: Dr. Willis's Comments on Sir Harry Parkes." *Monumenta Nipponica* 39, no. 2 (Summer 1984): 147–61.

Cramer, M. J. *Ulysses S. Grant: Conversations and Unpublished Letters.* New York: Eaton and Mains, 1897.

Crook, D. P. *Diplomacy during the American Civil War.* America in Crisis, edited by Robert A. Divine. New York: John Wiley and Sons, 1975.

Cross, Coy F., II. *Lincoln's Man in Liverpool: Consul Dudley and the Legal Battle to Stop Confederate Warships.* DeKalb: Northern Illinois University Press, 2007.

De Leon, Daniel. "The Conference at Berlin on the West-African Question." *Political Science Quarterly* 1, no. 1 (March 1886): 103–39.

Dennett, Tyler. "American Choices in the Far East in 1882." *American Historical Review* 30, no. 1 (October 1924): 84–108.

———. "American 'Good Offices' in Asia." *American Journal of International Law* 16, no. 1 (January 1922): 1–24.

———. *Americans in Eastern Asia: A Critical Study of the Policy of the United States with Reference to China, Japan and Korea in the 19th Century.* New York: Macmillan, 1922.

———. "Early American Policy in Korea, 1883–7: The Services of Lieutenant George C. Foulk." *Political Science Quarterly* 38, no. 1 (March 1923): 82–103.

———. *John Hay: From Poetry to Politics.* New York: Dodd, Mead, 1934.

Deuchler, Martina. *Confucian Gentlemen and Barbarian Envoys: The Opening of Korea, 1875–1885.* Seattle: University of Washington Press, 1977.

Dougherty, Patricia. *American Diplomats and the Franco-Prussian War: Perceptions from Paris and Berlin.* Washington, DC: Georgetown University Institute for the Study of Diplomacy, 1980.

Doyle, Michael W. "Liberalism and World Politics." *American Political Science Review* 80, no. 4 (December 1986): 1151–69.

Dulles, Foster Rhea. *America's Rise to World Power, 1898–1954.* New York: Harper Torchbook, 1963.

———. *The Imperial Years.* New York: Thomas Y. Crowell, 1956.

———. *Prelude to World Power: American Diplomatic History 1860–1900.* New York: Collier Books, 1971.

Earle, Edward Mead. "A Half Century of American Foreign Policy: Our Stake in Europe, 1898–1948." *Political Science Quarterly* 64, no. 2 (June 1949): 168–88.

Edwards, Rebecca. "Politics, Social Movements, and the Periodization of U.S. History." *Journal of the Gilded Age and the Progressive Era* 8, no. 4 (October 2009): 463–73.

Endy, Christopher. "Travel and World Power: Americans in Europe, 1890–1917." *Diplomatic History* 22, no. 4 (Fall 1998): 565–94.

Fahs, Alice, and Joan Waugh, eds. *The Memory of the Civil War in American Culture.* Civil War America, edited by Gary W. Gallagher. Chapel Hill: University of North Carolina Press, 2004.

Fairbank, J. K. "Patterns behind the Tientsin Massacre." *Harvard Journal of Asiatic Studies* 20, no. 3/4 (December 1957): 480–511.

Fairbank, John King. *Trade and Diplomacy on the China Coast: The Opening of the Treaty Ports, 1842–1854*. Stanford: Stanford University Press, 1969.

Fairbank, John King, and Merle Goldman. *China: A New History*. Cambridge, MA: The Belknap Press of Harvard University Press, 2006.

Fairbank, John King, Katherine Frost Bruner, and Elizabeth MacLeod Matheson, eds. *The I. G. in Peking: Letters of Robert Hart, Chinese Maritime Customs, 1868–1907*. Cambridge, MA: The Belknap Press of Harvard University Press, 1975.

Ferrell, Robert H. *American Diplomacy: A History*. New York: W. W. Norton, 1969.

Field, James A., Jr. "American Imperialism: The Worst Chapter in Almost Any Book." *American Historical Review* 83, no. 3 (June 1978): 644–68.

———. *From Gibraltar to the Middle East: America and the Mediterranean World, 1776–1882*. Chicago: Imprint Publications, 1991. Originally published by Princeton University Press, 1969, as *America and the Mediterranean World, 1776–1882*.

Fiore, Jordan D. "'When General Grant to Ireland Came . . .': A Discordant Note in an Harmonious Journey." *Bridgewater Review* 3, no. 3 (December 1985): 18–20.

Foot, Rosemary, John Lewis Gaddis, and Andrew Hurrell, eds. *Order and Justice in International Relations*. Oxford: Oxford University Press, 2003.

Foster, John W. *A Century of American Diplomacy*. Boston and New York: Houghton Mifflin, 1900.

Frazar, Everett. *Korea, and Her Relations to China, Japan, and the United States*. A paper read before the New England Society of Orange, New Jersey, November 15, 1883. Orange, NJ: Chronicle Book and Job Printing Office, 1884.

Furer, Howard B., ed. *J. Garfield, 1831–1881, C. Arthur, 1830–1886: Chronology—Documents—Bibliographical Aids*. Dobbs Ferry, NY: Oceana Publications, 1970.

Gade, Gerhard. "General Grant in Norway." *American-Scandinavian Review* 21, no. 5 (May 1933).

Gleijeses, Piero. "1898: The Opposition to the Spanish-American War." *Journal of Latin American Studies* 35, no. 4 (November 2003): 681–719.

Goldman, Merle, and Andrew Gordon, eds. *Historical Perspectives on Contemporary East Asia*. Cambridge, MA: Harvard University Press, 2000.

Graebner, Norman A., ed. *An Uncertain Tradition: American Secretaries of State in the Twentieth Century*. New York: McGraw-Hill, 1961.

Grant, Jesse R. *In the Days of My Father General Grant*. New York: Harper and Brothers, 1925.

Grant, Susan-Mary, and Peter J. Parish, eds. *Legacy of Disunion: The Enduring Significance of the American Civil War*. Conflicting Worlds, edited by T. Michael Parrish. Baton Rouge: Louisiana State University Press, 2003.

Grant, Ulysses S. *The Complete State of the Union Addresses of Ulysses S. Grant*. (London?): Dodo Press, n.d.

———. *Personal Memoirs*. New York: Penguin Books, 1999.

Grant, U. S. "The Nicaragua Canal." *North American Review* 132, no. 291 (February 1881): 107–16.

Gyory, Andrew. *Closing the Gate: Race, Politics, and the Chinese Exclusion Act*. Chapel Hill: University of North Carolina Press, 1998.

Haffner, Sebastian. *Preussen ohne Legende*. Munich: Goldmann Verlag, 1981.

Hardy, William E. "South of the Border: Ulysses S. Grant and the French Intervention." *Civil War History* 54, no. 1 (March 2008): 63–86.

Harris, Daniel, "Facing the Unthinkable: Time for FCS to Merge with State?" *Foreign Service Journal* 90, no. 1 (January 2013): 15–20.

Harris, Jonathan. *A Statue for America: The First Hundred Years of the Statue of Liberty*. New York: Four Winds Press, 1985.

Hedren, Paul L. *After Custer: Loss and Transformation in Sioux Country*. Norman: University of Oklahoma Press, 2011.

Heinrichs, Waldo H., Jr. *American Ambassador: Joseph C. Grew and the Development of the United States Diplomatic Tradition*. Boston: Little, Brown, 1966.

Henrikson, Alan K. "Beyond Global-Regional Thinking." In *The Global Century: Globalization and National Security*. Vol. 1. Edited by Richard L. Kugler and Ellen L. Frost. Washington, DC: Institute for National Strategic Studies, National Defense University, 2001.

Herring, George C. *From Colony to Superpower: U.S. Foreign Relations since 1776*. Oxford: Oxford University Press, 2008. *The Oxford History of the United States*, edited by David M. Kennedy.

Hill, Michael. *Elihu Washburne: The Diary and Letters of America's Minister to France during the Siege and Commune of Paris*. New York: Simon and Schuster, 2012.

Hoogenboom, Ari. *The Presidency of Rutherford B. Hayes*. American Presidency, edited by Donald R. McCoy, Clifford S. Griffin, and Homer E. Socolofsky. Lawrence: University of Kansas Press, 1988.

Horstmann, G. Henry. *Consular Reminiscences*. Philadelphia: J. B. Lippincott, 1886.

Houchins, Lee, and Chang-su Houchins. "The Korean Experience in America, 1903–1924." *Pacific Historical Review* 43, no. 4 (November 1974): 548–75.

Hourani, Albert. *A History of the Arab Peoples*. Cambridge, MA: The Belknap Press of Harvard University Press, 2002.

Huffman, James L. "Edward H. House: Questions of Meaning and Influence." *Japan Forum* 13, no. 1 (2001): 15–25.

———. "Edward Howard House: In the Service of Meiji Japan." *Pacific Historical Review* 56, no. 2 (May 1987): 231–58.

———. *A Yankee in Meiji Japan: The Crusading Journalist Edward H. House*. Lanham, MD: Rowman and Littlefield, 2003.

Hunt, Michael H. *Ideology and U.S. Foreign Policy.* New Haven: Yale University Press, 1987.

———. *The Making of a Special Relationship: The United States and China to 1914.* New York: Columbia University Press, 1983.

Iriye, Akira. *Across the Pacific: An Inner History of American-East Asian Relations.* New York: Harcourt, Brace and World, 1967.

———. *China and Japan in the Global Setting.* Cambridge, MA: Harvard University Press, 1992.

———. *Cultural Internationalism and World Order.* Baltimore: Johns Hopkins University Press, 1997.

Janis, Mark Weston. *The American Tradition of International Law: Great Expectations, 1789–1914.* Oxford: Clarendon Press, 2004.

Jansen, Marius B., ed. *The Emergence of Meiji Japan.* Cambridge, UK: Cambridge University Press, 1995.

Jessup, Philip C. *Elihu Root.* New York: Dodd, Mead and Company, 1938.

John, Richard R. "Who Were the Gilders? And Other Seldom-Asked Questions about Business, Technology, and Political Economy in the United States, 1877–1900." *Journal of the Gilded Age and the Progressive Era* 8, no. 4 (October 2009): 474–80.

Jonas, Manfred. *The United States and Germany: A Diplomatic History.* Ithaca, NY: Cornell University Press, 1984.

Jones, Howard. *Blue and Gray Diplomacy: A History of Union and Confederate Foreign Relations.* Littlefield History of the Civil War Era, edited by Gary W. Gallagher and T. Michael Parrish. Chapel Hill: University of North Carolina Press, 2010.

Kasson, John A. "The Congo Conference and the President's Message." *North American Review* 142, no. 351 (February 1886): 119–33.

———. "The Monroe Doctrine in 1881." *North American Review* 133, no. 301 (December 1881): 523–33.

Kayaoglu, Turan. *Legal Imperialism: Sovereignty and Extraterritoriality in Japan, the Ottoman Empire, and China.* Cambridge, UK: Cambridge University Press, 2010.

Keating, John M. *With General Grant in the East.* Philadelphia: J. B. Lippincott, 1879.

Keene, Donald. *Emperor of Japan: Meiji and His World, 1852–1912.* New York: Columbia University Press, 2002.

Kennedy, Paul. *The Realities behind Diplomacy: Background Influences on British External Policy, 1865–1980.* London: Fontana Press, 1985.

Kennedy, Paul M. "The Tradition of Appeasement in British Foreign Policy 1865–1939." *British Journal of International Studies* 2, no. 3 (October 1976): 195–215.

Khan, Yasmin Sabina. *Enlightening the World: The Creation of the Statue of Liberty.* Ithaca: Cornell University Press, 2010.

Kuo, Ping-chia. "Caleb Cushing and the Treaty of Wanghia, 1844." *Journal of Modern History* 5, no. 1 (March 1933): 34–54.

LaFeber, Walter. *The American Age: United States Foreign Policy at Home and Abroad, 1750 to the Present.* New York: W. W. Norton, 1994.

———. "The 'Lion in the Path': The U.S. Emergence as a World Power." *Political Science Quarterly* 101, no. 5 (1986): 705–18.

Lamont, Jim, and Larry Cohen. "In the Beginning: The Rogers Act of 1924." *Foreign Service Journal* 91, no. 5 (May 2014): 26–32.

Large, Stephen S. *Emperors of the Rising Sun: Three Biographies.* Tokyo: Kodansha International, 1997.

Leung, Edwin Pak-wah. "The Quasi-War in East Asia: Japan's Expedition to Taiwan and the Ryukyu Controversy." *Modern Asian Studies* 17, no. 2 (1983): 257–81.

Lewis, Bernard. *The Middle East: A Brief History of the Last 2,000 Years.* New York: Scribner, 1995.

Lieven, Dominic. "Dilemmas of Empire 1850–1918. Power, Territory, Identity." *Journal of Contemporary History* 34, no. 2 (April 1999): 163–200.

MacArthur, Douglas. *Reminiscences.* New York: Fawcett Crest, 1965.

Mahin, Dean B. *The Blessed Place of Freedom: Europeans in Civil War America.* Washington, DC: Brassey's, 2002.

Marshall, Byron K. "Professors and Politics: The Meiji Academic Elite." *Journal of Japanese Studies* 3, no. 1 (Winter 1977): 71–97.

Marszalek, John F. *Sherman: A Soldier's Passion for Order.* Carbondale: Southern Illinois University Press, 2007.

Maruyama, Masao. *Thought and Behaviour in Modern Japanese Politics.* Edited by Ivan Morris. London: Oxford University Press, 1969.

May, Ernest R. *Imperial Democracy: The Emergence of America as a Great Power.* New York: Harcourt, Brace and World, 1961.

May, Robert E., ed. *The Union, the Confederacy, and the Atlantic Rim.* West Lafayette, IN: Purdue University Press, 1995.

McPherson, James M. *This Mighty Scourge: Perspectives on the Civil War.* Oxford: Oxford University Press, 2007.

Merli, Frank J. *The* Alabama, *British Neutrality, and the American Civil War.* Edited by David M. Fahey. Bloomington: Indiana University Press, 2004.

Merli, Frank J., and Theodore A. Wilson, eds. *Makers of American Diplomacy.* 2 vols. New York: Charles Scribner's Sons, 1974.

Meyer, Henry Cord. *Five Images of Germany: Half a Century of American Views on German History.* Washington, DC: American Historical Association Service Center for Teachers of History, 1960. Publication Number 27, 2nd edition.

Meyer, Lysle E. "Henry S. Sanford and the Congo: A Reassessment." *African Historical Studies* 4, no. 1 (1971): 19–39.

Millard, Candice. *Destiny of the Republic: A Tale of Madness, Medicine, and the Murder of a President.* New York: Doubleday, 2011.

Mo Guanting. "The Guangdong Government and the American Consular Service in the Late Qing: A Case Study." www.amstudy.hku.hk/news/treatyports2011/files/kennixmok.pdf.

Morgan, H. Wayne. *Unity and Culture: The United States, 1877–1900.* Vol. 4 of *Pelican History of the United States,* Robert A. Divine, general editor. Baltimore: Penguin Books, 1971.

Morris, James. *Heaven's Command: An Imperial Progress.* New York: Harvest/HBJ, 1980.

Morris, Richard B. *The Peacemakers: The Great Powers and American Independence.* New York: Harper and Row, 1965.

Moskin, J. Robert. *American Statecraft: The Story of the U.S. Foreign Service.* New York: Thomas Dunne Books, 2013.

Moss, Kenneth. "The United States and Central Europe, 1861–1871: Some American Approaches to National Development and the Balance of Power." *The Historian* 39, no. 2 (February 1977): 248–69.

Murase, Shinya. "The Most-Favored Nation Treatment in Japan's Treaty Practice during the Period 1854–1905." *American Journal of International Law* 70, no. 2 (April 1976): 273–97.

Nevins, Allan. *Hamilton Fish: The Inner History of the Grant Administration.* American Political Leaders, edited by Allan Nevins. New York: Dodd, Mead and Company, 1937.

Nichols, Jeannette P. "The United States Congress and Imperialism, 1861–1897." *Journal of Economic History* 21, no. 4 (December 1961): 526–38.

Nicolson, Harold. *The Congress of Vienna: A Study in Allied Unity, 1812–1822.* New York: Harcourt, Brace, Jovanovich, 1974. Originally published in 1946.

———. *Diplomacy.* 3rd ed. Oxford: Oxford University Press, 1963. Originally published in 1939.

Nield, Robert. *The China Coast: Trade and the First Treaty Ports.* Hong Kong: Joint Publishing Co., Ltd., 2010.

Ninkovich, Frank. *Global Dawn: The Cultural Foundation of American Internationalism.* Cambridge, MA: Harvard University Press, 2009.

Nipperdey, Thomas. *Nachdenken ueber die deutsche Geschichte.* Munich: Verlag C. H. Beck, 1986.

Notehelfer, F. G. "On Idealism and Realism in the Thought of Okakura Tenshin." *Journal of Japanese Studies* 16, no. 2 (Summer 1990): 309–55.

Oneal, John R., and Bruce Russett. "The Kantian Peace: The Pacific Benefits of Democracy, Interdependence, and International Organizations, 1885–1992." *World Politics* 52 (October 1999): 1–37.

Osterhammel, Juergen. *The Transformation of the World: A Global History of the Nineteenth Century.* America in the World, edited by Sven Beckert and Jeremi Suri. Princeton, NJ: Princeton University Press, 2014.

Owsley, Harriet Chappell. "Henry Shelton Sanford and Federal Surveillance Abroad, 1861–1865." *Mississippi Valley Historical Review* 48, no. 2 (September 1965): 211–28.

Pagden, Anthony. *Peoples and Empires.* New York: The Modern Library, 2001.

Paullin, Charles Oscar. *Diplomatic Negotiations of American Naval Officers, 1778–1883.* Baltimore: Johns Hopkins Press, 1912.

———. "The Opening of Korea by Commodore Shufeldt." *Political Science Quarterly* 25, no. 3 (September 1910): 470–99.

———. "President Lincoln and the Navy." *American Historical Review* 14, no. 2 (January 1909): 284–303.

Pease, Donald E. "Commentary: Imperial Discourse." *Diplomatic History* 22, no. 4 (Fall 1998): 605–15.

Peffer, Nathan. "The United States in the Far East." *Political Science Quarterly* 54, no. 1 (March 1939): 1–14.

Perkins, Bradford. *The Creation of a Republican Empire, 1776–1865.* Vol. 1 of *The Cambridge History of American Foreign Relations,* edited by Warren I. Cohen. Cambridge, UK: Cambridge University Press, 1993.

———. *The Great Rapprochement: England and the United States, 1895–1914.* New York: Atheneum, 1968.

Perkins, Dexter. *A History of the Monroe Doctrine.* Boston: Little, Brown, 1963.

Perkins, Susan G., ed. *Letters of Capt. Geo. Hamilton Perkins, U.S.N.* Freeport, NY: Books for Libraries Press, 1886; repr. 1970.

Pitre, Merline. "Frederick Douglass and American Diplomacy in the Caribbean." *Journal of Black Studies* 13, no. 4 (June 1983): 457–75.

Pittau, Joseph. *Political Thought in Early Meiji Japan, 1868–1889.* Harvard East Asian Series, vol. 24. Cambridge, MA: Harvard University Press, 1967.

Pletcher, David M. *The Awkward Years: American Foreign Relations under Garfield and Arthur.* Columbia: University of Missouri Press, 1962.

Reischauer, Edwin O. *The Emperor of Japan: A Profile on the Occasion of the Visit by the Emperor and Empress to the United States, September 30th to October 13th, 1975.* New York: The Japan Society, 1975.

———. *Japan: The Story of a Nation.* New York: Alfred A. Knopf, 1970.

Root, Elihu. "The Need of Popular Understanding of International Law." *American Journal of International Law* 1, no. 1 (January–April 1907): 1–3.

———. "A Requisite for the Success of Popular Diplomacy." *Foreign Affairs* 1, no. 1 (September 1922): 3–10.

Rosenberg, Emily S., ed. *A World Connecting, 1870–1945*. A History of the World, Akira Iriye and Juergen Osterhammel, general editors. Cambridge, MA: The Belknap Press of Harvard University Press, 2012.

Ross, Ishbel. *The General's Wife: The Life of Mrs. Ulysses S. Grant*. New York: Dodd, Mead and Company, 1959.

Runkle, Gerald. "Karl Marx and the American Civil War." *Comparative Studies in Society and History* 6, no. 2 (January 1964): 117–41.

Russell, Charles Wells, ed. *The Memoirs of Colonel John S. Mosby*. Boston: Little, Brown, 1917.

Russett, Bruce. *Grasping the Democratic Peace: Principles for a Post–Cold War World*. Princeton, NJ: Princeton University Press, 1993.

Rutkow, Ira. *James A. Garfield*. American Presidents, edited by Arthur M. Schlesinger Jr. New York: Times Books Henry Holt, 2006.

Sansom, George. *A History of Japan, 1615–1867*. Stanford, CA: Stanford University Press, 1963.

Sarna, Jonathan D. *When General Grant Expelled the Jews*. Jewish Encounters, edited by Jonathan Rosen. New York: Schocken Books/Nextbook, 2012.

Scaturro, Frank J. *President Grant Reconsidered*. Lanham, MD: University Press of America, 1998.

Schaller, Thomas F., and Thomas W. Williams. "The *Contemporary Presidency:* Postpresidential Influence in the Postmodern Era." *Presidential Studies Quarterly* 33, no. 1 (March 2003): 188–200.

Scott, Douglas D., Peter Bleed, and Stephen Damm. *Custer, Cody, and Grand Duke Alexis: Historical Archaeology of the Royal Buffalo Hunt*. Norman: University of Oklahoma Press, 2013.

Scott, James Brown, ed. *Texts of the Peace Conferences at The Hague, 1899 and 1907*. Prefatory note by Elihu Root. Boston and London: Ginn and Co., 1908.

Seager, Robert, II. "Ten Years before Mahan: The Unofficial Case for the New Navy, 1880–1890." *Mississippi Valley Historical Review* 40, no. 3 (December 1953): 491–512.

Sexton, Jay. "The Funded Loan and the *Alabama* Claims." *Diplomatic History* 27, no. 4 (September 2003): 449–78.

———. *The Monroe Doctrine: Empire and Nation in Nineteenth-Century America*. New York: Hill and Wang, 2011.

———. "The United States, the Cuban Rebellion, and the Multilateral Initiative of 1875." *Diplomatic History* 30, no. 3 (June 2006): 335–65.

Shepperson, George. "The Centennial of the West African Conference of Berlin, 1884–1885." *Phylon* 46, no. 1 (First Quarter 1985): 37–48.

Sherman, W. T. "General Sherman's Tour of Europe: In Spain, Italy, Egypt, and Turkey," *Century* 57, no. 93 (March 1899): 729–40.

Shinohara, Hatsue. *US International Lawyers in the Interwar Years*. Cambridge, UK: Cambridge University Press, 2012.

Sideman, Belle Becker, and Lillian Friedman, eds. *Europe Looks at the Civil War*. New York: Orion Press, 1960.

Silber, Nina. *The Romance of Reunion: Northerners and the South, 1865–1900*. Civil War America, edited by Gary W. Gallagher. Chapel Hill: University of North Carolina Press, 1993.

Silberman, Bernard S. "Bureaucratic Development and the Structure of Decision-Making in Japan: 1868–1925." *Journal of Asian Studies* 29, no. 2 (February 1970): 347–62.

Simon, John Y., ed. *The Personal Memoirs of Julia Dent Grant (Mrs. Ulysses S. Grant)*. Carbondale: Southern Illinois University Press, 1975.

Simpson, Brooks D. *The Political Education of Henry Adams*. Columbia: University of South Carolina Press, 1996.

Skidmore, Max J. *After the White House: Former Presidents as Private Citizens*. New York: Palgrave MacMillan, 2004.

Skowronek, Stephen. *Presidential Leadership in Political Time*. Lawrence: University Press of Kansas, 2011.

Smith, Jean Edward. *Grant*. New York: Simon and Schuster, 2001.

Smith, Theodore Clarke. "Expansion after the Civil War, 1865–71." *Political Science Quarterly* 16, no. 3 (September 1901): 412–36.

Snay, Mitchell. *Fenians, Freedmen, and Southern Whites: Race and Nationality in the Era of Reconstruction*. Conflicting Worlds, edited by T. Michael Parrish. Baton Rouge: Louisiana State University Press, 2007.

Snyder, Louis L. "The American-German Pork Dispute, 1879–1891." *Journal of Modern History* 17, no. 1 (March 1945): 16–28.

Spence, Jonathan D. *To Change China: Western Advisers in China*. New York: Penguin, 1980.

———. *The Search for Modern China*. New York: W. W. Norton, 1991.

Stead, Alfred, ed. *Japan by the Japanese: A Survey by Its Highest Authorities*. London: Heinemann, 1904.

Steinberg, Richard H., and Jonathan M. Zasloff. "Power and International Law." *American Journal of International Law* 100, no. 1 (January 2006): 64–87.

Stewart, Watt. "George Bancroft: Historian of the American Republic." *Mississippi Valley Historical Review* 19, no. 1 (June 1932): 77–86.

Stuermer, Michael. *Bismarck: Die Grenzen der Politik*. Munich: Piper Verlag, 1987.

———. *Die Grenzen der Macht: Begegnungen der Deutschen mit der Geschichte*. Berlin: Siedler Verlag, 1990.

Swartout, Robert R., Jr. *Mandarins, Gunboats, and Power Politics: Owen Nickerson Denny and the International Rivalries in Korea*. Asian Studies at Hawaii, vol. 25. Honolulu: University Press of Hawaii, 1980.

Taliaferro, John. *All the Great Prizes: The Life of John Hay from Lincoln to Roosevelt*. New York: Simon and Schuster, 2013.

Taylor, Marie Hansen. *On Two Continents: Memories of Half a Century*. New York: Doubleday, Page, and Company, 1905.

Thomas, William G. *The Iron Way: Railroads, the Civil War, and the Making of Modern America*. New Haven, CT: Yale University Press, 2011.

Thompson, Gerald. *Edward F. Beale and the American West*. Albuquerque: University of New Mexico Press, 1983.

Treat, Payson J. "China and Korea, 1885–1894." *Political Science Quarterly* 49, no. 4 (December 1934): 506–43.

———. "The Return of the Shimonoseki Indemnity." *Journal of Race Development* 8, no. 1 (July 1917): 1–12.

Wade, Alf. "The Prince Imperial." *Military History Journal* 3, no. 2 (December 1974): http://samilitaryhistory.org/vo1032aw.html.

Washburne, E. B. *Recollections of a Minister to France, 1869–1877*. 2 vols. New York: Charles Scribner's Sons, 1887.

Waugh, Joan. *U. S. Grant: American Hero, American Myth*. Civil War America, edited by Gary W. Gallagher. Chapel Hill: University of North Carolina Press, 2009.

Weinberg, Albert K. *Manifest Destiny: A Study of Nationalist Expansionism in American History*. Chicago: Quadrangle Books, 1963.

Weinstein, Robert A. "North from Panama, West to the Orient: The Pacific Mail Steamship Company, as Photographed by Carleton E. Watkins." *California History* 57, no. 1 (Spring 1978): 46–57.

Weisbrode, Kenneth. *The Atlantic Century: Four Generations of Extraordinary Diplomats Who Forged America's Vital Alliance with Europe*. Cambridge, MA: Da Capo Press, 2009.

West, Elliott. "Reconstructing Race." In *The Essential West: Collected Essays*. Norman: University of Oklahoma Press, 2012, 100–126.

Westad, Odd Arne. *Restless Empire: China and the World since 1750*. New York: Basic Books, 2012.

Wirtz, Horatio E. "General Ulysses S. Grant: Diplomat Extraordinaire." In *Ulysses S. Grant: Essays and Documents*, edited by David L. Wilson and John Y. Simon. Carbondale: Southern Illinois University Press, 1981.

Wong, Owen Hong-hin. *A New Profile in Sino-Western Diplomacy: The First Chinese Minister to Great Britain*. Kowloon: Chung Hwa Book Company, 1987.

Woodward, C. Vann. *Reunion and Reaction: The Compromise of 1877 and the End of Reconstruction*. New York: Doubleday Anchor, 1956.

Wooster, Robert. *The Military and United States Indian Policy, 1865–1903*. Lincoln: University of Nebraska Press, 1995.

Young, John Russell. *Around the World with General Grant*. 2 vols. New York: The American News Company, 1879.

———. *Men and Memories: Personal Reminiscences*. 2 vols. Edited by May D. Russell Young. New York: F. Tennyson Neely, 1901.

Young, Kenneth Ray. *The General's General: The Life and Times of Arthur MacArthur*. History and Warfare, edited by Arthur Ferrill. Boulder, CO: Westview, 1994.

Younger, Edward. *John A. Kasson: Politics and Diplomacy from Lincoln to McKinley*. Iowa City: State Historical Society of Iowa, 1955.

Zasloff, Jonathan. "Law and the Shaping of American Foreign Policy: From the Gilded Age to the New Era." *New York University Law Review* 78, no. 1 (April 2003): 239–373.

Zeitz, Joshua. *Lincoln's Boys: John Hay, John Nicolay, and the War for Lincoln's Image*. New York: Viking, 2014.

Ziebarth, Marilyn, ed. *California History* 57, no. 1 (Spring 1978), special issue: *The Chinese in California*.

Zimmermann, Warren. *First Great Triumph: How Five Americans Made Their Country a World Power*. New York: Farrar, Straus and Giroux, 2002.

Index

Index

Edwina S. Campbell is a former U.S. Foreign Service officer and a professor emerita at the University of Virginia, National Defense University, and Air University. She is the author of *Germany's Past and Europe's Future: The Challenges of West German Foreign Policy* and *The Relevance of American Power: The Anglo-American Past and the Euro-Atlantic Future* and a contributor to *Our First Glimpse of Japan.*

THE WORLD OF ULYSSES S. GRANT

Edited by John F. Marszalek & Timothy B. Smith

After the assassination of Abraham Lincoln, Ulysses S. Grant became the most popular American alive. He symbolized the Federal victory, the destruction of slavery, and the preservation of the Union. Grant remained a popular topic among historians who have written about those years, but over time scholars and the public removed Grant from his place in the pantheon of leading Americans. As the decades passed and attitudes toward the Civil War and war itself changed, the public's perception of Grant devolved: no longer a national idol, Grant was instead written off as a heartless general and corrupt president. In the early twenty-first century, however, Grant's place in history is being reinterpreted. Now he is increasingly seen as a success on the battlefield, a leading proponent of African American civil rights, and the first of the modern American presidents.

To further an understanding of Ulysses S. Grant through a close analysis of his life and work, this innovative book series provides a thorough examination of particular events and periods of Grant's life in order to present important insights into his generalship, presidency, influence, and reputation. Books in the series explore Grant's character as well as his role in American history. By delving into the deeper detail and context of what Grant did and saw, this series aims to break new ground and provide the historical profession and the general reading public with accurate, readable perspectives showing Grant's significant contributions to the world he lived in and to the years that followed.

OTHER BOOKS IN
The World of Ulysses S. Grant

Grant at Vicksburg: The General and the Siege
Michael B. Ballard

America's Hardscrabble General:
Ulysses S. Grant, from Farm Boy to Shiloh
Jack Hurst

The Best Writings of Ulysses S. Grant
Edited by John F. Marszalek

The Impulse of Victory: Ulysses S. Grant at Chattanooga
David A. Powell

The Personal Memoirs of Julia Dent Grant (Mrs. Ulysses S. Grant)
Edited by John Y. Simon

The Decision Was Always My Own:
Ulysses S. Grant and the Vicksburg Campaign
Timothy B. Smith

Interrupted Odyssey: Ulysses S. Grant and the American Indians
Mary Stockwell